SACRED FALL

by
JACK WEAFER

ISBN-10: 1482359138
EAN-13: 9781482359138
Library of Congress Control Number: 2013902767
CreateSpace Independent Publishing Platform
North Charleston, South Carolina

Dedication

To my parents, John and Genevieve, and all the ancestors preceding them who provided me the opportunity for this sacred life.

Reviews

There are many reasons that men put pen to paper and write the story of their lives. Some need to express publicly that which they did not have the courage to say directly and in person. Others write in order to leave for posterity their inflated sense of the value of their lives. Many record the events that they were privy to in the halls and offices of power. Jack Weafer has created a personal journal of his near death and rebirth that touches the essence of the human experience. Sacred Fall is the story of one mans near tragic accident that served as the vehicle for his awakening to the deeper truth of the universal and epic struggle of mankind; To see the meaning and value in the challenges of our precious lives. It is the unvarnished, naked, account of the pain, rage, fear, humiliation, devotion and love that for most of us remain hidden in the daily procession of our lives. His courage in exposing the deeply private feelings and intimate sensitivities that most of us spend our energy protecting serves as an unusual opportunity to learn how one man did not shrink from a challenge that would have killed many. In recording his journey, Weafer, has opened his personal secret door in order to illuminate the darker places of all people. His message is delivered in a detailed, riveting unflinching, open way that allows each reader to take the message to the level that his consciousness permits. If you can allow it, this story can change the way you see life, love and yourself.

—Rabbi Yehuda Pearl

Dr. Weafer displays the courage it takes to stand in the truth of one's being and discover a deeper meaning of life and love. Instead of succumbing to the chaos of trauma, he offers a way to turn into one's body without the protective layers of ability, function, personality and roles. The reader that allows his experience to enter their consciousness will initiate their own journey of discovery. Having

chosen to suffer both his pain and what it uncovered, his courageous story illustrates a path that restores dignity ,hope and meaning to one's life. I will enthusiastically recommend this book to both
patients and friends.

—*Michael Lowenthal, M.D.*

Sacred Fall is a powerful story of our ability to turn tragedy into
uplifting personal growth. Jack illuminates how turning into and
facing his worst pains and fears facilitated his healing process after
a traumatic accident. His journey is a testament to the courage in
us all and points us to the power we each have to live a deeper life
with a fuller engagement with the richness of the moment, whatever it may bring.

—*Ken Manning, Ph.D., Psychologist and President,*
Insight Principles, Inc.)

Jack Weafer's incredible journey reveals how physical trauma can
create an opportunity for the greatest healing of all–the journey
to wholeness through the healing of the child within. He credits
his survival and recovery to the grace and guidance of the Beloved.
His articulation of that presence in each of us is incredibly inspir-
ing. You will find this book a manual for living the conscious life.

—*Elizabeth Hallstrom, Ph.D.*

There are so many layers to each of us, and time, experience, living often bury some of them deeper and deeper. As invisible as
they may become, the background noise they produce wants to
be acknowledged and dealt with. This powerful book invites the
reader in, not just to Weafer's being and becoming, but to the
potential for our own.

—*Jonathan Goldberg*

Preface

"The Beloved is all, the lover just a veil.
The Beloved is living, the lover a dead thing.
If Love withholds its strengthening care,
The lover is left like a bird without wings.
How will I be awake and aware
If the light of the Beloved is absent?
Love wills that this Word be brought forth.
If you find the mirror of the heart dull,
The rust has not been cleared from its face."

Rumi (Mathnawi Book1, 34)

For 50 years, I had seen myself as the archetype of the Hero. There was no obstacle I couldn't overcome, no goal I couldn't achieve.

I had been a football player, a wrestler, weight-lifter, cliff-diver, race-car driver, sky-diver, marathoner, horseman and tri-athlete. I had cleared my own land, built my own house, landscaped my property with hand-built stone walls, and cut and split my own wood. As a psychotherapist my business thrived. I engaged my work, my role as a husband and then as a father, with the same passion, confidence, and drive that permeated every other facet of my being.

With great pride and passion, I embraced and tackled life. In every aspect of my being I strove to be the best that I could be. I overpowered obstacles and "played through the pain." The words "vulnerable" and "helpless" were not in my vocabulary.

I was the provider, self-made, self-reliant, and self-sufficient.

The journey that unfolds in these pages begins quite literally with the fall that shattered my body and my entire sense of that heroic image. It was a fall that by all accounts, I should never have lived to write about. It was a fall that brought me to "near death," but in doing so broke open a transcendent dimension of life that not only became the central healing Presence responsible for my eventual recovery but has sustained and nurtured me ever since.

For what turned out to be 2 ½ hours, but seemed like an eternity, I literally hovered in the liminal region between life and death. I floated above the ruins of my body consumed by a loving energy, which surrounded and embraced me, a nameless essence whose vibrating primordial presence permeated everything. This divine Presence was all-encompassing and, at the same time, so loving and unconditionally inclusive of "me," that I was completely intoxicated and transported to a new sense of being. It was as if all that I had attached value to in life, except love, simply vanished. It was clear to me in that moment that only love survives death. Love alone carries the essence of what I met that day and came to call (after Rumi's poem) the "Beloved."

And so, my life was transformed forever.

My journey has been one of suffering, healing, and above all else, awakening. Over the course of nine months it involved my struggles between abject suffering and hopelessness and the restorative energies of that Presence, the Beloved, which I had discovered while hovering so close to death. This existential struggle required all of the knowledge and insight that I had gained from all of my life's experiences. It meant breaking open my body and confronting a lifetime of traumas. It meant dark lonely hours when the physical and psychic pain was unbearable. It meant opening my heart and soul to the compassion of others in ways I had never dreamt.

It meant surrendering to whatever the moment demanded, remaining in the here and now, accepting my life situation of the moment, no matter how joyous or tragic.

I could never have imagined being more broken than when I lay on the floor of that ravine. Today, I have emerged more whole than I could have dreamed, with the blessing of an unwavering sense of the Beloved. On the journey, I discovered a process in suffering that allows for openness to the terror and pain of post-traumatic recovery. I found depths of compassion and love for and from my family, friends, myself, and even those I hardly knew.

I have learned to embrace the here and now in suffering and joy, in love and in pain.

I have learned to be in and live in the present.

We cannot control those fateful moments when our lives and bodies are broken. We can only control whether we will awaken or contract in response to the pain and fear that accompany those moments.

What follows is a story I could never have imagined telling, until I myself was awakened, and my mind and spirit broken wide open.

TABLE OF CONTENTS

CHAPTER 1
Falling Upward

My journey began on a clear, crisp blue-sky day in September. I remember that Tuesday morning perfectly. I had taken the day off from work and had planned to begin building a large screened porch enclosing the rear deck that extended over the ravine behind our house. I could hardly wait to get started.

The deck extended over the land below and was surrounded by trees, which had matured around it. My new porch would ultimately be like a tree house. I could just imagine the fun our family would enjoy in this new space. But before the building could begin, I had to deal with a potential hazard that hung directly over my deck and soon-to-be porch. A large limb had grown out from one of the surrounding trees. Climbing up and cutting that limb away would be the first step in the project.

The kids were headed off for school. My wife, Alice, had already left with our 13 year old 8th grader, Brendan. Devin, 8, a lively third grader, was waiting for me to drive him down the long rolling driveway and around the corner to the bus. I relished this time with him on the mornings I was home. That morning, the bus was late, so we pulled a soccer ball out of the back seat and kicked it around. My last image of Devin that morning was of his tiny and beautiful little body kicking the soccer ball back to me in a perfect pass, just before he bounded up the steps of the bus to join his friends.

When I got back to the house I took Walker, our short-haired pointer, for one of my favorite walks, a short trek to the crest of the mountain where we lived. It is one of the highest elevations in southern New York. The view from there is spectacular, and you can see for miles. Arriving there that morning I looked out over the densely packed forest of oaks, birches, maples, and evergreens and watched the light reflecting off the lake below. It seemed to be dancing along and through the mountain laurel bordering it. I thought of all the years I had spent clearing our 28 acres of dead trees so the forest could develop, and how often I had hauled tree trunks in the tractor and split and stacked the wood with my boys. I found myself smiling as I acknowledged how deeply bound I was to this land and our home.

When Walker and I got back, he went for the water dish, and I enthusiastically got ready to work. With that limb cut, my project could officially begin. I went to the garage to gather up the tools I would need. I collected my substantial 24-inch chainsaw, rope and a ladder, and I was only mildly annoyed when I remembered that I had lent my tree harness to a friend. Given the number of trees I had climbed, I hardly gave it a second thought. I wasn't felling an entire tree. This was just a quick surgical removal of a limb. Without a worry in the world, I took the rest of my equipment and headed off.

The deck wrapped around to the back of our house and was designed to connect with the birch trees and evergreens that surrounded it. It cantilevered off the back of the house and stood some twenty feet above the ravine below. The limb I wanted to remove was some twenty feet above the deck.

I looked up at the old black birch tree, sizing up the job. The limb looked to be five or six inches thick and extended out over the deck some fifteen feet. The only difficulty I foresaw was that I would need to climb up and actually sit in the tree to make the cut. Had it been maybe ten feet lower, I could have stood on the deck and cut it off with my pole saw.

I tied the rope around my waist and the other end to the chainsaw, which I left on the deck. I climbed up the ladder's ten feet and then into and up the tree. Once I reached the limb, I sat in the crotch of the tree. With my back to the ravine I took a few minutes to enjoy the view and sounds of the surrounding forest. The solitude that I felt in that moment seemed to be enhanced by the beauty of the trees and the stream that flowed forty feet below through the granite rocks. Then I got to work.

First, I pulled up the chainsaw from the deck. Then I assessed the limb. I had cut down or trimmed hundreds of trees over the years. I had long since learned that each tree responded differently to the saw. Each fell according to its own twist, its own lean. I started up the chainsaw. I assessed the limb again, its weight, and the way it angled off the trunk. Sitting in a crotch of the tree, I reached down and notched the limb beneath where I wanted to make my cut.

But just before I reached down to cut the branch beneath me, a subtle but strange feeling swept through me. I turned off the chainsaw and looked around thinking maybe I had heard a car coming up the driveway. I didn't, nor did I expect anyone to come home until school was out.

I shrugged it off, restarted the chainsaw and began cutting.

There was no warning to the limb's sudden erratic break. One second I was cutting, and then in one horrific instant the branch cracked and lurched back and up, toward me, driving into my chest and pushing me backwards out of the tree. In the same instant, the chainsaw also kicked back and roared upwards toward my throat. I jerked backwards away from immediate death, the fully powered chainsaw slicing through the air after me.

I was falling.

I extended my arm that was still holding the running saw and pushed the saw and its howling blade as far away from me as I could. To this day, I can still hear the metallic whistling sound of that running blade and feel its vibrations as its teeth brushed by me, coming within an inch of decapitating me.

Everything slowed. I released the chainsaw and continued dropping headfirst and backwards into the ravine. Instinctively, drawing on a forgotten instinct from my days as a cliff diver, my body kicked around and descended feet first, hands at my side.

I remained conscious right to the point of my impact with the granite ledge.

As I hit, my legs, then pelvis, back, ribs, hand and elbow exploded. My shattered body bounced, the impact throwing me backwards again, over the ledge, and further down into the ravine.

CHAPTER 2
In the Ravine

Everything stopped.

Everything came to life.

I have no memory of the impact. I remember the shock and the panic. I remember falling, turning, and plummeting down feet first. And then I remember a miraculous surge of energy that swept "me" up and out of my body. Everything that was "me" seemed to gather into an experience of light separate from my body. I felt as if the entire universe had embraced me in love and I was one with it.

I was floating up in the treetops, looking down at a seemingly lifeless body in the ravine below. I felt both a sudden surge of terror and an all-consuming sense of peace and joy. The fear came from the unknown and of looking down and seeing "me," and my horribly broken and crumpled body. The indestructible man that I had been lay almost unrecognizable and seemingly lifeless on the rocks. Twisted. Distorted. Bloody. Helpless.

Yet as precious as that body had been to me, it paradoxically no longer seemed part of me. I wasn't drawn to it. It lay there broken while I was the light; dynamic, vibrant, up in the tree-tops. Like the leaves sparkling in the sun, I too turned from green to silver and back again. I became the breeze and its source. I flowed unencumbered by form. My body lay broken apart, yet somehow, I had become whole. I felt united with everything in a euphoric sense of Oneness.

I was in God's presence.

As I floated, infused with a boundless sense of peace and completeness, I realized with unequivocal clarity that I had always been in this Presence, as had everyone and everything. Looking down on my body, I knew it had all been perfect: the pains, fears, suffering, rages, joys, loves, sorrow. I sensed and knew that within all humanity and all inhumanity there was perfection. Cradled in that rapture, in that light, I felt that the entire universe embraced me in love, and I was whole with it.

I have no concept of how long I remained aware of this blissful state, absorbed in this larger, ineffable reality. But for those precious moments, I had become a part of God. And in that experience, I awoke to the most essential truth I could ever have imagined. That Presence was not "out there somewhere" but resided within my innermost being. It was part of me, part of all of us, timeless and eternal.

With a jolt, my consciousness slammed back into my body, as if some remaining invisible ligament still connected us. I had the strong sense that I had died prematurely, and a scene began to unfold before me; an apparition of sorts.

I envisioned my boys coming home from school. They let Walker out, who after his usual excited greeting, started walking around, nose in the air. He began whining, catching my scent on the breeze. His whining intensified, and he ran around the back of the house with the boys in pursuit. They stopped at the deck railing and looked down. As the boys saw my body below, they screamed out, "Dad! Dad!" Tears flowed, streaming down their faces.

They screamed, "NO!"

Their "NO!" reverberated through everything.

The vision of their anguish reached me in a way my body's silent pleadings had not. Deluged by their grief, I realized instantly that while I could have left my body in the ravine, I couldn't leave my boys. Their lives and love had touched my innermost being, and an enormous wave of love, gratitude and grief swept through me.

I could see and feel God's love in their suffering. The Presence I was part of flowed through their brokenhearted cry.

In that pivotal moment, their love drew me back to life. I was near death, but not dead, and the choice to live was one I had to make. As intoxicated as I was in the light and peace of the Presence, and while I longed to remain a part of it, the love for my family drew me with an even greater force. I was unsure if I would carry the awareness of this Presence back into life. I wasn't even sure if I would carry a memory of it. But I was sure that I had to return to the ground, my body, and my family.

I don't remember saying "yes," only immediately becoming one with the sack of crushed bones that lay below. In an explosion of agony, I was again fully present and in my body. I lay on my back looking up into the trees and the sky. Pain surged within me at incomprehensible levels.

"Breathe," I thought, through clenched teeth "breathe." What I imagined were several broken ribs made each intake of air labored and agonizing, but each breath was also an affirmation of life. I fought to find a rhythm and then lifted my head a little to try and assess my injuries.

I looked down at my legs. My left one was propped up on a small boulder, impossibly twisted, as if it could have been detached. My right leg lay to the right, bruised but not broken, in the ferns beside it. Bones pierced through the skin of my right arm near my elbow. I had little sensation from my back down to my toes, and I could only imagine the internal damage, though I knew from the pain in my chest that several ribs were fractured. Fears of paralysis and massive and horrific waves of pain tore through me. I was overwhelmed with nausea.

But as I fought to remain conscious in that maelstrom of pain, the Presence I had been part of – was part of – ebbed and flowed through me. I had not lost my awareness of it. It was still part of me. As I slowly raised my head and looked over my body, the pain temporarily gave way to an unearthly calm. It moved through me, mixing with that sense of oneness and love I had felt up in the treetops.

Then like a tide, it receded.

My vision began to blur. I closed my eyes and lowered my head onto the ground. As the pain and the nausea swelled, I knew that if I didn't start to move soon, I would never move again. Sitting up was impossible. I could see and feel the catastrophic damage to my pelvis and legs. My only option was to crawl, which required the hellish task of rolling over. Using my left arm and hand, and drawing on the strength I felt from that mysterious Presence, I reached out and grabbed some ferns, and then the rock ledge, slowly pulling myself and turning onto my stomach. Then, over the course of what seemed an eternity, I carefully and painfully snaked my body around so that I was facing uphill and toward the back of the house.

My body screamed, "STOP."

I lay trembling with my face on the ground. The nausea rolled over me in incapacitating waves, and I could feel and taste the mixture of tears, sweat and blood that streamed down my face and onto the dirt and granite beneath me. As I looked up toward the house, the distance seemed insurmountable. The actual distance was only about 30 feet to the deck, but it was uneven and uphill, with rock ledges and boulders that dwarfed me. To reach the deck, I would have to somehow pull myself up and over those massive unyielding formations, zigzagging my way between slippery rock ledges that would be challenging to traverse if I had been in perfect health.

I began to drag myself forward, working with the only two parts of me that functioned. I clawed with my left hand and pushed feebly with my foot, moving several feet before I arrived at the foot of the first boulder. Its crest was about 6 feet above me, its face at least a sixty-degree angle. As I struggled desperately not to pass out, I slowly pulled myself to a near standing position clinging to the face of the rock, inching myself up its face, toward the house and the only hope I had to survive. It was the vibrating awareness of the Presence that pulled me along.

In my state, there was no earthly way I could have traversed any part of that hill. The rise from the ravine to the house was inaccessible by Humvee or even a horse, no less a shattered body. In my state, it would have been a miracle if I had managed to drag myself thirty feet across a level asphalt driveway. But ascend a near vertical climb? Over boulders and brush where there was no path?

Intellectually, I couldn't explain the force that sustained me. But instinctively and emotionally, I knew. I made my way up because that divine Presence worked through me. It engaged a life force within me that inched me up and toward survival. It ebbed and flowed as I fluctuated from blinding pain to its insulating light and vibration. There were moments I couldn't move or breathe through the agony of my injuries. And then came moments when I sensed everything in the forest was alive, directing me, sustaining me. It seemed that even the ledge and boulders vibrated with a sustaining energy; the air around me pulsated; wild ferns, lichen, moss supported me, all helping me to crawl.

I lost all sense of time as I struggled forward, drifting back and forth between the pain and the Presence. I was drawn by the love for my sons and lulled by the nurturing light that sustained me.

After reaching the apex of the first boulder, I had to move parallel to the deck to find an accessible route up. I snaked my way sideways over the rocky surface, finally finding another rock face I felt I could climb. Again I had to hoist myself to a near standing position in order to pull myself up, screaming with the pain of trying to maneuver my legs under me. I pulled and scratched my way up, held to the near vertical rock face by a combination of the barest thread of gravity and the little traction I could gather through my left hand and right leg. If the angle of ascent had been a single degree higher, I would never have been able to keep from sliding down that boulder. I reached for the crest of the boulder to pull myself onto the ledge above, and as I did, I suddenly lost my tenuous hold and started sliding on my belly down toward the ledge below and back into the ravine. The fall was only 12 feet or so, but I knew in my condition, I wouldn't survive it. I stopped abruptly as my left leg caught on something, snapping the head of my femur back into my shattered pelvis. I saw a huge flash of light as the pain exploded through my body. Unimaginable agony again coursed through me, and I had no choice but to endure the moment. To pass out, to drift into the Presence, would mean another fall and the end of life.

I pulled. I climbed. I willed myself toward life.

At the top of the boulder, I just lay there, writhing in pain that seemed to have no beginning or end, tears flowing, trembling from the shock and the excruciating pain.

Then, lying on the rocky ledge looking sideways through the ferns, I saw a squirrel out of the corner of my eye. Scampering along not five feet away, bushy tail in the air, he stopped. He cocked his head in my direction and his big brown eyes met mine. Then he bounced off to search for more acorns, driven by instinct to prepare for the future, as I'd always done. He too drew me to life, down from the trees to the earth. Thick tears rolled down my cheeks as I reaffirmed my choice to endure this suffering – to live. As I did, I again had the acute awareness of the sustaining power of the Presence that flowed through me and all of life.

I continued to crawl. The Presence flowed through me as I inched ever closer to the deck, the stairs, and a phone. I pulled myself up onto a small fern and moss plateau and stopped, looking around to get my bearings. To my surprise and encouragement, I could see the deck supports and footings nearby.

God, I was so close.

I wiped the blood and sweat out of my eyes. It had taken me over 2 hours to reach this bluff, and now I was within fifteen feet of the stairs. But between me and any hope of rescue, was a dangerously narrow surface forming a granite bridge between me and the foot of the deck. I would have to pull myself up onto that ledge and transverse that narrow lip. If I slipped off I would fall into the gully that separated two huge rock formations. If I could get passed it, I would reach the base of the deck, the stairs, a phone.

My first move was to again pull myself up several feet and onto the ledge. To do that, I had to once again get my legs under me. But this time, given the narrow lip of the rock, I would also have to swing my pelvis under me first, in order to get situated squarely on the rocky ledge. Shaking violently from the pain, I looked to my left and saw the sheer vertical drop. If I ended up down there, no one would see me from the deck, and it would take days for anyone to find me. I paused and thought of my boys and Alice. I drew from them the courage and strength to pull myself up off my knees and slide my pelvis onto the outcropping. But as I lurched up, I lost my balance and abruptly slipped. In terror, I grabbed a rock with my broken right arm, and pulled desperately with my left. My twisted left leg, bone still protruding from my hip, hung off the ledge's edge. I was 10 feet from safety, yet within an inch of again falling to my death. The pain muted my terror. My breath came in violent spasms, but I dragged myself up and then along the ledge, trying to shut out the horror of how close I had come to careening into the gully.

I pulled, moving with great caution, finally reaching the relative flat underneath the deck. The stairs were within 10 feet of me. The pleading in my head to "stop" had quieted. At some level, the pain began to seem normal, and I focused on the final few feet I needed to cover to get to the stairs.

And then the forest became quiet, as if it and the breeze and all of its creatures were holding its collective breath. As I listened, I thought I heard a car coming up the driveway. I remembered back to the premonition I had had just before cutting the limb and wondered if I was actually hearing anything at all. I waited. My breathing had become shallow. I was exhausted.

But I had heard a car, and it had stopped. As it did, a hawk shrieked loudly overhead. With all the strength I could muster, I cried out.

"Help me." And then louder, "Help me."

I heard a response and called out again. It was our housekeeper, Lorraine. She scrambled to the back of the house, and looked down at me.

"Oh God!" she said, "Oh God! Oh God!" She ran to me.

"Lorraine. I need you to call 911." I could see the shock in her eyes and face at seeing me.

"You need to tell them I have several shattered bones and serious internal injuries." It was hard to speak.

"Please hurry," I gasped.

She ran into the house and returned a few minutes later.

"The police want me to run down to where the driveway meets the road so they can find the house," she explained. "OK?"

"OK," I said.

I watched her disappear around the back of the house. I was alone again, but the promise of help overtook me and was almost too much to bear. I was alive. I began to cry.

Lorraine ran. She ran 1/3 of a mile down our gravel driveway to ensure the police didn't miss the driveway. By the third rise in the drive, Lorraine was having problems of her own. From the stress of running, compounded by the shock of finding me in that broken state, she was overcome by an asthma attack. She had to crawl the last 50 feet to the main road. She arrived just as the first squad car had passed. But on one knee and with one hand waving frantically in the air, the second car saw her, and help was finally on the way.

"I need to call for more help." A policeman was kneeling beside me. With great compassion, he held my good hand in his and surveyed my condition.

"I promise I will be right back," and he started to stand.

"Please don't leave," I pleaded. "God, please stay."

He knelt back down. "OK."

His partner went back to the car and radioed for help. Not long after that, I heard sirens. An ambulance arrived with yet another police car, and in a matter of minutes, a group of people had surrounded me. Someone carefully cut my clothes off to get a better look at the damage.

As they looked at me, everyone fell silent.

"We need an immediate emergency helicopter transport." The radio crackled an acknowledgment and the location was relayed, and then they got to work getting me out of the woods to the evacuation site.

As gently as they could, they placed me on a stretcher and carried me up onto the deck and out to the ambulance. I appreciated the blankets they had draped over me as I had begun to feel uncomfortably cold. The ride in the ambulance was short, just over 2 miles, but every bump, lurch and turn was agony.

The extraction point, of all places, was the parking lot at my kids' school. Devin would tell me later how all the kids had run to the window as the helicopter set down in the lot. Not knowing it was me, they had seen the ambulance, a person wheeled on a gurney to the helicopter, and then the roar and excitement as the copter lifted up and raced back to the hospital.

My anxiety and pain elevated as they lifted my stretcher and loaded me into the helicopter. I had never felt so dependent and helpless in my life. A helmeted, uniformed nurse busily hooked me up to monitors and various life-sustaining apparatus. But as we took off, the thundering loudness of the turbine engine and rotors mixed with and amplified the terror that was growing within me. I had left the ravine and, I thought, any contact with the Presence that had sustained me. Outside of the ravine, in a helicopter, how would I ever connect with that Presence. I would be lost. My fear and pain started to consume me, and I began to spiral into panic.

"I'm so sorry I can't give you anything for the pain." The helmeted medevac nurse was shouting to be heard. She held one of my hands.

Her eyes locked onto mine and her face radiated the most beautiful and compassionate expression I had ever seen. She seemed to grasp the very essence of me and the tenderness of her voice riveted me in the present moment.

"The emergency room doc says they need you not to be medicated. I'm so sorry, but I'm here with you."

My rising demons of pain and panic dissolved into the loving sadness in her eyes. She and I breathed together in an intimacy few humans share. She seemed to shoulder the weight and knowledge of what lay ahead for me and appeared to mourn in the present moment for the loss that I was facing.

I simply surrendered to her presence as I had surrendered to the divine Presence I had experienced in the ravine. I recognized and felt that Presence, that boundless love, through her.

To be sustained – in abject need – by the loving presence of another person, as I was in that helicopter, is one of the most moving experiences we can have as human beings. That moment still endures as one of the most indelible moments in my life.

She didn't shy away from my injuries. She wasn't jaded by her profession of dealing with victims of trauma. She was present. She knew what lay ahead for me and held that with infinite compassion and tenderness. Despite my hellish pain, while in her care I felt fully alive and present, once again fully aware of the essential truth of life - that love sustains us.

The helicopter touched down and jolted everyone into action. I was being hustled out, and my angel of mercy was about to depart. I felt I was being orphaned once again, left alone at that abyss of pain and terror.

"You're going to be OK," she said.

As the rotors roared, and as I was hurried to the emergency room, I could sense the pain and fear begin to circle and close in again. But I also felt a seed had been planted in my awareness. Though I was not close to even remotely comprehending it, I had experienced an undeniable divine Presence that had sustained me in that ravine. That same Presence had been manifested and affirmed through the complete and unconditional compassion of a medevac nurse.

Everything stopped

Everything came to life.

As the gurney rolled toward the emergency room, I imagined countless and horrific scenarios of how broken I was physically. But I never could have imagined how the awakening I had experienced would evolve and eventually transform every facet and nuance of my life.

CHAPTER 3
Moment to Moment

I was no longer Jack.

Horribly broken and completely helpless, I was hurried from the helipad to the emergency room, an anonymous trauma victim. Handing me off from air to ground, a team of highly efficient hospital workers immediately reduced me to a series of data points - a male Caucasian in his fifties with multiple traumas to his legs, spine, ribs, arms. They shouted out my vitals. No one reached out to me.

"He's critical." I heard, as the lights raced by overhead.

"Fell over forty feet onto a rock ravine. He fell three hours ago."

"Jesus. He's lucky to be here at all." Nameless doctors, nurses and technicians spoke around me and about me as if I wasn't there.

Any shred of the transcendent energies and calm I had felt in the ravine and the compassion of the medevac nurse evaporated in the swirling chaos of the emergency room. I was slipping into a literal Hell as I was swept up into a stark and frenetic maelstrom of activity and a swirling maze of surgical green. I felt only pain and dread as they rolled me down the halls, faceless strangers pelting me with questions, and eyes and hands sweeping over me with vacant and impersonal professionalism. They swarmed, focusing on my injuries as if they existed as something completely detached from me. I was part of a process, part of a daily grind, and I would be forgotten the moment any of their shifts were over, other than fodder for a story that would begin, "Holy crap, there was this guy who fell over 40 feet onto the rocks..."

I had lost any sense of the Presence in the maze of the ER. Pain, panic, and fear consumed me. Like sunlight through a magnifying glass, the confluence of intense agony that cascaded from different regions of my body was magnified and intensified to unimaginable degrees through the lens of my frantic imagination. There were so many points of intense pain that I literally felt my body was on fire. I could feel the bone beneath my left hip protruding through my pelvis. My back was exploding in pain. Bone and bloody muscle stuck out of my right elbow. I could taste the blood in my mouth and wondered how many organs were at risk of shutting down.

Would I ever walk again? How serious was my head injury? Did I have brain damage? Would I be paralyzed? Would I live?

But worst of all, like a raging demon from some hellish nightmare, the pain terrorized me. I lay rigid, teeth clenched, every muscle taut, barely breathing, and fear raging in my head that all my pain would never stop growing. I was afraid I would die. At other times, when the gurney was jolted or a doctor moved me, I was afraid I would never die and that the tempest of pain and horror would continue to devour me forever.

They had different questions from mine. For them it wasn't so much about me as it was about process. What was my name? Could I talk? Did I have health care?

"Please help me," I moaned.

"We're doing everything we can," said the voice behind the mask.

Did I know where I was? Did I know why I was there? Could I remember my social security number? Could I feel my feet? Could I see? Was there anyone they should contact? It was dizzying, and elevated every fearful thought that had ignited in my head.

I heard tests being ordered, doctors summoned, and IV's requested. I felt like a floating piece of debris on a turbulent sea, hopeless, helpless, and with pain and fear that was exponentially amplified with every motion of the gurney and every impersonal prod and poke.

So much activity, so many people, and yet in that swarm, I had never felt so utterly alone.

"Please help me," I repeated.

"We'll do something for the pain as soon as we can," said a new face. He was looking into his chart as he spoke.

"But first we need to determine just how badly you're hurt."

"REALLY BAD!," I shouted.

He looked up from his paperwork. Someone had finally seen me.

"Look," he said. "You fell a long, long way onto a rock ledge. It's amazing you are alive, but you are. Right now we're worried how badly you're hurt inside, and until we can learn the extent of the damage to your bones and internal organs, we can't give you anything for the pain." He paused.

"We will send you down for some x-rays, an MRI and some other tests. We will do something for the pain as soon as we can. You have to hang in there." And he was gone.

Doctors came and went. They asked more questions. They gave no assurances. They offered no relief. They explained they would be taking me downstairs for more tests and x-rays soon. Time slowed, and I waited for what seemed like an eternity, with no reprieve from the wounds and breaks of my body. And as I waited, the pain took on a new dimension and became literally suffocating. With so many broken ribs, each breath felt as if a huge Boa constrictor had wrapped around my chest and was slowly crushing the life out of me. I struggled to take what were at best shallow breaths, and the sense of having my breathing constricted only added to my cycle of pain and panic.

As far back as I could remember I had always looked inward for strength. I played through pain. I never surrendered. I never made apologies. I never showed weakness or let myself be vulnerable.

I don't think I had uttered the words, "I'm sorry" since I was 7 or 8 years old.

But when Alice entered the ICU, I felt my old armor shudder and almost crack. Tears flooded from me, and while some part of me wanted to shout out "I'm sorry," it was the paralyzing fear that had been consuming me that found words.

"I don't know if I am big enough to handle this," I whispered with great intensity, tears pouring down my cheeks.

Alice kissed my forehead with infinite tenderness and gently held my head in her hands. She told me she loved me and whispered that we would deal with this one moment at a time.

"What happened?" she asked, after a long silence.

As I whispered the details of the accident, I became even more aware of the reality of my situation, and a huge wave of grief and guilt convulsed through my body. I could see my freefalling fears and emotions reflected in Alice's face. I was shattered; not only my body, but my entire identity. Everything I had been, I was not now. The fearless, all-American athlete, father, healer, provider, husband, invincible hero, now lay crumpled, terrified, and absolutely powerless. What was left of me? What would that mean for our family?

"Jack," Alice whispered softly, "We are here for you. You *will* get through this."

She held her hand on mine, and while the physical pain still raged, I found a way to take a breath slowly. Lying still with Alice soothed me beyond words, and for those moments, I saw how my tenacious resistance to my injuries and everything that was going on in the ICU had only magnified my pain and terror. Alice's presence was the first comfort I had felt since those moments the medevac nurse had cared for me in the helicopter.

Those moments and the comfort they brought me passed in what seemed like a heartbeat. My battery of tests was nowhere near to being over and two orderlies wheeled me from the ICU, explaining to Alice that they would return me as quickly as they could. As they shuttled me downstairs to the dark and cold x-ray and MRI rooms, they talked to each other, sharing their evening plans and joking about a party they had attended. I was less significant to them than a pile of sheets they might be taking to the laundry room. They were pain free and carefree, and I envied them for it. I was enraged by their indifference to me. I was furious with myself for my sudden surge of self-pity, something I never wallowed in.

"You are lucky to be alive, a lucky man." I repeated to myself what so many of the doctors and technicians had told me.

And I *was* alive. I would see my sons grow up. Others would not be so lucky. As the orderlies continued their banter about their evening plans, I willed myself to push self-pity aside and quiet the cacophony that raged in my head. I made a vow on that gurney to take what was left of my life and live it as fully as I could. I tried to focus beyond the pain to promise myself to learn whatever lessons this experience imposed on me.

But, as quickly as I had embraced those thoughts, my chatty orderlies distractedly hit the wall with the gurney. With the jolt, I saw a flash of white light and screamed with an intensity that must have been heard throughout the floor. I gritted my teeth consumed only with thoughts of the pain and the bitter resentment that came with it.

All I wanted was to be still, to be untouched. But for the next several hours there was nothing but relentless movement. I was wheeled, lifted, rolled, turned, and with every x-ray. MRI, and CAT scan, I was ironically asked to remain as still as I could. The pains intensity blew my mind, and I passed out several times during the process. And after every image that was taken and each film that was analyzed, I was moved again, and wheeled to the next test. I had screamed and moaned to the point that my throat was dry and raw. I had cried so much my eyes were swollen.

Slowly in that maze of motion, scans and diagnostics, information trickled in, and the doctors finally pieced together the full extent of my injuries, which read like a laundry list.

The bulk of the impact had been absorbed in my pelvis, sending an explosive wave up my spine, ribs, scapula, shoulder and out my right arm and side. I had a crack in the humeral head of my femur. The left side of my pelvis was pulverized; no bone fragment remained larger than 1/8th of an inch. My femur had burst through my pelvis and protruded from my butt. Six vertebras were fractured, three were broken. Had it not been for the dense muscle mass along my spine, the spinal cord would have been cut or severed rather than simply parts of vertebras fractured and broken off.

Eight of my ribs were broken and on my right side I had a broken scapula, broken shoulder, and a compound fracture of my elbow. My right hand was broken, and I had a crushed brachial plexus, the large bundle of nerves beneath my right shoulder blade which allowed movement for my right arm and shoulder.

But despite the dramatic lacerations to my scalp, I had no injury to my brain. None of my internal organs were severely injured. And to the awed disbelief of many of the doctors, I had suffered no paralysis.

"Looks like you will walk again," was how one doctor so encouragingly reported it.

I must have been quite a sight for Alice and our two dear friends, Alycia and Lorraine, who were waiting for me back at the ICU. It had been over ten hours since the fall, and no one had bothered to clean me up. In addition to the tubes running into my arms, my grimaces, moans, and contortions from the pain, and my obvious exhaustion, my hair and face were still caked with a gruesome combination of tears, leaves, dirt and blood.

"I am so relieved." Alice had heard my diagnosis.

"There was so much blood," she said, "I was scared over everything else how badly your head was injured."

Lorraine, who looked as if she hadn't breathed in since she found me by the deck, looked nearly as shaken as I felt.

"I was so scared," she stared, and took in a few breaths before she could continue. "I am so happy they say you will walk again. When I saw you, I didn't think you would even make it to the hospital." Their time with me was brief, but their compassion and empathy meant everything to me.

At the doctor's urging, Alycia and Lorraine said their good-byes. I had fallen at around 8:30 that morning. As they left the room, it was now close to 9:00p.m., and other than a light sedative, I had still not received anything for the pain. The doctors were anxious to settle me down and prepare me for the night.

Alice still sat by my side.

"I want to stay with you." There were tears in her eyes now.

Part of me couldn't bear for her to leave, but so much of me was consumed in a vortex of violence and pain and the incessant catastrophic scenarios that were playing in my mind, that an almost primordial instinct drove me to retreat alone to a cave and wrestle with my suffering entirely by myself. I was desperate to gain some measure of control.

"The boys need you." I said. They had been picked up from school and taken to a friend's home. We both knew how frightened they had to be and the pain and worry they would feel without one of us there to reassure them.

"I know," she said, "but I also don't feel like I can leave you here alone."

"Seeing the pain I'm causing you and the boys is only making it more difficult for me to manage this insufferable agony. Go tell them I'm talking and I'll be OK."

I had resurrected myself somewhat with Alice by my side. But as she reluctantly left my room, all of the pains and fears flooded back to their full intensity. I couldn't quiet the rising pain or stem the flood of thoughts that a lifetime of dreams and independence had been snuffed out of me. I was a ruin.

Darkness had fallen outside, and I was alone with all of these demons. I began to think I would lose my mind.

CHAPTER 4
Dreams and Nightmares

They started a morphine drip the moment Alice left. They placed a "booster" in my left hand, which enabled me to increase the morphine dosage if I needed it. While it took some of the bite from the pain, the drip essentially had no effect on me at all. The adrenaline that coursed through my veins still overrode most of the effects of the morphine, and I lay in bed wide awake, still wracked in pain with my imagination running unchecked, reluctant to boost the drip. And amplifying all my fears were the sounds that emerged from the trauma ward as the night progressed.

Hell, as it turned out, can be a shared space.

As I lay there, I became aware of the tormented cries of the other trauma patients that began to increase in intensity as the hours wore on. Darkness. Pain. Loneliness. Fear. I could hear it in every voice. But eclipsing all others were the cries that came from the bed nearest to mine. From the woman in that bed came a cry so heartbroken, so forsaken, so heavy with what sounded like a lifetime of grief, that it frightened me. After 25 years of having a psychotherapy practice, I thought I knew all the sounds a human being could make. But the cries I heard that night had me wishing I could put my hands to my ears to shut it out.

She wept in the darkness and literally howled in her despair. I had heard some of the staff whispering earlier that she had tried to commit suicide by hurling herself into the Hudson River from the highest point of the Tappan Zee Bridge. But instead of killing herself, she had severed her spinal cord and lay paralyzed from her neck down. Her ear splitting screams sent ripples of unrest and sorrow from our room across the entire floor. The sounds were heart wrenching feral cries for help and relief. Her anguished shrieks haunted me throughout the night. I boosted my drip and then finally drifted in and out of very brief periods of opiate-induced sleep.

At one point she jolted me from a troubled sleep by a scream for God's mercy, a scream which faded into an endless stream of sobbing. As I listened, still burning in my own pain, I prayed for us both. Trying to escape whatever torment had driven her over that bridge, she had become more trapped and pained than ever. Her pleading reminded me of my own broken state, and I wondered if either of us could find the courage to confront what life now demanded of us.

The night was endless. Toward dawn I was ripped from sleep by yet another horrific scream. It was my own. I had been dreaming.

I was in a jungle, trapped in a crib from which I couldn't move or escape.

Tigers circled me. I screamed for help, my own voice echoing back to me through the jungle.

The tigers circled closer, growling, their predatory sounds terrifying. I could smell them, sense their hunger. I was frozen with fear and panic.

Then I heard and felt the ground shake and a huge elephant thundered out from the trees. The enormous elephant trumpeted loudly scattering the tigers, then reached down with its trunk and put me, crib and all, on its back.

Heart pounding, eyes now wide open, sweat pouring from my body, I struggled to wake fully and pull myself out of my opiate haze.

It took me several moments to even realize where I was. I looked around the room and slowly, regrettably, realized where and why. And as I awoke, pain almost immediately coursed throughout my body, triggering an avalanche of fear and dread. With the images of the dream still fresh in my mind, I tried hard to focus on breathing and not let the pain and fear completely overtake me. I clung to the sounds, smells, and images of the jungle.

For more than a decade in my own Jungian analysis, and even longer in my private practice, I respected the sacred, transforming power of dreams. I knew that in the ocean of my unconscious, dreams had always been fashioned and sent like transformative and restorative waves to the shores of my personal consciousness. Their images had always enriched me and had brought meaning and growth. They were healing images sent from the very core of my soul.

With my forehead bathed in a cold sweat and my heart still racing, I tried to check my physical discomfort and replay the dream before it dissipated into nothingness under the light of my being awake. Remembering a dream could be like painting a picture out of mist, and I closed my eyes and concentrated on reliving those moments in the crib and the messages that they brought.

With my eyes shut, I revisited the jungle scene. I saw clearly that in my pain and with my injuries, I lay as helpless in that hospital bed as any infant in his crib. And circling and threatening to devour me with the same horrific intensity as those tigers, was my own fear, panic and pain. But the heart of the dream beat for me in the presence and action of the elephant. From riding elephants many years ago when I was in India, I knew just how tremendous and awesome a force they were. They dwarfed any image of me I could ever conjure up and had instilled in me an immeasurable sense of strength and safety.

As I replayed the images in my head and relived the force of the charging elephant, I realized it had been an embodiment of what had transcended and sustained me in every way. It was the Presence from the ravine. It had rescued me and carried me up that impossible climb to the house. It was the compassion of the medevac nurse. It was the love of Alice, my boys, the policemen, nurses, Alycia and Lorraine. Without it and all of them, I would be devoured in darkness and the abyss of terror and pain that now defined my life.

I was overwhelmed with gratitude, and the image of my rescue soothed my broken heart and body. It restored my sense of hope and guided me through the night. My pain had been matched and overshadowed by the sense of love I experienced. Somehow, in my fall, I had pierced through a veil and been immersed in the Presence whose force, like the elephant in my dream, sustained me unconditionally.

Before that day, I thought I knew God. I was raised Irish-Catholic and traveled and lived in the Middle and Far East. I met priests, sheiks, yogis, shamans, and holy men and women. I'd felt touched and uplifted in their presence. But I had never felt the awesome power of Spirit as I had in the ravine. It was almost as if God remained unconscious to me until I became unconscious to my own personality and a part of the sea of Oneness I had experienced.

I lay in the ICU, the dream still vivid in my mind. The pain swirled but my profound sense that I had been lifted and carried to safety sustained me, and I recognized that there might be a blessing inside my intense suffering. In that moment of clarity, I knew that staying present with that Presence was the only way that I would ever fully heal. I had to surrender to what was, totally. There were no partial surrenders, I had to accept unconditionally and with an open heart that my life as I had known it was over. Any thought that wasn't acceptance would only increase the pain and terror.

In the days that followed, it was impossible for me to maintain that sense of clarity. As it had since the ravine, my awareness of the Presence ebbed and flowed. I was awakening by degrees, in short concentrated bursts. In the next couple of days, my condition had stabilized and the doctors were preparing to operate to set the breaks in my arm and pelvis. My awareness of opening to the pain and stop resisting was clouded by the surgeries and the constant drive by the doctors to shut off the pain with drugs. Managing the pain, they explained, was the first part of the healing process. So, I languished in bed connected to a morphine drip that ushered me into what I first blissfully looked on as the "forgetting room." It was a delicious place, far, far away from the relentless pain. Step out of and away from any suffering. Stop the pain. Their siren song was almost impossible to ignore.

But even in my drugged state, I sensed that the morphine, while it numbed me out, also robbed me of my greatest ally, my awareness and capacity to choose; to be present. It took me days to fully realize that "healing" was not something that would come from the hospital. It was something I would have to achieve from a source deep within myself.

When people came to visit in those first days, I tried to move up through the pain and morphine haze, yet I never completely surfaced. But on the third day, Alice came with Brendan. It would mark the first time I had seen either of my children since the accident. Shackled to the morphine drip, I lay motionless beneath the white sheet that covered all but my face. I have no idea how long the two of them stood there before I opened my eyes. Alice was next to Brendan, her arm around his shoulder. When I looked at him, nothing could have prepared me or Brendan for the look each of us found in the other's expression. I could see in his face and eyes that his innocence was violently torn away. He saw helplessness and pain. I watched a kaleidoscope of emotion pass across his face and felt my heart breaking as I saw the fear and disbelief that radiated from his eyes. I could tell that life as he had known it was over. He saw it in me, and I saw it in him.

I had not only never shown Brendan or Devin any signs of weakness, I had never even suggested the possibility. They had seen me compete as a Triathlete, build, provide, coach, and even rescue a teenager from treacherous surf. To them, I had been a veritable superhero. But at that moment, I lay before him broken, completely vulnerable, and barely conscious above the haze of my medication. I tried desperately to recover some version of "dad" for him, but my words were swallowed under waves of emotion. From my very core, I felt an intense sense of guilt. I had nourished my son's innocence his entire life, and now I had destroyed it. I could see the fear, uncertainty, grief and even dread clouding his world that had been so carefree, joyful, playful, and imaginative. I had destroyed the one thing that was sacred in childhood, his innocence. It was the reason we lived in the forest and not in suburbia. I had lost my sense of security and innocence so early, I had been determined to preserve and protect my sons'.

I was crying again, something else he had never seen. I finally broke the silence between us as I choked out the words, "I love you Brendan."

I wondered if he would be able to forgive me or if he would harbor an unspoken anger. I wondered if we could ever talk about this grief-filled moment we now shared. I prayed he would not resent me.

Over the next couple of days, when I wasn't in the haze of the "forgetting room," the guilt I felt rekindled and fanned my fears. I found I couldn't stay connected to the Presence, and was back to resisting, once again suppressing any thoughts of surrendering. Between the pain and the morphine, I drifted between not thinking at all, to the suffocating panic of wondering what I would become and how I was going to survive

Rebuilding my pelvis was the most intricate and worrisome procedure my doctors had to face.

"There's not much left to work with," was the portrait they had painted.

The surgery, which took place toward the end of my first week there, due to scheduling problems and other incoming emergencies, took over 15 hours. As they detailed for me later, they used wires, screws, mesh, plates, and even bone fragments from cadavers to put me back together again. But when I awoke in recovery, the optimistic accounts all labeled the surgery a success.

The next day, however, a new twist was added to my prognosis, as if the injuries I had already sustained weren't enough.

"You have the onset of pneumonia," the doctor said. "It's not serious, but to prevent it from getting worse, we are going to need to start a series of breathing exercises."

From the moment I had entered the hospital, I had learned to minimize my movements to the barest of essentials. Every motion hurt, and with so many broken ribs and fractured vertebra, that was especially true of breathing. So I had learned to take short shallow breaths, which had unfortunately led to the onset of the pneumonia. Now, in order to avoid a critical case of pneumonia, I was told I would need to breathe deeply. And with "logic" only possible in a hospital or Congress, they gave me narcotics to counter the new agony wrought by my breathing exercises, narcotics that had the minor side effect of – suppressing my respiratory system.

And so a new wave of pain began. Even with the drugs, tears crested my eyes as I expanded my lungs more fully in an effort to ward off the pneumonia. I tried to accept this new condition, to move into the pain, make room for it, and accommodate it mentally. I knew from my years as an athlete how to manage pain, but this was compounded on top of so much.

"What next," I thought, as I braced myself for every agonizing deep breath.

Crisis is opportunity. I had always been a firm advocate of that philosophy. But this crisis had developed too many layers and left me totally overwhelmed.

The doctor responsible for rebuilding my pelvis was Dr. Asprinio. He was about forty, well-tanned ,with a face and temperament that were open and inviting. He was the most likable of doctors who had operated on me. He stopped in to check on me one afternoon and carried with him what seemed to be a toy, four balls encased in plastic with a hose attached. He explained that I had to blow into the hose and ultimately try to raise all four balls.

It was "a game," he explained, that I needed to indulge in several times a day, not for the purpose of exasperating my pain, but to keep the pneumonia at bay. I put the tube to my mouth and blew for all I was worth. The pain would suggest that my lungs and ribs had exploded and that I may well have blown the roof off of the ICU unit. As I moaned and my ribs screamed, I opened my eyes to see one ball barely lifting off the plastic case. The other three were still.

He encouraged me to keep trying and felt I would have all the balls moving in no time. As for my pelvis, he let me know that he had done all he could, and that time and my body's ability to heal would determine what I would be able to do or not do in the future. I thanked him for his time, and kept my "toy" next to my left hand, the only part of my body I was able or allowed to move. Every fifteen minutes, whenever I was conscious, I blew. It was something to focus on, the only thing I actually felt I had any hope of gaining control over, making four plastic balls move on the strength of my breathing.

Friends and family continued to visit, but I felt less and less comforted by them. Aside from the relentless pain, I felt ashamed. I spent my life denying the state of helplessness and dependency that now defined my life. Like my father before me, I detested weakness and vulnerability, and now it was the only trait I could recognize in myself. At the time, I was sure it was all anyone else could see in me. I couldn't get four balls to stir in a plastic chamber. I couldn't pee without help. I couldn't bathe myself. I hadn't had a bowel movement since the accident, not that anyone would have been able to get a bedpan under my broken back anyway. Hell, I couldn't even feed myself. I didn't think I could sink any lower.

The night after my surgery I lay in a bit of a morphine haze as an aide fed me dinner. She not only had to cut the beef for me, but she needed to feed me each individual bite, like an infant in a highchair. My throat was dry from the surgery and morphine drip, and when I swallowed, one of the bites I had just taken got lodged in my throat.

I couldn't breathe. I couldn't call out. I wasn't able to gesture. The aide, who was busy cutting up my meal didn't notice a thing.

She just thoughtlessly placed the next bite in my mouth, oblivious to my then bulging eyes and beet red face. I clenched my teeth and tried to signal with my one good hand for water. She looked at me angrily mistaking my motions as some tantrum and my dissatisfaction with the meal. She threw down the fork and stormed out of the room.

I laid back and went into spasms, finally generating enough force to cough up the lodged and nearly fatal cut of beef. It was five or ten minutes before the aide returned with the head nurse. I started to complain, but the nurse talked me down like I was a troublesome child.

"We don't tolerate behavior like this," the nurse told me, sternly. "If you are going to be difficult, there will be repercussions. Don't forget, I am in charge of replacing your morphine." She ignored my protests, dismissing me with a flick of her hand. Lying there, helpless and dependent, I could only feel like the troublesome child they had felt I was.

They left and never returned to replace the morphine.

Fifteen hours of surgery, and soon there would be nothing for the pain. Yet at that point, I had been humiliated to such an extent, that I didn't care. I would take physical pain over their abuse and my need to depend on them to make it through the night. I made the decision then and there not to go back on morphine or any other drug that altered my consciousness, though I still thought, at the time, that the nurses would return to replenish my morphine drip. And while I had made the decision to stay off the drip, I never would have opted to do it all at once. I would have preferred to do it gradually, but the act of violence those nurses caused me gave me no choice.

The pain through the night had been beyond anything I could have imagined. I passed out several times during the course of the night. At 5:15a.m., when the first nurse of the day came by to take my vital signs, I was awake, in agony, and in a rage. There were no dreams, no medicated haze, just the clarity of my pain, humiliation, and rage.

"At 1:15 this morning, that morphine drip ended," I pointed at the empty bag. "Not a single person looked in on me all night. I know. I never slept." I demanded to see the hospital administrator and the nursing supervisor.

I had simmered all night, the intensity of my rage building exponentially as the morphine wore off. I may have been physically helpless, but that did not justify indifference or abuse. My mental facilities may have been hindered by the medication and my voice may have been weakened to a whisper, but I was still a voice, with coherent thoughts, feelings, and a lifetime of experience to separate me from a temperamental infant.

The supervisor was extremely apologetic and assured me she would personally instigate an investigation about the night nurse's behavior. She asked the attending nurse to immediately administer a new bag of morphine.

"No more morphine," I said flatly. I firmly refused their insistence that they restart the drip.

"We need to treat the pain. We have to get this drip going again if you are going to heal."

"No." I refused the medication unequivocally. I had survived the night without it, and I would survive moving forward without it.

I had been awake all night and again battled the pain that rose steadily as the morphine was depleted. But as it faded, I became more acutely aware. I felt intense shame and humiliation that drew me back and started to unravel memories of my infancy. My anger found a way through the haze. I drifted into and out of my intense memories of the Presence and clung to the image of the elephant that had lifted me above the ravenous tigers.

Through all of the complexity and cacophony of those emotions and thoughts, my struggles between anger, surrender, resistance, and the unconditional love I had experienced in the ravine, one truth became ultimately clear. If I were to truly heal, the process would need to extend well beyond my body.

I would need to be entirely present.

They moved me to another floor. My rage gradually ebbed to anger, and through the pain my thoughts begin to turn from fear to understanding how I might truly heal.

That night I blew into the plastic container and saw three of the four balls rise freely into the air.

CHAPTER 5

The Sacrificial Altar

When I was 21, I graduated from military college. One of my closest friends was a second lieutenant heading off for Vietnam. I wasn't. I was not commissioned due to injuries I received playing college football. With a couple of months ahead of us before he was called into active duty, Chuck and I took off to Europe, bought an old beat-up VW Camper in Munich, and toured. When our time together came to a close at the end of that summer, and Chuck had to report for active duty, we made a pact. In what made perfect sense at the time, he and I agreed to meet in Vietnam. He would fly, courtesy of the United States Military. I, on the other hand, set off on an overland trek that began in Italy and took me through Greece, Turkey, Iran, Afghanistan, Pakistan, Nepal and India. It wasn't a plush and pampered overseas tour, booked courtesy of a Frommer's handbook and a Eurail Pass with funding from mom and dad. It was unplanned, unsanctioned, seat-of-the-pants, off-road, and off the grid. It never occurred to me at the time how insane attempting that journey might be. I just did it.

By foot, horse, bus, train, logging truck, and even elephant, I made my way to the Far East for what would end up being almost a year. I was alone. I neither spoke nor understood any foreign language. Yet, there wasn't a foreign city, a mountain path, an ancient village or even an armed and hostile Afghani tribe that I couldn't find my way around or through. I worked the black market. I lived cheaply. I survived and thrived.

I was invincible and fearless.

Images of that journey flashed in my head as I looked over my broken body the day after surgery. Forget trekking for days in the Himalayas or confronting an armed Afghani, I couldn't even get out of bed. I couldn't wash my own body. I needed a bedpan and a nurse to relive myself. I needed someone to cut my food in order to eat. I lay smoldering in the pain of the previous day's surgery, my anger festering each time I thought about the violence of the nurses who had brutally left me without morphine.

"What more do You want of me?" I thought.

"Did You save me only to torment me? Was it your hand in removing the morphine?"

And then that afternoon, as if in answer to my question, a series of welts started to appear on my back and legs. These large raised red blisters hurt like hell and itched incessantly. Having almost no mobility, scratching them was nearly impossible.

"What next?" I demanded. "What else?"

Within two days, they had blanketed my entire body. They were in my mouth, on my ears, between my fingers. There wasn't a millimeter of my skin outside of my feet, that wasn't on fire. I couldn't sleep, and the fingernails of my left hand were black from clawing at myself at the few places I could actually reach. My pain had become multidimensional, broken bones on the inside, hives on the outside. There was no relief, no sense of safety.

"Please GOD, stop this." Beaten helpless by pain, rage, fear and sorrow, I pleaded for relief or understanding. But my prayers went unanswered. God, I thought, had abandoned me, again.

A battle raged within me.

I fought against the pain and humiliation.

I cursed and railed at God and the Universe.

And in moments of exhaustion when the fear abated, I yielded, and then started the whole cycle again.

And in this cycle of struggle, rage, and surrender, the layers of my personality began to unravel. Everything that had been me was being peeled away and exposed. My pain, humiliation, and complete vulnerability were like beacons shedding light into the dark and forgotten recesses of my subconscious, churning up vivid memories and hurtling me backwards through years of development. The powerful, armored, controlled man that I had become was slowly burning away, leaving the angry adolescent to re-experience his humiliation, and the little boy to express his isolation and longing. The heroic and self-sufficient man, the confident and fearless young adult, the delinquent adolescent, the temperamental and hyperactive boy – each was experienced, engaged, and sacrificed at my altar of suffering.

The sensible option was to continue to yield to the inevitable, but old warriors die slowly – fighting, yielding, struggling in humiliation and defeat, only to fight and then yield again. Ultimately, all that was left was the innocent child, unprotected, completely helpless and vulnerable.

Primary issues of safety, security, trust and love had opened up scars from long ago that had been hidden by time and hardened by life. I knew from many years of clinical practice that all of our experiences in life are organized, and stored in the unconscious until those unresolved moments can once again be realized and resolved in daily life. My day had come, and my psyche, like a volcano, was sending up from my depths earlier hardened parts of me, softened by my ongoing suffering.

Pain. Rage. Humiliation. Fear. Frustration. Surrender. As the hives burned across my body, I cycled through all those emotions and reactions. I felt at some deep level that when I yielded to my suffering and accepted my vulnerability, I felt in it, the Presence, the Beloved as I had come to call it, sustaining me. But it was so hard to hold onto it. During the day especially, it was impossible to concentrate, calm and focus my mind. There was too much going on around me. I preferred the night, when there were fewer prying eyes and hands. I wanted to be left alone.

As a child I learned to let the night and its sounds soothe me as I often stared out my window. Although I now had a roommate, I had the bed by the window. I looked to the stars, and once again felt the darkness and stillness quiet me. The night itself became like a prayer, and in it I felt compassion not just for others, but for myself. I didn't know the meaning of all of my suffering, but I knew I had to accept it and accept the person I had become.

"This was it," I thought. "This is my life." I had to trust in myself and let go into the fear, into the unknown. I had to choose it moment to moment. Staying in the here and now, with my heart open, I yielded and my prayers manifested themselves as tears, as the Beloved flowed within me and through me, lifting me again to safety as it had in the ravine and in my dream.

I thought of all of the patients on that surgical floor and listened to their cries and sobs echo through the dimly lit hallways. So many of us were being stretched to our limits and reshaped by our suffering. My instincts were to find a foothold, cling to something that could pull me from the torrent of fear and pain. But there was nothing in that room or those halls to cling to and like a drowning man, the more I struggled, the more rapidly I sank. So on that floor and in that sea of vulnerability, I breathed deeply and let go, surrendering, cast adrift in my own fear and torment. But rather than being pulled under, it was in those moments that I was buoyed by the Beloved and my pains were eased.

My roommate's moaning erupted into screams. A nurse rushed into the room and closed the curtain that was laughably meant to somehow separate the two of us. It may as well have been made of gauze or even air for all the good it did. His screams poured over me, and I could hear his every movement in the bed, every gasp for air, every word and movement of the doctor and nurse that tried to sooth him.

"Breathe," I said as I looked out the window, focused on the stars, trying to stay open to this new onslaught of suffering. I felt my own pain, and embraced the sorrow I felt for my roommate and myself. As I opened myself to those moments, I felt a great

surge of kindness and an unfathomable sense of my own humanness.

———————

"How are you doing Jack?" Dr. Asprinio was by my bedside
bright and early. His obvious compassion was always very soothing
to me. I wished his energies were more common amongst the staff
in the ICU.

How was I doing? It was hard to know where to start. Sleepless, broken, covered with hives, no bowel movement since I had
arrived, the screams of my roommate still reverberating in my soul.
Other than that, Mrs. Lincoln, how was the show?

"Dr. Asprinio," I started, hardly recognizing my own voice,
raspy with sleeplessness, a sense of desperation, and hives boiling
in my mouth and throat.

"These hives are pushing me off the edge. They're everywhere.
I'm telling you, you have to help me." I was surprised at the despair
I heard in my own voice.

"Jack, your pelvis was so pulverized that rebuilding it took a great
deal of hardware. I just hope your body isn't rejecting it." He paused.

"You hang in there. I'll give the chief of dermatology a call and
get him to come by and see you. We'll figure this out."

Trembling and perspiring, all I could say was, "Thank you."

With the morning, I had cycled back to struggling, the pain
and discomfort of the hives magnifying my fears. But I noticed that
Dr. Asprinio's words had calmed me. In his presence, my breathing had become softer and deeper. His empathy and concern had
allowed me to regain some compassion for myself.

My healing fed on that energy.

Conversely, the Chief of Dermatology strode into my room
later that afternoon. He seemed annoyed as he announced himself.

"Mr. Weafer, I'm Dr. Clark, Chief of Dermatology. Dr. Asprinio
wanted me to look in on you."

He was curt, distracted, and seemingly a little put out that Dr. Asprinio had asked him to make an unscheduled stop. He stared at me as if waiting for me to point out what was wrong. He had nothing to say about the welts. He had nothing to say about my obvious distress. He basically had nothing to say.

"Thanks for seeing me, Dr. Clark." I tried to control the anger boiling up inside me.

"I've been trapped inside a blistered mass of burning welts for two fucking days. If I could get out of this bed, I'd get a gun and put it to my head. I'm literally clawing my skin off, and there is still no relief." I felt like I was begging, and I felt even more humiliated by having to explain what I felt should have been obvious.

Dr. Clark continued staring.

Every cell in my brain blazed as I glared at him.

"Sorry," I tried hard to calm down.

"I've been able to distract myself or somehow numb myself from pain, but this is over the top. There's no escape!"

Dr. Clark was apparently a man of few words. I felt no sense of being cared for in his presence, only exposed and disconnected as he mechanically examined my upper body. It was hard to imagine anyone could be more disinterested. I was railing now and flung off the covers with my left hand.

"Look at this." I shouted. As a final plea to him and an affront to any sense of dignity I had left, I lay there balls to the wind. He stared down at my testicles which were red, blistered, and literally the size of grapefruits. He actually said something.

"You sure you're not allergic to any medications?" He asked me almost accusingly.

"I've never been allergic to anything in my life. NOTHING!" I was livid, and could feel every muscle in my body tighten.

He cocked his head, looking at me suspiciously, as if to gauge my mental status.

"I'll leave an order at the nurse's desk for an ointment for you." And then in a final show of empathy and compassion he added, "This is one of the worst allergic reactions I have ever seen. I'm doing rounds later on with a group of physicians doing their residence in dermatology. Do you mind if we stop by and have a look at you?"

When he left, I found my breathing was shallow and tight and my anger at the boiling point. There was nothing about that encounter I could associate with healing. I lay back feeling resentment at feeling so utterly needy, and exhausted at the roller coaster of emotions that buffeted me. I was losing myself and becoming less and less able to recognize who I was with all of my armor stripped away.

Naturally Dr. Clark returned with the residents long before any ointment arrived. And rather than coating me with a balm that would sooth the blisters, they covered me with impersonal stares. They gawked. In their silent but wide-eyed reaction to my blistered flesh, they diminished me even more, reducing me to a collection of freakish symptoms, wounds and welts. Not one of them saw a man. Certainly no one saw me.

"I'll give the dispensary a call and get that ointment for you," and Dr. Clark and his entourage were gone. No new diagnosis. No words of encouragement. No support.

Twenty minutes later, a tube of ointment the size of my index finger arrived, just enough to barely cover my ears and my grapefruit.

"Your father is coming to visit."

I had fallen asleep, enraged and exhausted after the degrading encounter with Dr. Clark and his flock. The nurse had been standing near me when I awoke and relayed the message from Alice about my father.

I hadn't seen him since the fall and didn't want him to see me this way. Raw, exposed, weak and helpless was unfamiliar ground for either of us. The "Jack" we had known was unrecognizable, lying feebly in a hospital bed without a shred of dignity. Seeing dad would be too intense, especially given how agitated I felt following my humiliating encounter with Dr. Clark and his pack of residents.

I just wanted to disappear.

"I personally went down to the dispensary," the nurse added, "and I told them how ridiculous one tube of ointment was for someone whose whole body was one massive welt."

"They had six tubes. They gave me four" She said.

And with that, in what was the first relief I had had in days, she started gently spreading the ointment over my blistered body.

The rawness of my vulnerability amplified every stimulus to my mind and body. Dr. Clark's apathy and indifference hit me with such force and intensity that it elicited what seemed even in my own mind to be a disproportionate rage. But that same sensitivity made me equally aware of this nurse's compassion. Her act of kindness, her care, and her willingness to connect with me filled me with an intense sense of gratitude and compassion. Tears of appreciation rolled down my face. In that moment I again clearly realized how the hidden treasures that seek to be rediscovered in life can be found in the experience and expression of suffering. We simply need to open ourselves to them.

The four tubes of ointment covered a little less than half of me. It afforded me some relief physically, but it was the nurse's kindness that truly healed. I was still flailing in a confused sea of emotion, gentleness and fierceness alternately coursing through me. But in the wake of her care, I felt more accepting of myself and my condition.

My anxiety waned. I began to look forward to my father's visit.

———●———

A show of emotion was never high on my father's list of positive attributes. As an Irish- Catholic, he was steeped in the traditions of discipline and hard work as the solitary requirements for prosperity. As a soldier, highly decorated for service in the Pacific Theater in WWII, he had internalized unimaginable traumas and ran his family and business with the same rigor, precision, and toughness the military had bred in him. Without a father of his own (he was three when his father died from the influenza epidemic in 1921), his role model for a healthy father-son relationship was the army. Intimacy, sensitivity, and overt expressions of love were not guiding principles for soldiers. On the contrary, they signaled weakness, laziness, and, as the Parochial schools in those days were quick to point out, "willfulness."

I was born in 1947, and as the years progressed, it became obvious that I didn't fit my father's mold. I was sensitive, imaginative, somewhat hyperactive, and on top of everything else, had an undiagnosed learning disability. At home, if I showed emotion or cried, I was a "sissy," or a "crybaby."

"I'll give you something to cry about," was a phrase I had heard often.

And at school, I was labeled "willful." And willful kids needed to have their wills broken before they could be taught.

Since my father only associated emotions with shame, we drifted apart, our differences hardening after we moved every few years, from Boston to Philadelphia, to Baltimore, to Pittsburg. In the shadow of my unknown learning disorder, and in a brand new Catholic school, nuns humiliated me in class. My seventh grade teacher would emphasize her label of me as "stupid" by boxing both ears with erasers. And without the openness and intimacy of a mother or father who could understand my fear, unhappiness, and shame, my armor continued to harden and form. I got tough, and then tougher. I constantly fought with other kids. I pulled hateful pranks on abusive teachers. I became a petty thief. My adolescent rage hit a pinnacle just before we moved from Pittsburg to Scituate, MA. A "friend" had given me up for stealing several cars. After being marched through school in handcuffs, I will never forget the officer tipping my head sideways and down as I entered the squad car and looking back at what seemed to me the entire school witnessing my humiliating arrest.

I straightened out, but never softened. Strong. Self-reliant. Unapologetic. In those ways in particular, my father and I had become very much alike. As I lay there, reflecting on our years together, it occurred to me that I had only seen him cry once. Dad and I went to a hospital to visit his mother who was dying. I was sent out of the room just before she died. He came out a few moments later, walked into a telephone booth, closed the door and cried. I was 20 years old. As I watched him, I wondered if it would take the death of a loved one for me to cry.

"Jack, your dad and Alycia left here about a half hour ago. They should be there soon. I have to take the kids to soccer, but we will be in tomorrow."

I thanked Alice for calling, and I found myself getting tense and anxious again. I was trying hard to gather my strength and recreate some semblance of the Jack my father knew from the heap of bones, welts, and pain that lay in that hospital bed.

And then, dad and Alycia stepped into the room. In that first instant, his gaze seemed to completely encompass the horrific state I was in. His dark brown eyes actually filled with tears. He looked at me, speechless. I could see his concern and pained reaction to my ruined state etched clearly on his face and in his eyes. As he walked towards me, he continued to read my face with judicious solemnity. I watched his eyes continue to patch together information from the bits and pieces of me that were exposed.

The pain in his eyes pierced my heart like lightning striking a tree at its roots and running all the way up to its crown. We looked deep into each other's' eyes. His shoulders softened. There was no judgment, only acceptance.

Dad was nearly eighty. He stood beside me, steadying himself with his left hand on the bed's guardrail, his lustrous white hair still had just the faintest hint of red. His mouth relaxed a bit before he said.

"How are you doing son?" There was a closeness in his question that I had never felt before.

My throat suddenly hurt as I choked up and said. "I'm glad to still be here."

"Is there any part of your body that is not in pain?" my father asked.

"My feet," I said with a smile.

"For some reason they're the only parts of me not covered with those hellacious welts."

After a pause, Alycia spoke.

"Could we touch your feet?" she asked with the softest most comforting smile.

"OK," I said, letting go of my self-consciousness of being so helpless.

They each now stood at opposite sides of the foot of the bed. Tenderly they looked down at my feet. "I brought massage oil," she said.

And so they gave to me the only way they could, connecting through the one part of me not under siege. The stoic soldier, quietly crying, was comforting me without reservation, a father gently massaging the foot of his broken son.

I closed my eyes and surrendered completely to their compassion. I thought to myself how miraculous it was that in this troubled place, with its cold, pain filled rooms and empty space, there was still love, and how powerful that love could be.

For the first time I could remember, my father was with me in my pain and humiliation, rather than being the source of it. My old anger, blame, and guilt were now neutralized by our mutual suffering. Long buried emotions were unearthed by the healing fires of the moment. There was no posturing. My condition opened both of us to the sorrow that for so long had separated us, not only from each other, but equally from ourselves. Our wounded selves had surfaced, were finally heard, held, accepted, loved and embraced.

All my defenses were being burned away, and I was healing.

CHAPTER 6
Bittersweet Love

That night I slept for four consecutive hours, the longest stretch of uninterrupted sleep that I had enjoyed since my fall. The sun wasn't up yet, and in that predawn light, as I slowly awoke, I felt a dream slipping away, dissipating just beneath my awareness. Just before it scurried away into my subconscious, I had a vague notion that it involved my feet. And then the images of yesterday afternoon came back to me in full force. I thought about my father and the profound moments during which we had shared an openness and love unlike anything we had experienced together before.

But there was also a vague sense of anxiety within me. It took me a moment to trace, but as the morning light started to fill my room, I remembered that Alice and the boys would be coming to see me later that day. It would be the first time I had seen the three of them together, and the first time Devin had seen me since the accident.

Again I felt an intense sense of vulnerability, this time compounded by my worry about what my brokenness would mean for our family. This was no longer about how I would deal with my own helplessness, or how my father might view it. In the light of this day, Alice, Devin, and Brendan, the people I loved most dearly, the people most dependent on me, would see me for what

I had become. How would they see me? How would they manage the enormity of what had happened?

Part of me again wanted to disappear and not be seen. Another voice within me focused on the pain, the loss, the fear, and lashed out angrily at the unfairness of it all. As I had with my father, I tried to find ways to muster all of my strength and to recreate from the ashes a sense of the father and husband they knew. But in the turbulence of all of these thoughts, the strongest voice within me shepherded me toward keeping my heart open to the moment and accepting whatever sorrow, pain or fear we might feel. If we were to get through this crossroads and grow, I would have to be present, free of any resistance.

"Stay open. Stay present." I told myself. Surrender to the moment, whatever it might feel like, whatever it might bring.

"Hi Dad!" My heart skipped a beat as Devin greeted me. There wasn't a single sign of pain or worry in his face or voice.

"Hi Dev."

And there we were, all together, fully exposed to our labyrinth of familial suffering. Alice was cautious, Devin light as a feather, and Brendan was as he had been when he had visited several days earlier, tense, confused and withdrawn. I could immediately see in his face and posture that he was re-experiencing the feeling of grief and helplessness he'd felt during his first visit. The tension of his body language reminded me of his appearance just before he was going to compete in Tae Kwan Do. Having successfully competed in state and national tournaments, he knew how to manage both fear and pain. His fragility as a child was entwined within his protective, self-sufficient emotional structure.

"Dad, look!" Devin broke the silence.

"All the boys on the soccer team made pictures or cards for you. I did too! Here's mine!"

Devin had drawn a picture of himself with me waiting for the school bus kicking a soccer ball back and forth. The message was "Come home soon." The memory of waiting for the school bus and kicking a soccer ball back and forth brought me to tears.

Ignoring my tears, Devin charged ahead.

"This picture is from Bobby, this one is from Stephan, Kyle, Justin, ..." He took out the cards and paintings and one by one put them on my chest. Alice read the messages out loud. Brendan watched, taking it all in.

"So how did the game go on Sunday?" I already knew from Alice that Devin was upset about the outcome.

"We lost."

"What was the score?"

"6 to 1"

"Who got the goal?"

"Me."

"Well good for you Devin. You must have made yourself and the team proud."

"No!"

"No?" I said.

"We lost. We haven't ever lost. Not in three years."

"You and I talked about that and I told you that Division 1 was very competitive, that we would lose more than we won. Did you play as well as you could?"

"Yes."

"Well, that is all that matters. I'm proud of you."

"I saw the police cars and ambulance go by," Devin said.

"When?" I hadn't heard about any mishaps at the game.

"The day you fell. They went right by school. I saw them through the window. We all watched the helicopter in the parking lot."

And for a moment, time seemed to stop. In the turn of a sentence, bubbling to the surface with the unexpected spontaneity so wonderfully typical of an eight-year old boy, we were talking about the shattered elephant in the room. I wanted to reach out and hold him and Brendan, and shelter them all from a day that must have been so horribly frightening.

"Did that scare you?"

"No. I thought it was for someone else. Somebody I didn't know."

Devin came closer, and I gave him a hug with my good arm.

"I sure wish that ambulance had been for someone else, old buddy, but it was for me, and I guess we have to face it. We'll do the best we can. My operations went really well."

I had no map for this place we had come to as a family. Lying in that bed, weak and handicapped, I didn't see what kind of a father I could be anymore. As I held Devin and looked up toward Alice and Brendan, I sensed I had reached an ending but had no clue what a new beginning would look like. I was awash with guilt seeing how much pain I had caused them. But in that pain, I also felt an overwhelming sense of love. While I couldn't tell you exactly what a new beginning meant for our family, I knew it would rise from that love.

"We've got another game next week," Devin said.

And just like that, we were back to soccer and a myriad of updates about school.

What a road our family had traveled. From the moment Brendan had been born, I felt the euphoric richness of being a father, a richness only intensified with the birth of Devin several years later. They had engaged the child in me and helped me to understand and overcome a sense of incompleteness I had carried from my childhood. Brendan and Devin always brought me back in touch with my boyhood self. We played together. We explored the great outdoors. We learned. And throughout it all, they healed those incomplete parts of me, and nurtured the child within me that had for so long struggled to earn the approval of his warrior father.

They made me whole, and fatherhood became a cornerstone of my life.

"Visiting hours" weren't hours at all. And while I longed to remain with them, my time with any visitors was strictly limited. It seemed like no time had passed before the three of them were gently kissing me good night and good-bye.

"OK Dad. See ya." Brendan hadn't been able to say much more than that. I could see the hurt and hesitation in his eyes, a shadow that I had cast.

"Good night," I said, with the closest thing to a smile I could muster. It was so hard to give him the space I knew he needed.

I said good-bye with a heavy heart and with tears blurring my vision and choking my words. I made no pretense of being strong and let myself swell with the longing I felt for their love. And then they were gone.

I lay helpless in that bed, separated from everyone I loved, and everything I had been. I turned off my light, and I wept. Through the window, I watched the moon race in and out of the clouds, casting ghostly shadows on the helipad in the distance. I remembered falling, the ravine and that vision I had of my boys shouting "NO," finding me lifeless on the rocks below the deck. My love for them had drawn me back to life. And as I lay there in the pain of broken bones, surgery, hives, and the guilt that overwhelmed me, they were drawing me back to life again.

Clawed by pain.

Carried by love.

I couldn't see my way out of that jungle of opposing forces, but I knew that in being open to both, I would heal. I vowed from the love I felt for my family, that I would stay open, that I would heal, and that I would return to them a father more complete and present than they had ever known.

CHAPTER 7
Moving Walls

"You built a wall." Alice was smiling, but it was a nervous and tense smile.

When Brendan was born, I remembered the instantaneous bond I had felt from the moment he entered the world. All was right with the universe. I had Alice, a son, and could not have imagined any greater sense of joy and happiness. If you had asked me, I would have told you I had never been more present or connected to the moment and to life.

It took me a few moments to remember what Alice was talking about.

"You were laying that stone wall in the property. You would come into the house blissfully covered in sweat and dirt, make sure we were OK and that we had everything we needed, and then back out you went."

"Do you remember our wedding day?" she asked, with a definite edge.

"Of course I do." I said, my anxiety rising the more I sensed Alice's anger.

"At 8:30 in the morning you were outside clearing the brush behind the house with a chain saw. All those people coming at 1:00 and you're outside clearing the forest."

She, of course, was right. I had completely forgotten about the wall and the morning of our wedding. The intensity of both of those days was a bit overwhelming. I didn't know what to do with all that energy – certainly not talk about it. So on the day of our wedding I cleared brush to clear my head. On the day Alice and Brendan came home from the hospital, I was overflowing with joy. I looked at her, that miracle she held in her arms – my son – and I launched into a project.

I went outside, lifted stones, and started building a wall.

"I loved you and Brendan and those days were more meaningful than you could imagine," I said, defensively.

"I know you did the best you could. I know it was hard for you to take everything in."

My love for Alice and our love for each other had sustained me during those interminable days in the hospital. In fact, the longer the pain seemed to devour me, the brighter my sense of love burned from within. As we talked about those first days with Brendan, I thought how the wear and tear of our daily lives had cheated us from the fullness of the love we had shared in those early days of our relationship. It was all still there, just muted by the myriad responsibilities of life, kids, work, bills, school, soccer and everything else that comes with parenting and family life.

But in talking about the boys, their feelings, and all that had happened and was happening, Alice was opening her heart. She was in pain, and she was angry. I could see it in her face and eyes. The intensity of her anguish was discomforting, so I listened quietly. And for perhaps the first time in our lives, I was able to hear her in a way I never had before, and not all of it was easy to "hear."

"Your falling shook me to the core, Jack." She took a breath as the tears began to run down her cheeks. "You could have been killed, or paralyzed, or suffered some unimaginable brain injury. I've asked you not to do things like that when I wasn't home, but God Jack, you can be so single-minded." Her anger was palpable.

Alice put her hand lightly on my chest. It was a gesture that may have relieved her anger, but it compounded my guilt.

"I can see how much you're suffering. I can't imagine how much pain you are in, but the boys and I are suffering too. I'm sorry if I sound angry. I don't mean to be. I'm really just so very sad."

We were both crying.

"I know how much you love the land and the joy you get in designing and building, but this terrible fall made me raw to the fact of how often I feel shut out and excluded from your bigger-than-life presence. Too many times I feel like I take a back seat to your work, projects or dreams."

As Alice opened her heart to me, part of me wanted to say "stop," and "not now," but her suffering was alive and present, and I struggled to open my heart and my ears.

"I knew that someday something like this was going to happen. So did your brother and your friends. Last year in the Outer Banks, you jumped into that hurricane driven surf and saved that teenager. As I was dialing 911, the only thing any of us could think of was that you were going to drown. Your brother Kevin still tells the stories today of the time you nearly killed yourself parachuting and how he thought you had vanished forever when you swam offshore and got lost in the fog. Both times he thought he would never see you alive again."

As Alice claimed her unacknowledged truth, my respect and love for her grew even more. Yet, what little that was left of my self-worth collapsed again in honoring her truth.

"I love you so much," I said. "I never set out that day to deny you when I climbed the tree. I was simply swept up in the moment. I never fully realized until now how my instinctive movement in life came at the expense of a deeper, more loving relationship with you."

"We came *so close* to losing you." Her anger was an exclamation point. "Nobody who has stopped by the house and looked off the deck, down into the ravine can believe you're still alive. Only you could have survived that fall." She took a breath and checked herself.

"I love you because you are who you are, but it is not always easy to live with you."

Whirling experiences of remorse, physical pain, as well as an endless loop of memories spun through me. Alice gently placed her head on my shoulder and whispered:

"Thank God you didn't die and that you're still with us. I don't know what the boys and I would do without you. I love you Jack, but something has to change."

I felt broken open again. For over 15 years I had loved Alice and she me, but I had imagined that I had some control over the love that flowed between us. I wanted to cry out for mercy – less pain not more. There was no control here and that continued to be the truth of the moment. We laid there in silence, her head on my shoulder, as I began to grapple with her suffering and the question of how or even if I could become a different man. But I was letting it all in, yielding to her words, her pain. Having already felt that I had lost just about everything, it was a brutal realization that our marriage was perched on a precarious slope. I had always asked so much of myself and of life, but now I realized that apparently I had of Alice as well. Now Alice was asking more of me. In the stillness between us, I felt waves of love and sadness, gratitude and guilt, fear and anger, churn within me. Trying to breathe, I struggled to remain present and find the compassion for my and her suffering.

Lying there I realized I had never known what enough was until I had gone beyond it, to "more than enough." I had pushed the envelope many times, and while the mistakes I'd made, and the consequences of poor judgment had been painful and difficult, never before had they reached this magnitude. I wanted to fix the pain that I caused. I wanted to stabilize our marriage in any way that I could. But at that moment, I realized there was nothing I could do but listen and let Alice know that I had heard her.

And then the words came that I hadn't spoken in what felt like a lifetime.

"I'm sorry," I said, and I felt it to the core of my being.

"I'm sorry that I've caused you and the boys to suffer like this. I love you all so much. It wasn't my intention when I climbed the tree to cause any pain, but I understand the impact that choice has had for all of us."

So we continued talking. I told Alice about my near death experience in the ravine, the angel of mercy in the helicopter, and moments since when I experienced what I called the Beloved. I tried to put into words how the accident had wakened in me an acceptance of my vulnerability, a longing for love and the preciousness of life.

"Every time the pain reached an absolutely intolerable point, that Presence held me and pulled me out of my body. I have never experienced a greater sense of peace, oneness and what I can only describe as love. I know that probably sounds odd coming from me."

"I saw you that night," Alice said. "It was terrifying to see you that way. I remember wondering how you could endure all those injuries and how you ever made it up the ravine to the deck."

"I didn't make it out of that ravine by myself. I couldn't have," I explained. "The Beloved worked through me. When the pain become too much, it lifted me from my body. Once I was back in my body, its energy moved through me, and I was able to claw my way up those rocks. I prayed for the pain to stop, but somehow being present and yielding to all those injuries enabled me to survive."

"You know me," I continued. "Since I was a pissed off teenager, I haven't been able to tolerate feeling weak, helpless, or dependent. Can you imagine a more agonizing situation for me, to be bedridden like this? But during those first few hours in the emergency room, I started to glimpse that fact that struggling made everything worse. When I tensed up and the fear took over, the pain became unbearable. When I surrendered to it, that Presence seemed to work through me and carry me."

From the depth of my heart I told her, "I can't explain it all, but I believe this experience is changing me and healing me in ways

I could never have foreseen and never would have chosen. It's as if parts of me long asleep are awakening, and I pray every day for you, the boys and for myself to find the courage to choose what's asked of me, moment to moment."

Alice sat next to me quietly for some time. I let her love, her fear, and her pain in with an open heart. And in facing and accepting her pain and mine, I felt a glimpse of hope and perhaps the energy for crafting a new person from the ruins of the man I once was.

She stood up and got ready to leave.

"You know," I said, "When I got back to the beach after that swim in the fog, I found Kevin running around on the beach going out of his mind looking for me beyond the waves. He was sure the sharks or the fog had taken me for good. When he saw me, he was so pissed off, he punched me in the stomach."

"So he tells us," Alice smiled.

"When the chute tangled and didn't open properly, and I sailed into the trees and nearly hit all those wires, Kevin was running across that field going out of his mind with worry. When he saw me standing by my chute without a bruise on my body, you know what he did?"

"Punched you in the stomach." Alice leaned forward and gave me a gentle kiss good night. It carried her love and her pain, just as Kevin's punch had.

"I love you," she said.

I spent every waking and sleeping hour in that hospital on my back. My legs were slightly separated by a wedge shaped cushion, my right arm in a brace suspended by wires. I was basically rigged not to move, which given the pain that even the slightest tremor caused was fine with me. The hives had subsided pretty quickly once they discovered I had been allergic to the medication designed to keep my body from rejecting all the parts they had used to repair my pelvis. But sleep in that claustrophobic position was sporadic at best, and as a consequence, no dreams reached me to guide me. And that night, in addition to the pain and general discomfort, my thoughts swirled with Alice's words and the memories of our lives that they had triggered.

"Something has to change." Long into the night I replayed Alice's words in my head. From the depths of my being I knew it already had. But where this change and journey were taking me, I still didn't know. I still cycled between worry, fear, and acceptance. I had lived life to the fullest, always risking and giving myself totally to life as I found it. But now I realized there had been a "counter dependent" quality to my existence – a slightly manic search for that "rush" that came with abandoning myself to the moment. It was almost as though I sought out potential trauma in order to master it. And now I was going to have to face the trauma I'd been both running from and towards – the trauma of my early boyhood, its fears, its shame, its humiliation and the dependency I felt in my need for other people.

Fight. Yield. I was alternately being assaulted or uplifted by the wrath or mercy of the gods. The physical and emotional cycle I was in was confusing, but from deep within me, terrible pain and shameful feelings stalked my body and mind like those tigers in my dream. Their fiery appetite insatiably devoured what was left of my heroic armor. They had become daily predators that slowly transformed what lingered of my pride, tearing and grinding it, leaving the child within me raw, exposed, and now unquestionably a part of my life.

It seems God had waited for a torn-open cry from that child within me before sending in celestial relief to mitigate the pain. It was melting away my armor and opening my heart. Hearing my physical and mental agony, the Beloved nourished me and quenched my suffering. Family and friends reinforced the effect by extending compassion, empathy and support. My interactions with them were now wet, intimate, intense and deep as the little boy inside was touched and soothed.

Late at night, alone, while all others were asleep, the pain and fear often overtook me. I would call out "why?"

The only reply was the pain's insistence that I yield fully to its teaching. It seemed to say, "Leave everything behind…this is the only way out. Let me be your companion and guide."

The next morning, I was jolted out of my troubled sleep by my brother Kevin.

"I thought you were dead!" He looked as white as a ghost and was angry.

"Five minutes ago I walked into the room you were in yesterday and the bed was empty and covered with blood! I ran to the nursing station in a panic. The nurse thought you had been moved to a different room. On the way here, I kept repeating to myself, the blood is not Jack's, he's alive!"

Kevin wore that same look on his face the times he had found me on the beach and after I had landed safely in the drop zone.

"You're not going to hit me, are you?"

I started to laugh even though it hurt. After a few moments of silence he started laughing too.

"I think a punch in the stomach at this point might do me in," I added.

Through the tears of laugher I could also feel a painful echo of the earlier times when I had scared Kevin half to death. He was taking my accident very hard.

"I feel like I've lost my life-long hero," he told me as he sat by my bed. "Seeing you like this has made me feel like I'm adrift at sea." He recalled for me how he had gotten the news, as if he was still absorbing it.

"When I drove up the driveway after work, the kids weren't outside playing, and San was standing there alone. I instantly knew she had bad news. I held my breath as she walked over and told me, 'Something very bad has happened.' She quickly added that dad was OK and Jane was OK but you had been very badly hurt. Instantly, I was both numb and whirling with images of our youth: madness, sorrow, love and family. Forty years of instamatic pictures shot through my mind. I felt so badly for you, Alice and the boys. What I imagined that day didn't come close to the horror and fear I felt when I first saw you."

"Well, I'm still here, though I'm afraid the hero part of me was D.O.A.," I said.

Alice had told me that "something has to change." With Kevin, I could sense from the way we were talking that something had already profoundly changed. He reminded me of how I had tormented him as an older brother, and replayed for me those fateful days when I swam off into the fog and when I had trouble with my chute. As we spoke, I remembered just how I railed against his, mine, or anyone's vulnerability. I had no way of experiencing my own helplessness but to externalize it, feeling the fearful, painful states through Kevin while we were "playing."

Kevin and I spent hours recounting those times. While we could look back and laugh, there was still a lot of pain and rawness that lingered. I had frequently been caught up in bouts of fearless energy, and Kevin often bore the brunt of it. But, no more.

"I've never felt I had to rely on anyone. Now I can't eat, bathe, or even pee without a helping hand or two. I know I looked bad when you first saw me, but I feel even worse. Some hero, huh?"

"Well," he said, "as long as I have you, that's all that matters."

Saying good-bye, Kevin kissed me gently on the cheek. I was again flooded with the healing waves of love, and a deep sense of gratitude for the life we'd shared.

After Kevin left, I languished in the wellspring we had tapped of love, tenderness, forgiveness, and appreciation. As thoughts and memories of our childhood replayed in my mind's eye, a woman walked into my room. I knew her instantly, and an enormous wave of emotion swept through me.

"My angel of mercy," I said. She was wearing a flight suit, and smiled at me. Even before she was able to officially introduce herself, I started speaking.

"I will never forget you or the compassion you radiated that fateful day in the helicopter." With tears flowing freely, I went on. "I can't tell you how profound your presence was to me during those horrifying moments in the helicopter. You really saw me and offered me your heart, and that compassion relieved my fear and pain more than any medication possibly could have." I was so overwhelmed with gratitude it was hard to find the words. "You saw me, not just a mass of injuries, but a human being. Your compassion literally saved me. Thank you."

She stayed with me for a short while, sincerely happy to see that I was recovering. I thanked her again, and as she left, I added, "I will never forget you or the sense of peace you brought me."

I had cleared land on my wedding day. I had built a wall in the days following my son's birth. And now, in a state of unimaginable brokenness, the love from Alice, my brother, and my angel of mercy were gently washing away barriers I had built throughout my life, one stone at a time.

CHAPTER 8
Holy Commode

"Hey, what's the rush?" I yelled, as pain exploded through my body.

Hospital rooms flashed past me in a blur as I was bumped and rumbled down the hall on a gurney. The only comfort I felt in that hospital came with being completely still. The slightest motion was agony. Yet Al Unser Jr. was propelling my gurney around with the apparent goal of trying to set some sort of land speed record in getting me to the orthopedic floor. There was something other-worldly about being in a hospital and being pushed through a labyrinth of hallways on my back, glimpsing lights above me, doors to my side, and up and to my side, an orderly whose eyes flickered with what seemed to be a definitive lack of emotional stability.

"Slow it down!" I yelled.

The man looked at me, throttled back slightly, and then never looked at me again. My anxiety had skyrocketed, as my mind raced back to my fall and that first afternoon and night in the hospital. Bouncing around on that gurney unearthed fears of a loss of control and what I imagined would be some impending impact. I clenched my teeth and braced for the explosion of pain that I feared would come at any second.

When we reached my new room, a petite, athletic-looking nurse greeted me. Treating me with the care and dignity that one might afford a large slab of beef, she and the orderly who had driven me there slid my legs and then shoulders from the gurney to the bed. I saw white lights as I tried not to pass out from the pain.

"Now that was easy," the nurse said.

Easy. Holy shit. I took several long deep breaths as the pain slowly subsided. My driver and the gurney departed, but my anger and fear were coiled tightly in my chest and throat.

"You are lucky to be alive." She was familiar with my accident and my history. "I am wondering why you chose to discontinue the morphine."

"I need to make clear choices. When I am on the morphine, I am not as conscious or as present as I need to be. For example, if I were on morphine, I wouldn't have had the presence of mind to tell that idiot to slow down"

She seemed to understand and had a way about her that soothed me and helped reduce my anger and vulnerability. But being transferred from my old bed to the gurney and then from the gurney to this new bed had brought back unsettled memories and experiences of being in the ravine. The flashbacks to the fall were compartmentalized memories that became unearthed and were moving up and out of my body. There was the blissful experience of being out of my body juxtaposed with being trapped in it and consumed by the fevered, exhausting struggle to survive. The flashback seemed to coincide with the fear of being dropped when moved from the gurney to the bed and the red, hot, intense pain that accompanied it.

When the nurse left, I was glad to be lying still. No movement eased the fires. As I felt the pain and fear that was still coursing through my body, I softened my heart to it. I didn't tense up. I yielded. As I did, there was a subtle sense of aliveness that began vibrating within me emotionally. In the moment that followed, I noticed a sense of hope moving through the smoldering ashes of my life. I began to contemplate this change in my interior. It had been more than two weeks since the accident had torn off the innermost doors of my mind and sent me on this journey. Initially the accident obliterated the boundaries that defined my identity as Jack, as I dissolved into something much larger than my known identity. But slowly, as my recovery proceeded day by day, my ego seemed to take back some of the psychic space it had yielded up. I now wondered if the depression I was struggling with was the result in part of my ego's continued reemergence. Had I needed something this traumatic to push me to the point where I was forced to let go and wake up to the love that was always here?

The infusion of energy from the transcendent dimension had been most intense and noticeable when I was shattered, helplessly yielding to the moment and uplifted by the influx of this nourishing Presence. I thought of the prayer I had read in which a man walks with the Lord on a beach. As the scenes of his life flash before him, he looks back and notices that when he experienced the greatest sorrow and pain, that only one set of footprints can be seen. He asks the Lord why, when things were at their worst, was he left to walk alone. The Lord responds:

My son, my precious child, I love you and I would never leave you.

During your times of trial and suffering, when you see only one set of footprints, it was then that I carried you.

It became obvious to me that there was just one set of footprints in the ravine, and I had been carried. As the sun came in the window and painted me with light, I felt a curious loosening and stretching sensation in my chest that was both painful and exciting. I prayed that my heart would never harden or my ego overpower the experience of love that I'd found in the ravine when my body was "crawled," and I was carried.

I brought the sunlight into my body with my breath and let its warmth mingle with the hot, electric pain. I must have dozed off because the next thing I knew a man was standing beside my bed.

"Hi. I'm Richard your physical therapist."

Richard was dark-haired, about five feet eight, and seemed very young. But there was something about his demeanor and warmth in his dark brown eyes that gave me a sense of trust and honesty.

"Are you ready to sit up and see the world from a different vantage point?" His question surprised me, and I shifted my position in the bed.

"Hi," was all I could say before I was immediately swept up by the pain moving through my body. My lips parted as if to say more, but that was as much as I could get out.

Richard saw the look of surprise in my eyes. He was empathic and direct. "Did anyone tell you that your doctor had scheduled you for physical therapy today?"

"No," I responded, still in pain and surprised. "I guess I should have figured it out since I'm now on an orthopedic floor. What about all my broken vertebras? Is sitting up such a good idea?"

"Well, you're not going to be in a sitting position for long. We have to work towards getting you to transfer into a special reclining wheelchair that's been ordered for you. But that won't happen for a few days," he said with a smile. "Are you up for the challenge?"

"I guess so," I lied. Until that very moment I hadn't given a thought to what a treatment plan would look like for someone in my condition. I was having a hard enough time just trying to lie still and manage the pain.

And then, without further direction, I promptly tried to sit up.

"What are you doing!?" Richard reached toward me obviously surprised at what I was doing.

I immediately collapsed back on the pillow as the pain caused Richard and the entire room to start spinning. What was I doing? I knew. I was ashamed that I needed the help. I had impulsively risked my own well-being in order to regain my sense of self.

"Hold on, my friend." Richard was up and standing by my side in a heartbeat. "This is not something you do alone! That's why I'm here. We'll do this together."

"OK," I said. And so, we began together, taking it very slowly.

But even slowly and together, each time I managed to reach a sitting position, white flashes of pain burst in my eyes. Having weight shift onto my fractured pelvis and vertebras was excruciating. As the pain flashed, I held my breath, and several times left my body. The altered state I entered was familiar, as if I was in the leaves again, looking down on my body. And each time I reentered it, there was a rush of fear and helplessness unlike anything I had ever known.

We practiced a few more times, and he finally laid me back down. I was sweating profusely, and it took me several moments to come back down from the intensity of the pain. As I caught my breath and the pain eased, he talked to me about how the next days would pan out.

"Jack, we need to get you to a point where you can transition from your bed to a wheelchair, to the toilet, and back again. If you can do that, you'll be eligible for home care. If you can't, we are going to need to send you to a rehab facility."

"I'm going home," I said. I knew enough about the rehab center to know to steer clear of it. "How about we practice a little more later on today?" Another experience of fear and shame overwhelmed me at the thought of just how broken I was.

"Fine. I'll be around later." He gave me a few exercises to try on my own, and left me.

After I was fed lunch, I did my exercises. Movements I had always taken for granted were difficult and infused with searing pain. I concentrated, focused my energy and tried hard to breathe through it. Memories of college football came back to me and of all the pain I had learned to "play through." This was different. Then, I had access to the wild aggressive energies of my youth, the angry refusal to give in to tears, the 'Stony' strength that never let me give in to pain. Now there was no stone left in me. I felt weak, vulnerable, and dependent in the physical realm. I was stuck until I was able to stop resisting. Fight or yield, I had to find my way. I wondered what was the direction of love, and I prayed it was home, with my family.

People feeding me. People cleaning me. Now I needed help just sitting up. I felt for the first time in my adult life the hidden shame and the secret longing to depend on another that was cloaked beneath my independence. The realization blistered my consciousness just as the hives had my body. I could almost hear the heroic boy's voice inside me saying, "I can do it myself." That voice was eclipsed by the angry, shamed adolescent saying "I *will* do it myself! I don't need anyone." I had spent decades walking with confidence, without needing people. I had it all figured out. I had always felt powerful and totally self-sufficient. But in fact, I realized at that point that I was actually scared, anxious and distrusting. The impact of living that way had cut me off from others and left me feeling lonely at times and not able to give people access to me so that they could support me, or me them.

Richard said he would be back, but I could tell he was frustrated. I could see that my protective need and drive to "do it alone," had left him feeling somewhat negated. I also realized that the impact my willfulness had on others was that they felt judged or negated by me instead of being affirmed. As a result, people sometimes distanced themselves from me, and I often felt alone.

But the policeman in the ravine and the angel of mercy in the helicopter had met my pain and helplessness with caring and kindness. In those moments of extreme dependency, I had rediscovered the young child within me, as well as an open, loving man who had learned how to remain relational while being vulnerable. His trust had not been betrayed. I didn't want to lose contact with that man. I realized now that the trauma was re-engaging my past, liberating parts of me back into existence, asking me to accept what once had been too painful to tolerate in life.

I was developing a sense that I had to learn how to depend on others, trust them to be there for me and at the same time be self-sufficient. This wasn't an "either/or" situation of being independent or dependent. It was both. It reminded me of riding a bike for the first time. I just had to commit to it and pray I'd find a sense of balance.

When Richard returned, he helped me sit up amid the sparks, roaring pain and vertigo. I had learned to manage my pain by being passive and receptive. But moving meant I had to find different means of managing the pain. At one point the pain triggered an unexpected emotion – anger. It caused me to move instinctively in a way that I previously had not been able to. I had certainly witnessed how destructive it could be and how it could undermine healing. But it had also helped me find a way to move. I could see how anger was a storehouse of energy. If correctly engaged, it could be a powerful force in healing. Without it, the pain or fear of more pain immobilized me as it did so many other patients.

In the authoritarian atmosphere of my family background, assertion was seen as disobedience and a threat to my parents' authority. I learned to associate feelings of aggression with shame. Self-assertion was answered by their punishment and my guilt. Over time, I learned to repress that side of me, which had driven my anger underground, where it developed a private life as a wild creature which both attacked and protected me. That assertive part of me had been relegated to my subterranean realm in an effort to protect me. When I chose to "suffer" my fiery wild self in a constructive way, as in athletics, I could engage his energies in a powerful manner.

Engaging that aggression now would take discipline, but it seemed a far better option than repressing it. If I repressed my assertive and aggressive side, I would be too dependent on others to get into the wheelchair. I would also be cut off from my own source of strength.

I had to face myself. I realized yet again the only way out of the pain and the terrifying place I had found myself in, was to go through it. I had to commit to the lesson I'd learned a hundred times since the accident; to say "yes." Acknowledge and accept the intrusive feelings, fears and pains that were my daily companions and open my heart to all of it in a compassionate way. I needed to engage my will to carry these broken parts of myself back to life.

After dinner that evening, I asked the nurse if she could locate and bring me a dictionary. She brought one just before she went off duty. I looked up the word aggressive: "full of enterprise and initiative, to move forward toward a goal without undue hesitation, doubt or fear". I smiled to myself. I really was starting to link up the past with the present, integrating the old me with the new me. Taking the initiative was not so hard because I had my fear pushing it. The hard part was moving forward WITH hesitation, doubt and fear. Maybe that was the definition of courage.

When Richard arrived the next day, I could tell from the look on his face that something was wrong.

"What's the matter?"

"Well," he began, "the good news is that by the end of the week, you'll be off the orthopedic floor." I waited.

"And the bad news?" I asked.

"The bad news is that unless we can get you fully ambulatory by week's end, you'll be on your way to a rehabilitation center. If you become ambulatory, you can be sent home and receive physical therapy and nursing care there."

"By the end of the week!?"

"Yes, by the end of the week," he confirmed. "It was written in your chart this morning. Your insurance company is only going to cover your hospital expenses for three weeks, and we're coming up on three weeks."

Anger. There was certainly no repressing it at that point.

"How's that possible?" I shouted. "I can barely sit up in bed! I still have people feeding me and washing me. Every damn movement is a nightmare of pain."

"I'm just bringing you the news. I'm sorry, but I'm just the proverbial messenger."

"So some faceless case manager fifty miles away has made a decision, totally removed from my condition?"

Shattered, riddled with pain, still wondering if I would ever walk again without the use of a cane or walker. Of all the methods of healing that had coursed through my mind, informing a patient he wasn't worth the cost of the care was something I had never considered. I was as faceless as the day they wheeled me into the emergency room. No H.M.O would ever meet me. They would never care or track the outcome of their decisions. I was faced with yet another barrier to recovery. My possible failure and its implications terrified me.

"Well, let's get to it," I said.

"OK."

I was angry and emotionally tight when we began. It was a combination of pain and fear in the moment. I took the time between exercises to explain to Richard what was going on within me.

"I get it," he said. "You tell me what you need, and I will give you whatever support you want."

Richard did his work with me, and I did it with him and myself. The process was unpredictable. Most of the time when the pain came up, I would hold my breath and push forward. I would feel constricted and cut-off, or alone and not relating to the physical therapist at all. It was just me, my pain, and the wild man within me. The pain was continuous and intense, and there were several times that I thought I would either pass out or throw up.

Yet, other times I remembered to stay conscious of the moment, and I connected with what was going on inside of me, with the internal forces. I linked up with Richard either visually, or verbally or by feeling his supportive strength. I remembered to breathe, anchored the breath in my body and prayed I could trust him not to let me fall. At these times I noticed that the more committed I was to the effort, the more energy came.

I struggled from the bed, to the wheelchair, to the commode, and then back. Such a simple series of tasks had become a monumental hurdle. And to what end. It had been nearly two weeks, and I still hadn't had any serious use for the toilet. That had been a blessing the first week, but at this point, it was causing me noticeable discomfort and added a new serious wrinkle for the doctors to fret about. I was stopped up, and a barrage of laxatives and suppositories had proven useless.

But in the face of proving myself capable of getting to the commode and back, my ticket to going home, I filed any concern about terminal constipation several levels behind getting through the pain, getting off that bed, and getting beyond my horrifically palpable fear of falling to the floor.

To get to the wheelchair, I needed to use a "transition" board. In essence, I literally used a board to help me make a slow and theoretically controlled move down into the wheelchair. I experienced white flashes of pain from my broken back, from my pelvis, my ribs, and my arm as I slowly situated myself for the move. Merely adjusting my position in a bed was painful, but moving to that extent was excruciating. Again, my fear magnified the pain, and in my mind, I felt as if I was sliding down the face of Mt. Everest. I tensed and strained, bracing myself against the pain and trying desperately not to fall, though I knew intellectually that Richard would never let that happen.

If my own personal analogy of reverting back to infancy wasn't complete enough at that point already, the unthinkable happened. As I became closer to vertical than I had in close to two weeks, and as I strained to protect myself and ease into the chair, a week's worth of laxatives assaulted me with a vengeance. For a split second it occurred to me to hold back, but there was simply nothing I could do but remain focused on getting into the chair. Richard and his staff couldn't have been nicer, treating the whole incident as the most minor of inconveniences.

"It happens," they said. "Don't give it a second thought."

But as they cleaned the floor, the chair, me, and brought me a new gown, I could not have felt more shamed and humiliated. As I lay back in bed afterwards, resting a bit before getting ready to take another shot at getting into the chair, the child in me resurfaced again. I recalled vividly the image of my mother walking me to what must have been Kindergarten. On the way, I had an "accident." Without anger, fanfare, or consternation of any kind, she walked me home and helped me clean up and change. I had felt safe. Her compassion and tenderness had completely diffused a potentially humiliating morning.

And then we were back at it, Richard at my shoulders and an aide at my legs.

"Well, at least I'm a little lighter," I joked.

I made it from the bed to the chair, and then from the chair to the commode, which at that point I had absolutely no use for. But getting back into bed was worse. Moving up and across that board, I felt like I was clawing my way back up from the ravine. My back and pelvis were roaring. My ribs exploded with pain while my nerve-damaged right side hung limply.

I couldn't help the recurring flashbacks to the day of the accident, the most palpable being the complete loss of control and falling. Richard was vigilant, supportive and affirming, but still the very thought of falling terrified me. I tried hard to relax my breathing, and trust in Richard, but it was tough to let go. My central nervous system was lit up like a Christmas tree.

"That scared the Hell out of me," I told Richard. "And the more I try to move, the more I realize just how much physical capability I've lost. Dominant aspects of my personality have been peeled away, and I am not sure how I am going to get through all of this."

"We'll get through it together." Richard said with more compassion than confidence.

And I accepted that. In my pain and uncertainty, I acknowledged just how vulnerable I was. I said "yes" to needing the help and compassion of those around me in order to survive and recover. I believe the old version of me would have tightened up completely, resisted any help and shouted a rousing "NO," to any suggestion of vulnerability. My identification with my beliefs had imprisoned me. But at that point, I was embracing what I had spent my life denying. Though I didn't realize it fully at the time, my awareness and willingness to yield and accept saved me, both physically and mentally.

It opened me to the process of healing and redemption. I was finding the worthiness to consciously suffer, and in doing so, I was growing closer to myself.

Had it not been for my accident, I would never have known that my body and mind could fully enter each other and illuminate each other. And each time they came together, compassion was created which allowed a pathway for life energy to flow into the moment, guiding me forward.

By the end of the week, I could get from the bed, to the wheelchair, to the toilet and back again. Although humble aspirations, they were accomplishments that opened the doors to the next stages of my journey of healing.

By the end of the week, I was on my way home.

CHAPTER 9
Coming Home

I didn't leave the hospital with any sense of triumph or jubilation. I was happy to leave, yes, but I left still very broken and in unrelenting pain. I was wheeled out reclined and strapped in a special wheelchair, completely helpless. The slightest jolt of the wheelchair was agonizing, and I knew that with all the motion, turns, and bumps, the ride home in the ambulance was going to be nothing short of agonizing.

In a world in which insurance and health care systems were actually based on health and care, no one would have moved me in my condition for at least another month, but I was gone.

And the most unsettling thing about the fact that I was going home, was that I had no idea of who "I" was, or what "home" meant under my disabled circumstances.

As I was carefully loaded into the back of the ambulance, my head was inadvertently slammed into the rear door frame. I screamed, as much out of anger and shock as from the physical pain. I had never felt so small and helpless.

As the ambulance pulled away from the hospital I saw the helicopter bringing in another emergency. I looked out the window and said a prayer, my anxiety stirring as I thought of my flight just a few weeks earlier.

I was at the mercy of those around me, feeling small and helpless. I had been those things before, a long time ago, and as I lay
helpless in the back of the ambulance, feeling horribly trapped,
painful memories boiled to the surface.

I remembered how, from the ages of 7 through 10 years old,
my parents would yell and threaten me when they were really
angry with me. And when I provoked them past a certain point,
they would march into my bedroom, still shouting, and pack my
suitcase in front of me.

"We're taking you to the orphanage," my father would say. My
mom would then get into the car's back seat, while my dad pulled
me, kicking and screaming, out of the house and into the back
seat with mom.

Then I would plead, "I'll be good, I promise!" during the entire
10 minute drive to St. Mary's Home for Children. Sometimes, they
simply turned around when we pulled up to the gate. Other times,
they would take me inside, and I would wait while my parents
talked to a nun about my staying there. The visits we made at night
were the most frightening. When I saw the big gates, I would sob
and scream until I practically passed out.

I hadn't thought of those memories for years. But there they
were. And there I was again, this time literally strapped to a chair,
enduring the beating that every uneven stretch of the highway shot
through my body, unable to control any element of the journey.

I never before realized how bumpy roads are. Each jerk of the
ambulance caused pain to shoot through my body. I had my suspi-
cions that the driver was the same guy who had wheeled me around
so painfully on the gurney about a week before. I wanted to yell
at him and ask when, if ever, anyone had replaced the shocks. I
wanted to beg him to slow down, or even stop for a moment, but I
knew it would only prolong the agony.

"How did you get through it?" I asked that question over the
phone to a dear friend and colleague from my hospital bed, late
one night. I had been struggling not just with the pain, but my
inability to come to terms with the condition I was in. I was feeling

sorry for myself, looking at my broken self with resentment and disdain, unable to reconcile the sea of emotions that were churning inside me.

"The greatest gift Dove gave me," Shana said, "was her willingness to receive from me."

Dove was her daughter. She was born with a terminal genetic disorder called Hurlers. Children with this disease are missing an enzyme and the result is a degenerative process. For Dove this meant she became more and more physically and mentally regressed after about the age of 3 until she died at age 8. On a vacation we had taken together, I remember seeing Dove sitting in her stroller waiting for us to take her to the beach. She had a love filled smile and her curled fingers were clapping in anticipation. Her little skinny legs could no longer hold her up and she was more like a 2 year old than a five year old. Everything had to be done for her. I wondered how Shana and her husband Dan could so fully embrace life with their dying daughter as a precious gift instead of a tragedy as some might have thought.

They had wrestled through their anger, sorrow, and fear, and ultimately discovered the purest of heart connections that enabled them to experience this relationship with Dove as a blessing, valuing beyond measure every second they shared with her. It seemed to me that the disease had robbed her of what I thought it was to be a child. But Shana felt that Dove was liberated, living a life of true open-heartedness without ego needs to push away the love coming toward her. I repeated her words to myself.

"The greatest gift Dove gave me was her willingness to fully receive from me." Shana went on. "She taught me to be fully present in the moment and how to be purely receptive to love. Maybe you could see your condition as a gift to others that invites them to give to you and then feel affirmed in their capacity to express their love."

I had lain awake that night beginning to see parts of myself through Shana's eyes, as she had loved Dove through an illness that continually disfigured and disabled her. Perhaps I could learn to not only accept but find true compassion for the vulnerable and unrecognizable person I had become. Maybe through my fall I could find a way to befriend my brokenness and those disowned vulnerable parts of myself and make them an ally, rather than have them be persecutors I had spent my life avoiding.

As we turned into our driveway, the trip became more surreal. The closer I got to the house, the smaller I seemed to become. This had been our own private wonderland, but now everything was different. I was here by the grace of God. Tears welled up thinking of all the richness I had had in my life, of the dreams I had never pursued, and the love I had never completely expressed. I saw that no matter what we do, everything changes. Nothing lasts but the love we offer others. I began to cry for myself, and my family, friends, and even strangers. Was there no way to go through life without losing so much, and without leaving some part of the tapestry unfinished?

As Arnie and the driver unloaded me I saw for the first time how different things would be. There was now a ramp leading up into our front door. I asked Alice about it and she explained that a friend who worked with me building our house had foreseen the need and put in the ramp. I really like Al and appreciated what he had done, but I hated seeing that ramp. It assaulted and diminished me. Feelings of despair began to flood me as I was pushed up the ramp into our home. Small. Weak. Inadequate. Those words coursed through me and I could not find the means to embrace what I had become. I was nothing like the man who had created and maintained this home and property. I had put so much of myself into my home, and now it only reminded me of everything I had lost.

"Who am I?" my mind silently screamed.

Once inside I looked up at the light that cascaded into our main room through a large skylight in its center. The beauty of that light seemed to illuminate everything, especially the cedar ceiling. I thought, "Nearly five thousand feet of four inch tongue and groove cedar." I had selected each board, nailed, sanded and finished it. I could smell the cedar, taste the sawdust and remember feeling dizzy from the urethane fumes. But as I was wheeled into the room, all I could hear in my head were countless sentences that began with, "I'll never...." I'll never wrestle with the boys again. I'll never run. I'll never coach soccer again. I'll never compete in another triathlon.

I had desperately wanted to come home. I had looked forward to the moment when I was out of that hospital and back in the safety of my own house. I had not expected to feel so much despair at returning home. I had thought it would be the beginning of a return to "normal," but it wasn't even close.

When I saw the hospital bed set up in the next room and commode nearby, an emotional surge went through me that practically knocked me out. I hadn't left the invalid in the hospital, I just changed venues.

I was vaguely aware of three people getting me into the bed. I just lay there as it got darker and darker inside of me. That darkness consumed the courage I'd begun to find in the hospital where I'd learned to say "yes" and accept what the moment demanded of me. It consumed the compassion I had tried to find for myself as I reflected on what Shana had told me about Dove.

That night I stared out through a skylight above me and watched as the moon moved across the sky. Fragments of memories, like shooting stars, crossed before my eyes. As I lay there, I began to notice how all kinds of feelings would just cycle through my body, giving rise to thoughts which, when I concentrated on them, would solidify into moods lasting for minutes or hours. I began to watch how these moods rose or fell depending on whether I got entangled in them or let them go without moving into them depending on my attitude. I would ride them, or be ridden by them.

I had become so sensitive to those around me that sometimes the silence and the darkness brought me peace. Whoever was attending me had such a big impact on my mood. Whether it was a nurse or orderly in the hospital, Alice, the boys or a friend; that person's focus and mood had the power to make me feel better or worse.

If someone was distracted, I became vulnerable and anxious.

If someone was patient and present, I felt safe.

As the moon moved across the night sky, I thought again about Shana and Dove. "The greatest gift Dove gave me was her willingness to receive from me." As I had told so many of my clients, I needed to find compassion for myself and allow situations to unfold from my heart, not from my judging mind. "The heart," I would tell them, "doesn't label or distort, like the mind does. The judging mind is always busy trying to control our internal world, but we can't repress parts of ourselves and still be whole."

I knew it was time for me to embody this truth in a whole new way. In the ravine, I had let go of everything and somehow I had become a part of an ineffable Presence. That Presence had filled my heart with love and compassion. Rumi, the Sufi poet and saint, had called that presence "The Beloved." Now I knew why. As I lay there in bed, I decided I wanted to live in that state where I could know The Beloved. I decided I would accept my feelings and thoughts, instead of trying to hide from them or bury them. This would take more courage perhaps than any of the physical challenges I had created for myself in the past.

Holding my thoughts of The Beloved and my resolutions of acceptance were as hard to cling to in the dawn as the images from a dream. There were storm clouds brewing. I saw the tension, worry, and even anger in Alice's face as she brought me coffee. I felt it in her voice as we talked. I wasn't sure if it was concern, compassion, anger or disdain, and felt too vulnerable to even ask. I had been home for fewer than 24 hours, and already I was becoming an island unto myself.

By 9:00a.m. the storm was in full swing. The home care services Alice had set up fell through, citing the excuse that they couldn't provide service since we didn't live close to public transportation. Alice was undone and started working the phones to find friends that could come and help in shifts. Toward midday, the coordinator for the service called with his good news/bad news report. Hallelujah, they had found an aide who owned a car. Unfortunately for us, the aid couldn't start for another four or five days. Alice was back on the phone recruiting friends and family to take shifts to provide the care I needed.

By noon, the true force of the tempest was upon us. As my sister Jane and her husband Ed arrived for their shift, we received a call from our medical insurance representative telling us that we had no medical coverage for hospitalization or home care.

I could see the headlines. "Man survives 50 foot fall onto solid rock, dies of heart attack triggered by disastrous news from health insurance company." Jane and Alice worked the phones, making calls trying to clarify the disaster, but it was Saturday and there was not much they could do. This would have to fester over the weekend.

Once everyone started breathing again, we attended to more practical matters. During my hospitalization I had received only limited sponge baths. I still had blood caked in my hair, and I generally didn't smell very good. So everyone decided, if I was agreeable, to help me get into my special wheelchair and push me to the kitchen sink for a bath.

Perfect, I thought, more movement. I recognized that everyone wanted to be helpful. But movement frightened me and it intensified my pain. At the thought of climbing into the chair and wheeling to the sink, my body shouted out to me, "Are you nuts?"

But I wanted to move forward. I thought about the traumatized people who had come to me for counseling; so many of them had designed their lives to avoid emotionally stressful or frightening situations. As a result, their consciousness had narrowed, become rigid and restrictive, and gradually led to impoverished lives. I knew instinctively that if I stayed in touch with all my feelings and stepped forward anyway, I could expand my life and heal my body and perhaps become whole or at least I hoped so.

Alice, Brendan, Jane and Ed helped me get into my wheelchair while Devin, too young to be of help, looked on. I focused on my breath to stay open and not contract emotionally. I drew on the love around me for the support I needed. We made it to the sink without incident. Once there, we only had to resolve one simple problem: How to get me upright.

Ed and Brendan lifted me up, while Alice and Jane washed my hair and limp, rag doll body. I was racked with my fear of falling, and to my surprise, distrust also surged through me. I had no balance of my own. Suddenly I experienced a terrifying sense of falling backwards. A huge rush of adrenaline surged through me, but everyone around me held firm, and I remained safe. It took me a moment to realize it wasn't happening in the present. It was a flashback to the accident, falling and flipping around before I hit and was knocked-out.

We made it back to my bed without incident, and after thanking everyone for their care and help, I lay exhausted, reflecting on the day.

In my condition, there weren't many options while lying nearly immobilized in a hospital bed. Thoughts and feelings were floating in, and I let them. As I did, I experienced an amazing insight. I realized with sudden clarity, that I had engaged in all of my restless, risk-taking adventures to ward off all the vulnerable feelings that were now overwhelming me. When I was about to dive off a 60 foot cliff or skydive out of a plane, I would start to get an adrenaline rush that I liked (unlike the horrifying rush I had felt at the sink) and then I'd take off. At the moment when I leapt, I turned off all the fears and vulnerabilities. For the first time I understood that many of my athletic pursuits were unconscious attempts to master the feelings of powerlessness and helplessness I had so often felt as a child.

Again, I had the sense that my accident was an opportunity, a chance, finally, to embrace all the different parts of myself so that perhaps I could always be present with The Beloved, that force both inside myself and everywhere that I had encountered that day in the ravine.

My vulnerability was continuing to be a teacher for me. If I could just keep moving forward, face whatever was there, and include my vulnerability in my decision-making process, it would ensure that my life would improve.

It was my chance to heal a split that had defined my inner world for many years—a split between "Jackie," that vulnerable little boy who lived in the numb shell inside of me, and the armored, self-sufficient "adult" who lived in the outer world and carried much of my ego-identity.

CHAPTER 10

Putting the Pieces Together

Acceptance. Openness. Compassion for myself. A willingness to receive the help and love of those around me. In the hospital, on the ride home, and during my restless first night at home, I seemed to cycle through those revelations and resolutions, each time understanding them more deeply. But the reality of the day-to-day was jarring, and it constantly jostled me back into old patterns and fears.

I had been home for two days. Alice was simultaneously supportive, loving, anxious, and angry. Devin was concerned but filled with stories, questions and conversation. Brendan was all business. Did I need anything? How could he help? No small talk.

And I was a wreck, depressed by what I had lost, bed-ridden, and unable to get through the course of the day without help. I still needed assistance to get to the bathroom. I still needed to be fed. I was even a greater burden on friends and family until the aid could get there.

And now, the coup de resistance, financial ruin. I lay in bed estimating the expenses I had incurred to date because of the accident. The helicopter evacuation: $18,000. The hospital stay: $15,000-$20,000. X-rays, MRIs, cat-scans and surgeries were another $25,000. $63,000 was gone. And that was only the first three weeks. I still had months of home care with nurses, physical therapists and aides ahead of me. Then, there would be at least a year of physical and occupational therapy. Every week of missed income just put us deeper in the hole.

In the blink of an eye, our savings seemed to have vaporized.

Wasn't it enough to be crippled and helpless? Adding financial ruin to the picture, I began to drown in an ocean of sadness and despair. Everything I worked for during my life, was gone in the blink of an eye. There was nothing I could do and managing the physical pain consumed all my energy anyway. I felt weak, helpless and powerless to preserve or protect anything and had to simply let go. Staying identified with anything I <u>had</u> or <u>was</u> became unbearable. Grief was crushing.

As a long distance swimmer, I used to enter a space where my boundaries with the water dissolved and I just became my breath. There I connected the expansive ocean around me to the space within. That spaciousness was all that mattered when I swam. I just gave myself to that process and went with the flow. I found myself trying to find that same flow now, as I entered these unknown choppy waters.

Finally, several days into this new long distance journey, as I was learning to let go, the insurance company called. I told them my name, my social security number, our address. The date of my mother's birthday. My anxiety level had me gritting my teeth so hard I thought my jaw would break.

"Mr. Weafer, it seems we have made a filing error," she said.

"And?" I wasn't sure what shoe was about to drop.

"And, sir, it turns out you have been fully insured all along. Our mistake. We're sorry for any inconvenience we may have caused you." She wished me a good day and hung up.

Calls like that can make your head explode. I had wrestled with despair for five days, convinced that we were on the precipice of financial disaster. I was obviously hugely relieved, but frustrated beyond belief. They had exiled me from the hospital after 3 weeks. They had run me through an emotional mill for several days.

"Breathe," I told myself. "Breathe." There was nothing about health care that led to healing or health.

Soon after my call with the insurance company, my home health aide Antoine arrived. A tall, dark man from the island of Trinidad, he appeared to be about thirty years old and spoke softly with an endearing accent.

Things were looking up.

The first thing Antoine did was clean the kitchen. Then he turned his attention to me. "Do you want to take a shower?" he asked when he returned to my room. "I can wash the bed sheets at the same time." I agreed to this plan but with trepidation because any movement was painful.

Almost a week had passed since I had been washed at the sink. Antoine and I worked hard to get me into the wheelchair, but once there I began to look forward to a shower. We got to the shower, where I noted the handicapped bench that someone, probably Alice, had put inside. Antoine said he'd had a lot of experience helping bed bound people take showers. He turned on the shower, checked the temperature and helped me slide in. The cascading water was refreshing. But when Antoine let go of me for a second, I instantly tightened my grip on the bench. That put pressure on my fractured vertebras, sending hot, fiery embers of pain shooting up my back.

As my awareness began to clear, I moved beyond the pain and sat there transfixed. Antoine had put on large, black, industrial rubber gloves. His now hideous, giant rubber hands moved over my body. I felt mortified, objectified, humiliated. Why the need for gloves? My faint, lingering pride flowed down the drain. I gasped, helplessly inhaling water and began to weep as the water washed over me, taking my lingering pride with it.

The majority of my routine, outside of a trip to the commode or the infrequent and dehumanizing shower, was lying in bed. And in bed, I lay as still as I was able given the ever present intensity of my pain and discomfort. So I had plenty of time to contemplate the arc of my life. I could see that the accident was bringing up all kinds of memories and feelings, and I struggled to integrate them in a more comprehensive and profound way.

And through the pain, despair, and fear, I felt something surprisingly wonderful reaching towards me as I opened my heart more deeply to the process. Something guided my healing, something beyond anything I could consciously understand or orchestrate. I was utterly broken, yet moving towards a wholeness I never experienced. I felt a new and different kind of vitality coursing through my veins. This energy did not belong to me, yet it stayed with me as long as I accepted it and felt grateful for its presence.

I regretted that it had taken such a catastrophic accident to wake me up. I had been broken plenty of times before, yet none of those events had broken me open. I assumed they simply hadn't been severe enough. With particular regret, I thought about a motorcycle accident I had when I was 26.

I was traveling on an interstate highway on my way to work. As I came around a bend, the bike hit a patch of oil that had come from a previous accident, and it suddenly slid out from under me and into the guardrail. My body skipped across the highway like a rock across a lake. I heard the sounds of screeching tires as cars attempted to avoid running over me. I had several compressed vertebrae and spent three weeks in cervical and lumbar traction. I was so agitated that someone at the hospital sent the staff psychiatrist to see me. I barely gave him the time of day. I refused to let anything or anyone in.

When my parents came to visit, I was as stony and armored with them as I was with the psychiatrist. But as I lay there in my bed, I thought about how difficult it must have been for them to see me in that state and not be able to help. I wished I had been more open to their care, especially since it was only a few months after my recovery from that accident that my mother died from complications of a heart attack. I wondered what those last months of her life might have been like if I could have opened up.

On one of my last visits with her, as she lay dying in the hospital, I rubbed her back in an attempt to provide comfort and relief. Her lungs had filled with fluid and her heart was enlarged. Everyone knew it was close to the end. "I love you, mom," I told her. "You know, I finally understand why you and I were always struggling. We were just too much alike."

My mother let out a little chuckle and said, "You silly ass, I always told you that."

I was not with my mother when she died. I felt her loss acutely. But my defenses, my inability to open myself to the pain of her loss, congealed over the heart-break. I did not let myself suffer the grief and loss for long. But as I lay in my bed so broken open, I could hold my suffering and hers in a new way. I felt my mother with me as part of a warm, gentle, soft energy that flowed through my broken heart and around my pain.

I realized I wanted to share myself with my friends and loved ones from that point forward. If it was vulnerability that I had to share, I would. I would not exclude those I loved from my deeper feelings any more.

My armor was dissolving.

CHAPTER 11
Men

Men.

Throughout my life I had categorized them under "handshakes" not "hugs." In social and professional settings, while there was almost always respect, competition, virility and loyalty, there were subtle but significant barriers between us. We were alpha males in a pride. We were extroverted, hard driving, and iron-willed, with varying degrees of testosterone keeping us from getting too close. For many of us, certainly me, our bodies and minds had been formed growing up in the ambiance of threat, violence or aggression.

Once home, however, men circled me like a gaggle of male mothers, nurturing, supporting and affirming. Never in my life had I needed, accepted, or thoroughly enjoyed so much care and attention. I had male aides, therapists, psychologists, carpenters, friends, and fellow soccer coaches. They came laden with stories, expertise, medical devices, and compassion.

My aides bathed, shaved, fed and wiped me. My physical therapist manipulated my frozen limbs, slowly bringing my broken body back to life. My friends built ramps, refitted showers, split wood and even laid down winter rye in the garden.

But above all else, I enjoyed our conversations, and the stories they told me like only men could. We laughed, we cried, or just visited. It was as if my brokenness and slow process of recovery drew us away from the usual male world of accomplishment, power, and competition into a soft, gentle place where we could just <u>be</u>. There was an aliveness to this space which lacked the usual emotional tension. The competitive isolation I had experienced in my relationships with men was transformed into an open tenderness and compassion. I found myself enjoying relationships with men more now than ever.

I hadn't yet regained my bearings, and still struggled against being vulnerable, broken, and helpless, but I did like what it made available to me with men.

Women friends visited as well and were just as caring and giving, but surrendering to women who held, soothed and loved me had always felt natural. Surrendering to the care of men, on the other hand, had always felt uncomfortable. But it seemed that my accident had torn apart a complex system of self-protection with men that I realized I no longer needed. When men came to see me for the first time, their initial curiosity was invariably replaced by a deep, empathetic connection. Some friends even acknowledged that our visit had become the high point of their week! I knew the broken helplessness of my condition wouldn't last forever, but I secretly prayed that this tender, intimate connection with men would. We were free, like boys again, our hearts beating openly in the world.

After a couple of weeks, a man named Dennis had replaced Antoine as my home aide. Between his laugh and his build, he reminded the boys and me of Santa Claus. He was a gentle man with the incongruous bumper sticker on his Jeep, "NRA and I Vote."

Three times a week, Gary, a physical therapist, visited me always focusing on getting my "frozen" body moving again. It was called passive therapy, in that Gary did all the moving, manipulating different parts of me to break up the scar tissue and get me mobile again. As anyone who has been through physical therapy to recover from surgery knows, the pain is excruciating, every little motion feeling as if someone is trying to rip off whatever limb they are working on. The pain lead to tears, nausea, and several times, caused me to throw up. Often times, as he worked different parts of me, the pain would bring up a variety of emotions, thoughts or sensations. I moved into and with the pain and experiences as best I could, knowing my body was holding a lot of information I needed to retrieve.

Gary would call out to me as the pain began to overwhelm me and I'd start to space out. "Jack. Jack! Stay with me!" One day his words released another memory from deep within my cavernous body.

"Jack! Jack! Wake up! Don't you leave me Jack! Wake up. Stay with me Jack!" I was sixteen and had been playing linebacker in our annual Thanksgiving Day football game. I had been sandwiched, helmet-to-helmet between two halfbacks. My helmet had split in half, and I was unconscious with a severe concussion.

"Jack wake up!" My father was shouting at me, his face with a mixture of fear, anger and finally, relief.

Given the severity of the concussion, the doctors had wanted me to stay in the hospital for a few days. I didn't remember much until I was moved into a semi-private room with another man. I remember my father sitting there beside me, my shattered helmet on his lap.

"I thought we lost you Jack. You took a tremendous hit and scared the life out of your mother and me."

That night had been horrific. It was after midnight, and since I had slept on and off during the day, I was laying wide awake, noticing how the night-lights over the beds threw a ghostly shadow over the face of my roommate.

With a suddenness that startled me, my roommate started to convulse. His eyes popped open wide, his face became contorted, the sounds and image amplified by the silence of the night. Frantically, I pushed the call button. I was in a frenzied state and was still leaning on the call button when the man's arms flew out from under his covers. Reaching out, he seemed to be pulling himself up out of the bed. And then, he abruptly fell back, like a tree falling in the forest, his head smacking into the pillow.

Then nothing. He lay completely still and the room was filled with a profound silence.

The nurse arrived, put her hand on his neck and glanced at me and pulled the curtain. She hurried off. Sometime later she returned with another nurse and a gurney. Unceremoniously, almost gruffly, they slid his body off the bed and onto the gurney, covered it with a sheet and rolled it out of the room. I could still hear the gurney rolling down the hall when the nurse returned with clean bed sheets in hand. She stripped and remade the bed and walked out without a word to me.

I lay there in the darkness with the smell of my now dead neighbor covering me like a blanket all night long.

"Jack. Come back to me Jack." Gary was pulling me back to the moment and out of the pain.

"I'm OK," I said. "Your words just brought a distant memory to the surface."

The next day was Saturday. My neighbor Charlie walked in, and I was struggling with myself. I loved having my family around on the weekends, but I was also extremely aware of the added pressure on Alice and how anxious it made her. It was hard for me to see the meaning my suffering had for them other than just being an awesome burden. Dennis took weekends off to teach firearm safety classes and to hunt. This left Alice and the boys to care for me. They were wonderful caretakers who took their jobs seriously. However, Alice at 5'3" and 110 pounds and Brendan also at 5'3" but only 92 pounds, were anxious about helping me take a shower. We were all afraid of my falling. Although I had lost twenty pounds, I was still too big and heavy for them to get me safely into and out of the shower. So the job fell onto the shoulders of my neighbor Charlie.

"How are you doing today Jack," Charlie asked, his brown eyes as quick and friendly as his smile.

I answered by only shaking my head. "Not well" I whispered.

Charlie continued looking down at me. But as if from far away he said, "You'll come through this…but when you do you have to promise me you'll never, never tell anyone about my helping you take a shower."

I looked up to see his big, broad smile and eyes crinkled in their corners.

For that one moment, I stopped worrying and actually laughed, igniting a wave of additional pain surfing through my ribs.

"Since the first week in the hospital when Alice brought me this little dictation machine I've been recording my journey and the people in it with me. I'm trying not to deny anything, but if you prefer to remain anonymous, I'll protect your good name."

I had a smile on my face for the first time that day.

"Yea, you better do that 'cuz my wife is already curious about this shower thing we do, and she wants to know why I haven't taken a shower with her in years."

Now we were both laughing. The laughter woke me up from my trance of pain and worry.

Charlie prepared the transition board by securing one end of it to the hospital bed, the other to the arm of the wheelchair. He helped me sit upright and get on top of the board. Charlie guided my body on the slow, painful sideways slide down the board and into the chair. Once in the wheelchair my breath continued to whistle through my clenched teeth while the arteries throbbed in my neck and temples. I was aware once again of how dependent I was and helpless to protect myself. As my fear began to subside, I focused into my breath and body. With the body armor stripped away there was no tough guy to be found, only a raw, vulnerable, man who was extremely grateful to have friends in his time of need.

Charlie checked the shower, secured the shower bench in place alongside the transition board and turned on the water. He adjusted the water temperature, turned and looked at me. "You ready?"

I sat there in my nakedness. My right side hung limp like a stroke victim's. The rawness of the scars from the numerous surgeries left my body looking like red snakes were slithering up, down and across it. I couldn't trust my instincts here if I got in trouble. I'd only have my left hand on the wheelchair arm pad while Charlie stood behind me and lifted. As I pushed up and Charlie lifted, hot electric currents shot up and down my spine as each fractured vertebra moved along the transition board. I took a deep breath and exhaled with a shudder as I landed on the shower bench. The hot water hit my body and was instantly both painful and exhilarating. Charlie took his shirt off, so as not to get it soaked, and reached in. With one hand holding me steady, the other soaped and washed me.

After the final rinse he dried me off, helped me back into the wheelchair and then to bed. Mission accomplished, we talked a little more and Charlie walked down the driveway home.

Later that day, after his practice, Dan, a fellow soccer coach, came by. He coached the under ten year old boys while I coached the under nines. We often scheduled scrimmages between our teams. The boys were friendly with each other and generally everyone had a good time.

Dan sat across from me. His tan face, blond crew cut and athletic build made him look like he was in his twenties. He was good-natured and his coaching style reflected it.

"We were practicing on the field the same time your team was. Devin looked good."

"Thanks for saying so. I'm glad he's able to keep his focus but I'm concerned about him. Many of the boys on the team I've coached since they were five. They have become very dependent on me. I'm concerned Devin's taking on some of my responsibility. His athletic ability, commitment, focus, and skill make him a leader anyway, but I'm afraid he's struggling under the weight of this added responsibility."

"Last year the team showed so much heart in their determination to be the best team in Division 2. They trusted me and what I saw in them. That gave each of them the confidence to be the best they could be. It was a team with such bright dreams. Now they're turned upside down. It happened in the blink of an eye."

Dan sat there silent for a moment. "I can see in the kid's faces that they miss you and are struggling with Joe's coaching style. It's not yours, nor is he you. But kids are very adaptive and as disappointed as they are in losing you, they'll get over it."

"I know they will, Dan. But it hurts. My relationship with the boys was all about trust. They believed in me and my view of them. That's where the power came from to achieve beyond their natural abilities. I betrayed that trust. I'm not there to reinforce their belief in themselves in the face of failure. I can see with Devin how each loss generates more self-doubt. It narrows his self-image and restricts his full expression of himself."

Dan was shaking his head and looking at me. "That's deep Jack." He paused. "I just coach. The other coaches don't know what to make of you. You're so "intense" I guess you might say you're intimidating."

"Really?" I said, "I don't mean to be. I just bring who I am to coaching. I don't know how not to do that. I don't coach to win. I don't care about the score, really. I care about what takes place on the field; each boy risking being all they can be for themselves and their team. One for all and all for one. It's teamwork. I loved helping those boys. I miss them."

Dan sat there quietly. His concern for me was evident in his eyes.

Tears spilled, "I just feel really, really bad about it," I said. Sadness just seemed to flow out of the hole in the center of my chest. I breathed slowly and deeply. "The losses are that much more devastating because of the heights we attained last season." My words were raw with guilt.

"It will all work out Jack. Maybe I can help Joe with your team, or another coach. We'll get them the support they need."

"Thanks Dan. That means a lot to me. I want to somehow get to a game. Devin thinks the boys would be OK seeing me. What do you think?"

"I think you have to take care of yourself. That's what is most important."

After Dan left, I lay in bed continuing to feel responsible and helpless. Athletics had been the way I modeled emotional integrity, courage and persistence in the face of adversity for my sons and the boys I coached. What could I teach them from a wheelchair? Would I ever be able to coach again?

I recalled my surgeon Dr. Asprinio's, answer to a question I had asked him in the hospital. "Will my pelvis and back, once healed, stand up to my running a marathon?"

"No," he said looking at me as if I was crazy.

"Will I be able to run at all?"

"Jack. You were really badly injured. I did the best job I could under the circumstances, but let's take it one step at a time. If we get you walking I'll be happy. It's a miracle that your cord was only nicked. Be grateful that sometime in the future you'll walk again."

I remembered how selfish I felt at the time and how ungrateful I must have seemed, how disconnected I felt from the man that I once was. Now I was grasping again for what I once was to relieve the pain and fear. I knew it only made it worse, but I just didn't want to open to the palpable grief that now defined my life.

I was still struggling when Devin walked in. He had gotten home from soccer and stopped in to say hi. He seemed to be in a good mood. I pulled myself up out of my struggles and said, "Hi Pal. How was school today?"

"Good," he said looking at me, but then he looked away.

"How was soccer practice?"

"OK"

"Coach Dan stopped by. He left not long ago. We were talking soccer, and he said you looked good on the field today. He said he would talk with some of the other coaches and see if they had any free time to help out your coach."

Devin just looked at me; his mood seemed to have fallen into quicksand. He shrugged. "OK, if you think that will help. I'm going to get something to eat."

I felt it best at that point to give Devin the space he seemed to need to struggle with his own experience. I spent the weekend struggling with my life's responsibilities.

The weekend came and went, and on Monday Dennis stripped the bed and put clean sheets on it. He was helping to get me back in when Walker began barking. Once he got me in bed, he left me to see what the commotion was. He returned with Mike, a friend and an osteopathic physician. Mike had not heard of my accident until Alice had called him the previous week to see if he'd do a home visit.

I had met Mike several years ago after I'd taken a bad spill off my bike while competing in a triathlon. My body was twisted up, especially my neck and shoulders. He'd done great work with me and since that time I had referred several patients to him. We developed a good professional friendship. When he walked in, I could see in his eyes that his imagination had not adequately prepared him for the visual surprise of seeing me in the state I was in. Dennis lingered and I introduced him to Mike. I explained to Dennis that Mike was a primary care physician who practices a "whole person" approach to medicine, treating the body as an integrated whole.

Mike's enormous eyes seemed to be assessing my body's condition. Standing beside me he took my pulse. "How are you doing Jack?"

Dennis took the cue and walked into the kitchen.

"I'm struggling Mike. Thanks for coming out to see me."

"Had I known I would have been here sooner. Can you give me an overview of what happened and the extent of your physical injuries?"

As I began to recount the accident and the extent of my injuries Mike rolled my hospital bed out into the middle of the room. He then went to the head of my bed and gently lifted my head, resting it in his hands. Osteopathic physicians use their hands to diagnose injury and illness, and to encourage the body's natural tendency towards health and healing.

I told him about my struggles between fighting and surrendering to the pain and my condition. I talked to him about the Beloved.

"I end up feeling like I'm living in a physical, psychological and emotional combat zone. Fighting, surrendering, fighting, surrendering and then I'm gone. But there's something else," I said. "Inexplicably, something from beyond, much, much larger than me, sweeps me up, soothing and sustaining me. In those moments I don't have a sense of being shattered, just the opposite." While he held my head and moved his fingers under my neck, I continued.

"It's very similar to my experience in the ravine of being out of my body and then trapped in it in all the torment. Clinically, I used to see what resembled this state as a state of depersonalization, with patients feeling detached from their bodies or mental processes. Now I'm not sure. I stay conscious and present with both the physical and emotional pain that comes up. I don't feel like I dissociate, but when I least expect it I'm swept up and away from the pain and into an incredibly blissful state. I don't DO anything. I simply am, and then I'm gone. Maybe I just let go. For those hours before I was found in the ravine this invisible force held me as I moved into and out of my body, back into the light and a sense of oneness. It was as if the whole of me came into life that day."

Mike had moved down to my lower back and pelvic area. He carefully slid his hands beneath my back and the sheets. By now his facial expressions had melted into an impassive look of concentration, yet there was something tender and openhearted about his manner that helped relieve my anxiety. In the state I was in, I'd become hypersensitive to professionals' reactions or responses to me, scrutinizing both gesture and word in an effort to protect myself from statements that might tear me apart. I felt like I was fighting to stay alive, to love and be loved. The greatest gift Mike and others gave me was to simply see me, touch me and hear from me both what was and wasn't said.

Maybe it was just my imagination, but I felt as if Mike took me and my condition in with more than just his mind. I felt as if he took me into his heart, a heart that was open, receptive, active and expansive. When most people saw me, they didn't know what to say or do. They had to slow down, become more present, attentive and wait, which allowed the space between us to fill with something real, honest and genuinely caring. It's as if they were all loving witnesses to my suffering, and consequently dignified it. Mike's work was deep yet subtle. After about twenty minutes with his hands beneath my back I noticed sweat dripping down his forehead. He stopped a moment later.

Standing up, he looked directly at me. My breath caught in my chest.

"Jack, you know better than anyone that your body has been extensively traumatized. You're very fortunate to be left with as much functioning as you have. When your body hit the ledge there was a momentum of force that traveled through it shattering bone and tissue alike. The impact also fractured your body's systems and functions. The G-force that was released through your body when it hit is still in your body. Add to that the pain you are in, which further disorganizes those systems, and you can begin to understand why I can't do this myself."

"What do you mean?" I asked

Mike paused. The magnitude of the silence was deafening. I was exquisitely attuned to Mike's words. "I need your help."

"I can continue to come here and treat you, but if you are really going to recover you will have to stay in your body! It's as if I have to jump-start a very weak battery. Your system and its functions are very, very quiet. They are also, understandably, disorganized and not talking with each other. You have to stay in your body to keep it charged for optimal healing."

Despite all the heat and noise in me, I froze. I didn't know what to say.

"Together we have to set up a base line of functioning so that your body can get organized and all the different parts of it can begin talking so the unit can work as a whole. You have a self-observer that a lot of people don't, so when I say to you, 'I don't know where you are, that you are not in your body,' I see you understand."

"You were certainly thrown out of your body. I can see and feel that. Your body can self-heal, but it needs you. Pain and fear can take all of us out of the moment and at times out of our bodies. I know how conscious and courageous you are. You wouldn't be here if you were not that man."

Something in me resonated sympathetically with Mike's assessment, yet I could feel my resistance. I had no idea how I would stay in my body, but I told Mike I would do the best that I could.

We talked a little more, and he left. Waiting for Alice and the boys to come home I turned on my dictation machine.

"Holy Shit! Mike just told me I had to land in my body and stay there. I've been in a hospital bed for over a month and the friggin' pain has me tied to it. How am I supposed to not move with the energy that moves through me? The horrible pain is only manageable if and when I flow with it. At the same time, I'm afraid the pain will overwhelm me. Fear, or worse, may take over and annihilate my abilities to manage, my awareness."

Feeling frozen, my breathing shallow, I contracted into a big "NO!" I didn't like the images I was getting in my head. The anger gave way to a surge of emotion.

I slowed down my breathing and tried to reroute the energy. I was having a hard time finding the glass half full at that moment. I thought of my boys and Alice and how they needed me to find my way through this. I wanted the sacred breezes of the Beloved. I was dependent on them. It was the transpersonal energies that kept me alive and sane.

On some level, although I knew Mike really wanted the best for me, I was enraged. I knew the ramifications of allowing myself to get stuck in the pain, anger and fear. My thoughts became a downward spiral, driving me into the realm of self-pity. I didn't want to give in to this "poor me" place, so I began some physical therapy exercises and got into my breath and some purposeful pain.

Change.

How was I going to carve out space within my body for my "Beloved" and its benevolent breezes if I stayed within my body?

Endure the pain? My resistance was palpable and intense. I could see it, feel it, but deep down knew my resistance was really fear. If I really wanted to heal, I had to open to and flow with my body, staying in it. I had to make more space inside of me rather than soaring outside.

It became clear that I couldn't escape from being present in life. I couldn't find a way to stay in my body with the transpersonal energies and not "soar." Maybe I had been given my life to find a way to integrate the Beloved in my body and in life. I realized no possibility remained but to be present in my body and as aware of the pain, fear and grief as I had been of pleasure and power.

After we all had dinner, I asked Alice and the boys to sit with me. I explained my predicament to all of them and asked for suggestions. Brendan suggested I concentrate and push against something. Devin put his hand on my heart and told me to just be there. He also said he would hug me more. Alice simply affirmed my willful determination and her belief in me.

It took time, but I slowly developed an intention with a positive attitude. I would commit my energies to my body. Alice also reminded me that my will to live and heal was really strong, and that I could trust it would sustain me. The boys echoed each other's sentiments: "You can do it dad."

I rode the wave of their support, and as I contemplated my options, I realized what Alice said was true. The accident and my confrontation with death, had in some way really aligned both my conscious and unconscious will to live. It had brought the forces of life and death together in the same moment in the ravine. Something that was powerfully alive, vibrant with emotion and boundless with energy had been provided to me there. The awareness of coming back into my shattered body to choose life had been supported and sustained by divine, transpersonal energies. I had to believe that same divine presence would help me stay in my body. I knew what lay ahead would not be fun.

I looked out the window, and as the sun was setting I saw the light touch a huge oak tree and I said, "Please show me the way."

On Saturday of the same week Arnie came over to do some house chores that used to be mine. It was a warm, mid-October day and he had just come inside the house for a cold drink. He walked into the room smiling, sweat pouring off him. He looked at me with a glint in his eyes and said:

"I've taken the screens off your windows and put them in the basement. I've also cleaned the leaves out of your gutters, and before I leave I'll throw down some winter rye in the garden. Who do I submit the bill to?"

I enviously looked at him, standing there, sweat dripping.

"Get in line, pal. There's a lot of people ahead of you. I hope you have another source of income."

We both laughed.

"Thanks," I said, "for your help today. It makes things easier for both Alice and me."

Arnie looked at me, pulled a chair up next to my hospital bed and said, "Hey, what are friends for? But seriously, how are you doing?"

"That's the problem," I said. "I'm not able to <u>do</u> anything. I used to think I had great coping skills and that my destiny was clearly in my hands. I can't believe how dependent I was on physical activity to deal with stress. I'd go for a run, swim or workout at the club and by the time I was through my head was clear and my body relaxed. Now…?"

I paused. "Now, my body is so backed up with pain and fear that it makes my head boil. I used to be so busy with projects, care-taking and my practice that I never noticed the clashing of emotions really deep inside of me. I was a powerful and success-ful man whose life, I now realize, was designed around sustaining that experience of myself. Had I not been forced to be on my back nearly twenty-four hours a day I never would have come face to face with this other me…or this child in me."

Arnie was smiling, "You're all heart and gonads. I've known you for fifteen years and I've never seen you let up. You were a bit intimidating. Actually I'm kind of relieved you've become such a pussy. I feel a lot better about myself."

We both started to laugh and tear up. Arnie's simple openness, acceptance and support of me touched me deeply.

"I feel really isolated and alone in the pain. I resurrect my personality when Alice and the boys are around so they don't see how tormented I really am. I need to let somebody into it with me."

I could feel Arnie take me into his heart. In that moment we both opened into a more direct contact with each other.

"The friggin' pain in my pelvis and lower back is raging out of control right now. Any chance, Dr. Morgan, you might be able to relieve some of this?"

Arnie told me to focus on my breath and leave the rest up to him. I sensed Arnie's intense attunement to me as he slipped his hands beneath my back. As I breathed into his hands my body sent out sensations that were intense, vivid and frightening.

"Just follow your breath for a few moments and let the pain move into it and through it. See what the actual feeling of the pain is. Notice its temperature. Does it have a rhythm? Any pulsations? A color?"

"I'm noticing my breath catch. I'm afraid if I really enter the pain it'll sweep me away."

Arnie was now tapping different parts of my body.

"Just stay with your breath. Think of the pain as very alive energy. It's healthier to be with it. Notice how the energy is moving through you. Listen to the sound of your body. Don't resist it or make it something it's not. It's just energy."

"I keep spacing out."

"Where is the pain the hottest, the most chaotic?"

"My lower back and my right shoulder, before it travels down my arm, burning it up as it goes."

Arnie stopped tapping and slid one hand beneath my back.

"With an attitude of openness see what is here. It's moving, open to it. See what's inside, it holds the seeds of grace for you. Focus. Concentrate your energy. If you're spacing out you're everywhere and nowhere. I know how courageous you are. Don't meet it halfway."

Suddenly it felt like a bomb had been detonated in my pelvis as a surge of electricity convulsed up my spine, accompanied by a terrifying, beastly scream. The scream tore my throat open and I heard a voice saying "My body, my body, my poor, shattered body."

What followed was more animal than man sounds and my body continued to convulse, sending burning, emotional currents up my spine and out my mouth. The energy channeled through Arnie's hands ushered in a felt memory of the impact; a single image of shattering bones, jagged pieces exploding almost simultaneously as my body hit the ledge. Intense waves of emotion moved through me as I wept for this broken, pain-tormented body. I continued to cry and tremble as spontaneous discharges of energy moved up my spine and body and out my mouth and head.

Arnie, gently, and with tears in his eyes, placed his other hand on my heart. As he held my pain in one hand and my heart in the other, he encouraged me to continue to let go.

It might as well have been my soul as I surrendered it all to him. He helped me as I had helped my boys when they were hurt and frightened. I would hold them and tell them to breathe into the loving heat of my hand that lay on their diaphragm. I would gently say "Let go. Turn it over to me. You can trust that little boy to me. He's safe with me."

Now it was my broken body that was being held by a man. I was letting go into his strength and the protection of his caring compassion. I realized I could be, and needed to be, "fathered" at this time of my life. Trusting men with my heart, as my boys had entrusted me with their hearts, healed a wound deep inside of me.

My grief was as great as my pain; my relief now as deep as the despair that flowed through me. I had begun the day in such isolation and darkness, longing to be alone in the pain, my struggle hidden. Now I desperately needed hands to touch me, to hold me.

The mystery had been delivered. I now knew what it was like to be in my body, pursuing the healing from the inside-out. The resolution of this mystery had been my mission, and now perhaps it was my redemption. In all my life I had never been in the grip of such fear, pain, grief and longing. At least, not since I was a child. The pain was intense, hot, vivid, frightening and suddenly it started changing. I flowed with it. The brief sweet terrifying madness had stripped off an even deeper layer of protective armor, one that I now realize I'd been clothed in since childhood.

"Jack, when you initially told me about the accident, I didn't ask you if at any time after you hit the ledge you ever felt this terrifying fear or pain."

I thought back to my time in the ravine, now more than six weeks ago. "No, only wet, sad tears seemed to move through my body then. There were brief moments of anger…"

I paused, thinking, "No. The pain and fear, at least at the depth I felt it today, had been carried for me. I just went back up into the embrace of the light. There, I was simply wrapped in a kind of isolating cocoon, and I wasn't sure where I was in that."

Arnie smiled and nodded. "Well, you might not yet be a butterfly, but welcome back to this world. I've done a lot of energy work with clients over the years but I've never felt, seen or for that matter heard anyone ever move into, then out of, and then back into their body the way you just did. I'm still in some kind of contact high with you. That was incredible. Not only do you look different, but your body looks and feels very different."

Arnie's words reverberated through me until I began to tremble. My body shook and vibrated as if it was plugged into a 220 volt current.

Arnie sat silently with me, his hands holding mine. "There's depth in your eyes now that wasn't there when I walked in."

A deep sense of appreciation for both Arnie and the work we had done together moved through me for having suffered into life the terror, pain and grief that had pervaded my mind and body since the accident. It was held for me by my Beloved, I now realized, until I could suffer it all back into life. I fully understood that only if I did that could I remain conscious of the Beloved's overtones from within my suffering consciousness.

"Thanks, Arnie. I don't think there's anything I could say that could possibly convey the depth of my gratitude."

"Jack, I am grateful I've been able to help." He smiled at me. "And, don't worry I'll add it to my gardening bill."

All that deliberation and concern about staying in my body, and it happened with Arnie. I left a message with my news for Mike, and he returned my call on Sunday.

"You cannot organize what is going on in your body if your awareness is somewhere else," he explained. "All the parts and systems of your body "talk" with each other. When I put my hands on you, I felt that many of these parts or systems of your body were quiet or operating very faintly. Jack, your consciousness, as you now realize, has to be within your body. Then you will be able to engage the healing energy that remains in you."

"Stay in my body." I reiterated those thoughts to myself as he continued.

"I am sure you know, Jack, that there is a knowingness, a power that resides in you. It sounds like you became aware of this presence with Arnie. If you can stay in your body and contact that knowingness, from within your body and trust it, it will help rejuvenate as well as rehabilitate those lost parts of you."

Mike paused, allowing me to take in what he had just said. "One last thing," he added, "Do you remember being knocked out of the tree and how instinctually you repositioned yourself in mid-air so that you landed feet and butt first, not head first?"

I said, "Yes, I remember that part, just not the impact. At least not until yesterday."

"That same instinct wants to help you heal, but your consciousness has to be grounded in your body. You know you can't keep spending your days floating around outside of your physical reality and expect to fully recover. You're going in the right direction. Keep it up. I'll see you at the end of the week."

After I hung up, I felt a sense of hope take hold inside. Maybe there was something I could do after all. Maybe just having the courage to be in my body in a loving and compassionate way was the most important thing I could do right now.

Men.

Something had awakened within me and brought me to a new place, an awakening. That night, as everyone else slept, I thought that as my pride had died, a profound love was born and was blossoming. It was as if my vanity had obscured something that connected me to others.

This "something" inside of me was growing. It was nurtured by my embrace of the vulnerable boy within me, and for today, anyway, it had been nourished and strengthened by the loving attention of men – men who helped me take possession of my body and in so doing, my life.

CHAPTER 12
Soccer Sunday

It had been two months since my accident, and aside from taking a shower or using the toilet, I hadn't once left my hospital bed. But that cold autumn Sunday, I was not only out of my bed, I was headed to the car and Devin's soccer game. Brendan and Alice cautiously pushed my wheelchair, and Devin had run ahead to open the car door. The three of them helped slide me across the transfer board and into the front seat.

The day was as unsettled as I was. The sky was filled with dark grey clouds, and there was definitely a storm brewing in the west. My anxiety was intense and my sense of vulnerability was palpable. This was my first time out, and I was anxious not only about the physical ramifications of being out of bed, but the emotional ones associated with being seen in public for the first time since the fall.

But as anxious and vulnerable as I felt, I was also absolutely committed to attending Devin's soccer game. Although Alice drove slowly and carefully, I found my teeth clenched and breathing restricted. Every little bump was still tremendously painful. But despite the pain, I was smiling. The physical trauma took a distant second to the concerns I felt about my soccer team's struggle. I intended to relieve that today.

Alice had not wanted me to go. However, the previous afternoon, Devin had come home from soccer practice very discouraged and upset. He stopped at the foot of the hospital bed for a minute. He looked at me with his handsome, expressive face and said, "Soccer is just no fun anymore." He dropped his head and turned to leave the room.

I called after him, "Dev, do you want to talk about it?"

"No thanks, Dad," and he continued walking into the other room. As he walked out of sight, a cloak of guilt settled over me. I felt I had to confront this.

An hour or so later, Devin walked back into the room. He appeared to be in a better mood, so I asked him if we could talk for a minute.

"OK Dad," he replied. As he sat on the edge of my bed, a turbulent river of emotions began to flow through me, which both raised and deepened my mood. I launched into one of my paternal monologues.

"Losing," I said, "inherently holds many gifts for us, if we can learn from them and not get down on ourselves." I started to relate how being broken by my fall had opened so many amazing doors for me. "It has taught me life lessons I may have otherwise never learned."

I saw I had gone a little too deep, and was losing his interest. I switched topics.

"You, young man, are one heck of an athlete, certainly much more skilled than I was at your age. Somehow I think that our family's stressful year has had the side effect of sharpening your skills and general approach to the game."

And then I asked him a most difficult question for me. "Are you angry with me for not being there for you? Have I let you down?"

He shrugged his shoulders and looked down at the floor.

"I am so sorry," I began, but the emotions just broke through. He turned and looked at me, as a loving father or coach might look at a son. He put his youthful arms around my neck and hugged me. I tried to say something to relieve the tension, but no sound came.

My vocal cords were thick and tight. As tears began to roll down my cheeks, I felt his hair begin to mat and stick to my neck. Devin had begun to cry too as if his soul was breaking loose from his little body. It was as if all his hopes and dreams lay broken in this hospital bed with me, and that there would be no tomorrow for either of us.

We held each other and lay there separate, whole, broken, apart, yet melding together. As the sun set deep in the woods, the gifts of loss and darkness nourished both of us. I sensed Devin's unspoken sense of responsibility for the team; a responsibility that he had taken on in my absence. Perhaps it was one thing he felt he could do to ease my pain. Children can be so courageous in their willingness to sacrifice themselves in their love for a parent. But how long could I allow him to do that?

"When will you be able to come to a game, dad?" He was up and ready to get on with his evening.

"Soon," I said, "very soon."

Shortly after Devin left, Alice walked in. She and Brendan had overheard us and granted us time and space together.

"Our boys are amazing," Alice said. We shared a deep respect for both boys, but especially Devin in that moment, as he struggled with his overwhelming grief and loss. His willingness to be open and vulnerable with me had felt like a healing for each of us. In a deep and moist way, I felt much more present with my suffering and in my ability to witness and receive Devin's.

Later that night, Alice and I talked some more about Devin's sense of responsibility as well as mine for the team. "The choices we make" I said "are one of the most powerful things we do in life. I chose not to wait until I got my climbing harness back to cut off that tree limb. That choice had far reaching effects. I feel it's still my responsibility, not Devin's or some other coach's, to show up and deal with those consequences for the team."

Alice agreed, and I was out of the house, being driven to my first game in 2 months.

A couple of fathers helped transfer me into the wheelchair. It was a wonderful yet awkward feeling to have their hands and arms tightly around me, keeping me safe until I was firmly secured in my chair.

The two men pushed me, and as I was wheeled toward the field, all the boys stopped their practicing and conversations. Their eyes were transfixed on me and the wheelchair as if we were a magnet. Tentatively, they approached me.

"What are you guys staring at? I'm back. Let's go out there and play soccer like we know how to."

It took the boys a moment to break out of their trance but once they did, they shifted into overdrive, and were back on the field working through their drills.

As exhilarated as I was to see them, my brief encounter left me surprisingly very self-conscious and acutely aware of my vulnerability. It wasn't the boys that had triggered my apprehension, but the parents. I felt them looking, and could sense from many of their stares and whispers, that they weren't seeing my strength in being there. They were focusing on my weaknesses, my brokenness. I had become excruciatingly aware of what was in people's hearts since my accident. And while many were truly supportive, warm, and welcoming, many were judging and fearful. Those sentiments fanned my anxiety and made me acutely self-conscious and uncomfortable.

I redirected my attention to the boys on the field. My heart raced as I watched them. A friend graciously pushed me up and down the sidelines so I could follow the game. In the second quarter the team's level of play picked up. I became a part of each dribble, pass, defensive move or shot. The team was an intense emotional system, and I felt at the heart of it. Watching the boys play, I thought how soccer as well as life was a never ending story of choices and decisions that continually arise. It's our responses that define us and the ultimate outcome of the game.

At half-time the game was tied 1-1. The boys surged off the field wearing smiles from ear to ear. They gathered around me as if I were a lucky charm. I reveled in the moment and spoke to them, while listening to the sounds of the boys sucking orange wedges and spitting seeds, all the subtle nuances I had missed so dearly.

"No matter what the score." I said, "each one of you is a winner." Every one of you has given your all, and I know none of you
will have any regrets or think 'if only', when this game is done."

I focused on the boys, their smiles, innocence, and their won-
drous renewed belief. I felt an overwhelming sense of connection
to them and to the source of their lives.

For the first time in two months, I felt truly alive and a part of life.

They played with renewed intention and a growing sense of
confidence throughout the second half. When the game ended
we had won our First Division 1 game 2-1 and the right to believe
in ourselves again. The boys were thrilled, and as they lined up to
shake their opponents hands, I was pulled along with the tide.

But as things wound down, and as I was being pushed back to
the car, I felt a chill that came from a much more unsettling source
than the cold wind and approaching storm. Piercing the joy I was
savoring from the boys and most of their parents, I saw two parents
draw their sons away from the rest of the team, and from me. They
had had looks of disdain, and I instinctively knew there would be
repercussions from my being there.

As we surrendered the field to the oncoming storm, it was the
image of the big smiles on the boys' faces that burned brightly in
my heart. As some of the men helped me into the car, others folded
the wheelchair and put it into the trunk. Devin bounced into the
car still holding the game ball. I realized that today's greatest gift
wasn't the win, but rather the boys having found the strength, perhaps even the courage, to seize upon hope and turn away from
resignation and despair. It was a great lesson for all of us.

The ride home was wonderful as we recounted different exciting moments of the game. As we approached the house and the
ramp came into view we all got quiet. For a while on the ride home
it was just like old times, laughing and replaying what we remembered of the game. We had gotten free from the reality of my condition, if only for a while.

As Alice turned off the car and we prepared to transition me
back into the wheelchair, Devin said, "Thanks Dad. We just don't

play very good without you. You're the only coach we want to play for."

I felt like I was coming back as a coach in the only way that I could. I had gotten out of bed, and into a car, which was a huge victory. And I had shown up. In my broken condition, I had modeled for my soccer kids the "no-regrets" philosophy I had always taught them.

"Take everything onto the field," I used to tell them, "Your fears and weaknesses, as well as your strengths and desires." I had learned that throughout my life, and I was still learning it.

Bringing my fragileness onto the field Sunday had been much more painful and terrifying than any of the football games I had played in college. But, my imperfect presence aligned perfectly with messages I had consistently shared with the kids. Despite any limitations you might feel, get out there and do it. Do it with a full heart and regardless of your perceived limitations and weaknesses. The joy is in the doing.

I was on a high, right up until dinner. But as I lay back in my bed, and as Alice was getting dinner set for everyone, the vice-president of the soccer club called to relay a complaint from one of the parents. The nature and source of the complaint was irrelevant to me. The fact that anyone had complained at all wounded me deeply. It had been my love for the boys that brought me back to the field, exposing my handicapped condition. For me this was life, and what life was meant to be. The boys and most of their parents intuitively sympathized and supported me. But unfortunately, for a few of the adults in our soccer club, my willingness to re-enter the world in my broken condition seemed to threaten them to such an extent that they felt the need to extinguish my flame.

My presence and the team's relatively unimportant victory was a small triumph to me. But to a subset of parents, my presence had been offensive. To others who had envied my coaching style and my relationship with the team, I was a threat.

"Jack, people will try to define you by your wheelchair or your injuries." An old friend of mine had answered my call the following day and was sharing her experiences of being paralyzed from the waist down since a tragic car accident she sustained in college. Katy never looked back nor did she ever let her accident define her. She forgave the driver as she struggled back into life, fought back, graduated from college, and went on to have a highly successful professional career.

"People should have only seen the courage it took to be at that game, Jack. Don't let the shortsighted petty few define you by your injury." She was a treasure. In thinking about Katy's comments, it dawned on me that perhaps the difference between a meaningful, or painfully meaningless sacrifice was the intentional quality one assigns to the experience. Choosing to be a wheelchair coach didn't diminish me as a coach. I could still be an example for the boys about playing soccer or how to deal with adversity in life. This option, I knew, was fraught with conflict. I would stay open to the conflict and what it had to teach me, just as Katy had found a way to stay open to life and love.

I had a brief and restless sleep that night and was awakened by a dream fragment.

A child's heart is given to me, still beating.
The beating heart is throbbing with an enormous amount of love as I hold it.
Suddenly a voice says, "Why not reach out for the whole thing?"

I awoke, left with an image of reaching out and touching many hearts. As I replayed the dream that morning, I had an incredible sense of being connected with all of humanity through that child's heart.

My first thoughts were of my family, friends and Sunday's joyful, loving connection with the team. The accident had broken down not only my ways of relating to the world, but my identity as well. Perhaps my handicapped condition was the vehicle I needed to relate to the fragileness of the human condition in general.

The vividness of my own vulnerability, as I held this child's heart with such tenderness and love, stayed with me. Maybe this child's heart was the child in all humanity that longed for love and acceptance. I was drawn into thinking of my clients and the boys on the team and felt a force flow from me and back to me as I mentally made contact with each of them.

The dependency and helplessness of my condition, combined with the pain, had left me feeling both humiliation and humility. It had been the loving energy of my Beloved that had sustained me in this time of suffering and mortification of my identity. It was through this brokenness that I continued to remain in my Beloved's presence. The physical and emotional pain over the last two months had enhanced my vulnerability and had thrown open my arms asking for mercy. It pushed me out of myself to a place where I touched many hearts and now found a deep personal meaning in life and loving.

As I reflected on this process of being pushed out of myself by suffering and sacrifice, only to truly find myself, I thought of something T.S. Eliot once wrote:

> "In order to arrive at what you do not know
>> You must go by a way which is the way of ignorance.
> In order to possess what you do not possess
>> You must go by the way of dispossession.
> In order to arrive at what you are not
>> You must go through the way in which you are not.
> And what you do not know is the only thing you know
> And what you own is what you do not own
> And where you are is where you are not."

CHAPTER 13
Grandpa's Visit

It was the Friday the week before Thanksgiving. I was looking forward to Dad's arrival later in the day. He was going to have an early Thanksgiving dinner with us and spend the weekend, since he would be with his sister on the actual Thanksgiving night. Thinking about the festive evening ahead thrilled me.

But in the meantime, I was with Dennis en route to a scheduled check up with my doctors. As Dennis wheeled me toward the hospital, I thought how in many ways it had been an eternity since I was rushed into the emergency room nearly three months ago. It was still hard for me to fathom just how dramatically my life had changed. I was in pain. I was in a wheelchair. I still relied on the care of so many just to get by from day-to-day.

But I was alive and healing, and in so many ways, awakening. I thought how different this Thanksgiving would be. As Dennis pushed me toward the doors, the med-stat helicopter flew over. I instinctively tensed, and held my breath. When I finally exhaled, I said a prayer for whoever was being flown in, and thought to myself just how much I had to be thankful for.

"Jack, it's good to see you." Dr. Asprinio, my primary surgeon, greeted me in the waiting room with warmth and genuine interest in my overall condition. He told me he would see me again later in the afternoon after my many x-rays, an MRI, and visits with the neurologist and the other surgeon who was attending to all my upper body fractures.

"It only hurts when I'm awake," I explained to the neurologist, "which is problematic, because the pain is so incessant, I can't sleep."

The neurologist had completed his exam and was reviewing some of the films.

"The pins in your elbow may be in too deep," he said. "They may be exacerbating the nerve pain from your brachial plexus. But, then again, there are a host of things that can be contributing to all your pain." He paused to consider all of the options.

"It could be the pins. It could be that you tore away nearly three-quarters of those nerve root bundles beneath your shattered scapulae. There's a lot of scarring there. Then again, you have multiple fractures that are all healing. I'm sorry to be vague, but they are all contributing to the pain."

"The pain is incessant," I explained, "and makes everything else that much more difficult. Is there any chance that moving or removing the pins would make a difference?"

The Doctor was both attentive and sympathetic. "Jack, you might get some relief, but truthfully, nerve regeneration takes time. It may take anywhere from three to five years to regenerate new pathways from your back to your hand. Even then, what percentage will regenerate is unknown. Nerves grow very slowly if at all."

Six hours from the first time he had greeted us, I was once again sitting across from Dr Asprinio. I was feeling down. He had gotten all of my films and reports from my other doctors.

"I want to have my elbow looked at by another orthopedist I know. If he thinks the placement of the pins would diminish the pain in my elbow, I would opt for another surgery."

"I'll agree to that, Jack. I'll set up the referral." Then he went on to deliver a recommendation, which caught me completely by surprise.

"Jack, I've conferred with all of your doctors and reviewed all of today's reports and films. For a variety of reasons, there is a consensus among us that you need to begin to use a platform walker on a limited basis."

"A walker?" I was hopeful, excited, and anxious. "You want me to try and walk?" I wanted to be sure I had heard him right.

"With a walker, but yes. You need to begin to introduce pressure into you pelvis and back. Limited weight bearing shouldn't result in greater pain in that area." He paused, waiting for me to respond.

"Would you be up to giving it a try?"

"Of course," I said. "Yes. Absolutely."

He got a platform walker and demonstrated how to use it. With a combination of excitement and trepidation, I swung my legs off the table and my feet touched the floor for the first time in three months.

I grabbed the post that stuck up on the left side of the walker and rested my limp right arm on the platform on the right side. Stabilizing myself with the walker, I anxiously took three "steps."

Three steps.

Three months ago, no one knew for sure if I would walk at all and wondered how I had even managed to simply survive. And now I had taken three steps. A part of me lamented all I had lost, an athlete reduced to baby steps. But for the most part, a great sense of hope coursed through me.

That said, settling back into the wheelchair never felt so good. I had lost nearly thirty pounds since the accident and what felt like all my strength.

As I was wheeled out of the examination room, Dr. Asprinio followed, giving Dennis the walker.

"I'll follow up with the referral to Dr. Passick. Good luck if you decide to have the operation, and I'll see you in a month."

My arrival home was met with a lot of warmth and love. Brendan and Devin first gave me kisses followed by my Dad and Alice.

Just before dinner was ready I asked Brendan to go and get my walker. As he placed it in front of my wheelchair I felt like he was my older brother. I looked up at my dad and pulled myself up. Tears rolled down my cheeks as I felt like the phoenix rising out of its ashes. Taking a few steps towards him, I felt as if I were two years old and learning to walk again. He applauded my effort, and I recalled how many times Alice and I had done the same for our boys as they took their first initial steps. The circle of life was mysterious and wonderful, and I was thankful to still be a part of it.

The evening had a festive feel to it. Alice had made a great dinner, chicken parmigiana, one of my favorites, and both boys were excitedly telling grandpa some of the exciting things they had done since they had seen him last. It was a joyous dinner.

Following talk of school and sports, bedtime routines for the kids, and some afterglow conversation with Alice, Brendan and dad, it was time for me to call it a day.

It was just after Devin had gone to bed that I decided to undertake an adventurous "walk" of about ten steps into the back part of the house using my walker. I had designed the house so that the kitchen, living, dining and family room were all on one level, connected to a second wing by a step up onto an enclosed bridge. I had put the master bedroom, bath, library, and home office on the main floor of that wing and the boys' bedrooms, a bath and guest room downstairs.

I wanted to cross over the bridge and see Dad to the guest room. Given my injuries and the step that made wheelchair access impossible, I hadn't been to that part of the house for three months.

With Dad following close behind me, I slowly worked my way across the room. With great pride, I made it up the step and onto the landing of that wing of the house. But dad misjudged the step, and tripped. He fell forward and his head hit the doorframe, splitting it open as he fell onto me. I was catapulted forward and felt my upper body snap forward as my legs sagged under the weight of my father. The sound of my fathers' groan obscured my moan. Fearing he'd had a heart attack and collapsed, I struggled to pull my upper body towards him.

"Dad, Dad, are you alright?" I tried to raise myself, but my fathers' weight was too much on my legs. Terrified, I strained and heaved and tried to pull myself out from under him. Unable to move, I just lay there dazed.

Alice and Brendan arrived, shouting, "Dad, Jack, Grandpa, are you OK?"

My father lay there helpless across my lower body. Blood seemed to be flowing from several places on his head and face. Alice ran for towels. Brendan and I held his head as blood ran off him. Our hands were covered with blood and it soon spread across the floor. My father's face looked mangled.

He lay there, pathetically looking up at me with his brown eyes. I was struck how this bloody, gray haired, helpless man no longer looked like the World War II Infantry Major I had known as a child: the man I had both admired and resented, and finally learned to love. Seeing him lying there so vulnerable, fear in his eyes, I felt nothing but a deep sense of love and concern for him.

"Jack, are 'you' OK?"

"I think so. I'm more worried about dad than me." I was numb. Adrenaline was pumping throughout my body.

"Are you sure?"

"I'm OK. Let's get dad taken care of first." My concern was that my dad's skull might be fractured, or perhaps he had a stroke or heart attack. Praying I was wrong, I asked, "Dad, do you know where you are?"

A hoarse voice said, "At your house. I'm sorry, but I must have tripped."

"It will take twice as long to call 911 and wait for an ambulance." I said.

"I'll take him," Alice said. "Brendan will help. Are you sure you are OK?"

"Yes. You guys take Dad. If I have any problems, I can always wake up Devin."

"At least let us help you to bed, Jack."

"That could take more time than calling 911. Let me just sit here a bit and get my bearings. I'm OK, really. Please get dad to the emergency room."

As Brendan helped him out to the car, the last thing I heard was my father saying to him, "You are a fine medic."

Moments later I heard the car doors close, and they drove away. I was still lying there on the floor, trying to determine if I had been injured, if at all. I shook uncontrollably, and my heart was racing. Oddly, I found myself perversely fascinated by my father's blood on the floor, my clothes and hands. I was dazed. I heard myself mumbling, "My father's blood. My father's blood."

It was then that I noticed our dog, Walker, sitting quietly looking at me. From the first minute I was rolled into the house, Walker, a shorthaired pointer, had smelled me up and down, and after that had never left my side. He came to me slowly, smelling the blood. He first licked my face, and then, my hands. I held him for some time, and my trembling began to slow.

I knew I needed to get back into bed before the spasms began, and my body locked up. I crawled to the wall and pressed my back against it. Then I pulled my good leg under me and slowly worked my way up from the floor to a point where I could grab the walker. I have no idea how long it took, but it seemed an eternity before I made it back to bed.

Around midnight, Alice called. "He's going to be alright. He has some stitches but he didn't suffer a heart attack or a stroke. It seems that he just lost his balance. We'll be back home soon."

Eventually I heard them drive up the drive. The door opened, and my dad walked awkwardly towards me. When he spoke his voice was strained.

"Jack. How are you?"

"I'm OK, dad. I'm so glad you are too."

I held his hand. Weakly he held mine. Then Brendan took him off to bed.

Early that morning, I remember seeing the digital clock. At 2:48 A.M, I abruptly awoke to intense, searing pain. I breathed into it, and as I did, a dream fragment came back to me:

I was up on an altar, down on my knees, with two other men. In front of us was an enormous man with a huge sword or scepter. We were all to be executed.

I was the third in line. I looked at the first man. He looked terrified, and I felt a lot of compassion for him. He was shaking. His head was turned down, and he was not prepared to die. The 'executioner' walked up behind him and raised his sword. He was about to start the downward stroke when he saw me looking at the other frightened, kneeling man. He stopped, turned and walked over to me. He lifted my head, cupping my chin almost tenderly. He then lifted and stretched my neck out. When he touched me my fear and reservations faded. He walked behind me, and I felt him raising his sword.

As my neck is stretched, I slipped into another river of consciousness. I was welcoming death. I was connected with the other side. The executioner took his sword and swung down, but only grazed my neck. He came back around in front of me. A part of me was still on the other side, but another part of me was back in my body, feeling giddy. He stood me up and turned me around to see a temple that I didn't realize I was in. A large group of people were assembled. They seemed respectful and happy for me. He led me over to a sacred space, a sanctuary of some kind, resembling a garden. His sword was sheathed.

He said, "Wait here. Someone will take good care of you."

The change in my body and emotions following this dream was remarkable. The dream, like the sky above me, enveloped me in a sense of sacredness and hope. Deeply breathing, my body opened and a deluge of thoughts inundated me. Had the man who displayed such a frightened, helpless look been my father or me? His expression had evoked in me deep feelings of love and compassion. Was this my own traumatized demeanor afraid to suffer any more? Was it the look in my father's eyes as I cradled his bleeding head in my lap? Or, had the dream mirrored a remarkable transformation of my old heroic attitude from my experience with Arnie. My willingness to surrender had effectively transformed my sword wielding defenses into an ally, a partner in a much larger drama. What was demanded had been to sacrifice that which ultimately concealed the secret. I had made the choice. I chose to feel compassion for this brother on the altar with me. It had brought to me the ultimate choice to surrender my life fully to the moment, which brought to me a shift in consciousness and ultimately mercy. The mercy I had offered to my body in consciously, compassionately surrendering back into it with Arnie's loving help.

Was this the story of my accident? I thought of the ravine and recalled the amazing sense of love and oneness as I floated above the treetops. Gratitude rushed over me as I recalled the memory of sliding up and down that translucent filament that connected the "me" in the treetops with the body on the ground. Fetching the energy in nature for support, God's presence had assisted me. I was giddy that my life had been given back to me. Having glimpsed the temple's sacred garden and with the executioner's sword sheathed, I had waited for Lorraine to find me and the "angel of mercy" medevac nurse to "take care of me."

A prayer came to my lips and I heard myself say, "My desperate left hand had pulled while my right toe had pushed, and You then carried me along. Though I was shattered, You embraced me. Your breath dilated me, buoying me up. You, my anguished Father, had reached through death for the tender hand of your son."

A lonely tear made a path down my cheek. I looked up through the skylight into the night sky and said, "Thank you." I had much to be thankful for this Thanksgiving.

At breakfast, I told Alice that my body continued to feel alright, but I wanted to get an emergency consultation as soon as possible, just to be sure. In addition to worrying about me, we were both concerned about my father's condition, and we talked about his returning home to an empty house. Nearly eighty, he had been self-sufficient for nearly 20 years since my mother's death. He appeared to enjoy his life and had remained healthy and active. Though the examining doctor had assured Alice and Brendan that Dad would be alright, he was extremely bruised and would likely have some swelling and pain for a few weeks. We decided it would be a good idea to have a hot tub ready for him when he woke so he could soak and loosen up.

The boys soon joined us and Devin was surprised to learn all he had slept through. The 'medic' was concerned if Grandpa would be well enough to drive home the next day as he had planned. Devin was very curious to see Grandpa's battle wounds.

With great eagerness to see his grandfather, Devin slipped into his bedroom to take a look. Upon waking, Dad invited Devin into bed and recounted for him his experience, letting the caring child know he was "fine." He was stiff and sore, but Dad's attitude was good, too good. He got out of bed and gratefully slipped into the waiting tub. The boys gently helped him and directed his efforts to get the lingering blood out of his hair.

Later he came limping into the kitchen and announced that he was sore but otherwise felt fine. As he ate breakfast, he informed us that he was packed and would be leaving around noon as previously planned. Quietly I watched and listened. There was "Stony" in front of me once again. I empathized with his need to nurse his aches and pains in private. He wanted to protect others, as well as himself, from more of his experience. His will was engaged to seal the pain off so that he could get home. I looked at his swollen, stitched, bandaged face. So many feelings flooded me, but most of all I respected his desire to live his way. I saw myself in him, as he was a part of me and I a part of him. We had grown closer over the last three months, and I didn't want to lose that intimacy.

Through this ordeal, I had noticed something different. Something was hidden behind Dad's combat mask, and I could see its shadow. What was it, I wondered. Had he, for a moment last night thought he was dying? I could see his bloody face, frightened, lying in my arms trying to get his bearings. I wondered just how frightened was he. What thoughts had rushed through his head? Did his Beloved "visit" him in that moment when he was torn open and destabilized?

I sent out a few gentle probes, but he negated my attempts to touch or reach him. He had lived alone for nearly twenty years and was sustained by his habits and attitudes. Recalling again the moment when his mother died and how he had left the room seeking solace in the phone booth with the door closed, I felt sad with him then and for him now. I wondered what it had been like for him to have Alice and Brendan, the "medic", with him last night in his fear and vulnerability. At his age, his opportunities to experience love were fleeting. I knew how difficult the choice was and how thick the masculine armor could be.

I simply and gently told him that we would all be more comfortable if he would consider spending another day with us and then see the next day if he still felt like going home. Reluctantly, he consented. He appeared agitated and remained encapsulated for an hour or so before he made peace with the decision. The remainder of the day was enjoyable. He took it easy, and there were even moments when I thought he was glad he stayed to reap the benefits of being around people who loved him.

In letting us give to him, he not only was loved and nourished, but honored each of us and our love for him.

He and I were learning the same lesson.

CHAPTER 14
Thanksgiving

Dad had arrived at his home safe and sound and was relieved to be in his own house while mending. I, on the other hand, remained very agitated from the fall the week before, I couldn't be still, and I was looking forward to the following day's orthopedic appointment.

"Dennis, could you hand me the newspaper?"

I hadn't read the paper in weeks, and as Dennis made me lunch, it seemed as good an activity as any to burn off some of my nervous energy. I don't remember any of the so-called news I read, but I did notice the local supermarket was offering a free turkey with purchases over $100.00. I had a receipt from Alice's shopping trip from the week before.

"Dennis, tomorrow when we come back from our visit to the orthopedist, would you remind me to stop by and pick up a turkey? It's not much, but it will be my contribution to Thanksgiving and will take a little of the load off of Alice."

But even in the face all the excitement of a turkey pick-up and doctor's appointment, I felt completely flat. Dad and my mutual accident had left me both agitated and numb. Sometimes I couldn't shake the memory of falling or lying on the floor with dad's bloody head on my lap. At other times I felt preoccupied with the sounds of hitting the floor or of our groans. I couldn't shake the intense moments of that evening. I remembered smelling my father's body odor. I kept replaying the image of his blood on my hands. I tried to just flow with it, not identify with it, or repress it, but rather just let the turbulence run its course.

I had lost that growing sense of safety I had begun to gain when using the walker. My confidence was low, and I was hopeful that when I saw the orthopedist, some of the "noise" in my body and mind would be relieved.

The next morning, the same sense of agitation still gnawed at me. I tried some breathing exercises and somatic focusing. I tried self-hypnosis. Nothing worked. The transpersonal energies that I associated with the Beloved's presence had vanished. I felt alone and irritable.

When Dennis arrived, he was his usually bubbly self, which given my state of mind and body, I found uncharacteristically annoying. He helped me out of bed, into the wheelchair, pushed me into the bathroom and turned on the shower. With his help, I worked my way into the shower and onto the bench.

It was generally no longer painful physically or emotionally to be showered. I did what I could with my left hand and called to him to help with the rest. But as we worked our way through the shower routine, and he pushed me to the kitchen for breakfast, I began to feel a rising sense of being dependent, helpless and impatient.

"Here we go again," I thought to myself as I began to envision the day. Dennis would wheel me into the doctor's office. We would stop at the counter, where I wouldn't even be able to sign in, because in my wheelchair, my head would be at least a foot below the countertop. Most days I rolled with my condition, but that morning I felt as if the world was treating me like a 2-year old. I was having an acute sense of self-pity.

"Let's remember to pick up that turkey," Dennis announced as he brought over breakfast.

"I'm signing myself in today," I announced.

Dennis looked a little puzzled.

"We will leave the wheelchair at home and just take the walker."

"I'm not so sure that's the best idea," Dennis began, "You still get tired pretty quickly, and…"

"We're doing it," I interrupted.

"Well then," Dennis said. "Let's go see the doctor and go snag that turkey."

On the ride to the doctor's office, I felt better. It wasn't much, but I had taken back an inkling of control in my life. As I signed in at the doctor's office, I looked the receptionist in the eye. What a difference it made to be standing up! Any sense of exhaustion in getting around on the walker was dissolved by the seemingly miniscule achievement of looking at the receptionist eye to eye. And to top it off, the doctor was virtually on time. I only had to wait ten minutes to see Dr. Passick. The day was beginning to look better.

I hadn't met Dr. Passick before. He had received the referral from Dr. Asprinio and read the reports from the entire gaggle of doctors that had seen me previously. He inquired about the accident and reacted to it with the same astonishment most people did.

"Fifty feet onto the rocks, and you're not only talking to me, you made it into my office with a walker."

Clearly moved by the story, he continued enthusiastically, "You really should write a book."

"Maybe," I said.

"Seriously," he went on. 'Pain makes people feel miserable and helpless and most just want to give up. But you refused to become a victim. You ask about your condition and participate in the treatment."

"Early on in my practice, I used to consider people like you difficult. But I've since come to see that the patients who healed the best expressed their feelings freely and asked a lot of questions. I'm serious about the book. You, your story, your recovery could help physicians like me change the approach patients take to their healing."

"I will definitely consider it," I said, and thanked him for the thoughts.

"Now," I smiled, "you will be thrilled to know that I have a ton of questions about my condition."

And he gave me answers.

As the x-rays came back, the news I was most immediately concerned about, was good. My fall with dad had caused no damage.

"All clear from the other night, Jack. But…" I had sensed a "but" coming and tensed a bit, despite the great relief I felt knowing I hadn't injured myself with dad.

"But, now that I've heard the story of your accident and have a sense of the continual pain you're in, a little more surgery might be in order. Judging from the placement of screws and wires in your elbow, they could be putting more pressure on the nerves. You need to be realistic about the outcome, but I'll do a revision on the elbow and let's see if we can ease some of the pain."

As we talked about the pain, I told him that over the last few weeks the pain during physical therapy was so intense I became nauseated or blacked out. Gary, the physical therapist, had explained that it would take six months to a year to tear through the adhesions and approach the extensive scar tissue. Dr. Passick assured me that he would fully rotate the joints through a range of motion while I was under general anesthesia. He said that if I maintained the mobility after surgery the joints would not freeze up again. We discussed the equipment that could be rented and used to maintain the joints' mobility and scheduled a date for surgery two weeks down the road.

I left the office feeling somewhat calmer. I still had a long way to go, but I hadn't reinjured myself. The sense of relief I experienced was more the result of feeling seen as a person and affirmed as a man and a professional.

I thought about my dream the other night and how, at its heart, was the interplay between men, one frightened and one compassionately willing to stick his neck out. The dream allowed me to look at my life, as well as look out from it with a freedom I didn't usually feel. I felt the relationship within me between these parts of myself and the tension. Much like the elephant in my dream that first night in the emergency room, I knew I needed to pick up and carry with me the brokenness in my body and life out of the jungle and back into life. I was grateful for the dream's restorative connective role in my psyche and healing.

As we drove toward home and approached the supermarket, Dennis reminded me about the turkey.

"I'll park the car and run in and get it," he said.

"Just pull up in front of the store," I suggested.

"Why?" he asked.

"I want to go in and get the turkey myself."

Dennis was shocked.

"You can't do that."

"Why not?" I countered. "I may be handicapped, but I'm not helpless."

"Jack, you have already moved around a lot for one day and the wheelchair is at home."

"Listen Dennis, thanks for your concern. But this is something I really need to do. I'm not entirely sure why, but I need to go get that turkey." I checked my pocket and made sure I had the receipt from Alice's shopping trip the week before. I was set.

Dennis got out, walked around to open the car door and handed me the walker.

"You sure about this?" He asked.

"Not entirely," I said. "If I'm not back by nightfall, send in reinforcements."

He started to ask more questions, but I placed the walker in front of me and made a bead on the grocery store, surging forward 6 inches at a time.

I knew exactly where the meat department was, and holding the image of the turkey in front of me, I toe-touched along on my walker, one step at a time. Lifting the walker, my left hand gripping the post, I'd place it six inches ahead. Stepping with my right leg while my right arm rested on the platform, I'd shuffle along, finishing off with my left leg and foot lightly touching the floor. Deep inside an energy drove me forward towards the back of the store, one step at a time. Tunnel vision. Time ceased. Beads of sweat rolled off my forehead into my eyes. I dared not stop.

At the end of the aisle, turning left, the turkeys came into view. Like a magnet, they drew me forward. But when I reached them and looked over the entire frozen flock, it dawned on me there were no small ones. They all seemed enormous. Perched on my walker, I scoped out the least gargantuan of the bunch, and positioned myself in front of it.

Very cautiously, I reached out to grab it. Slowly my left hand pulled it to me, and as the label came into focus, my heart sank.

"18lbs 6 ozs."

"18 lbs," I repeated to myself. I grabbed a plastic bag and tried to slide the monster into it, using a single hand. It would have been easier to try to juggle a greased watermelon with one hand.

Patiently, I chased the slippery turkey around in circles. I tried a myriad of ways to get it corralled into the plastic bag. Then, in the frenzy of my turkey rustling, I paused, suddenly aware of numerous eyes staring at me. With even greater conviction, I pinned the turkey against the counter and slowly worked the bag over it. Triumphantly I pulled the bag out of the freezer case and hung it from the grip post of the walker.

Victory.

The walker immediately nearly flipped over.

Grasping the handle with the turkey hanging from it, I steadied it and attempted to move forward. But each step forward required me to lift the walker. And each time I attempted to lift it, I became precariously close to toppling over. After several attempts, I had become exhausted and moved a grand total of what couldn't have been more than 4 inches.

The turkey had beaten me. I had been bested by a dead frozen bird.

Catch and release.

I unhooked the turkey and dropped it back into the case and then slowly began working my way back up the aisle. My heart was pounding, and despite dancing with turkeys in the freezer section, I was sweating profusely.

Thinking things really couldn't get worse, I looked up and saw a neighbor, Lynn, and her two children standing in front of me.

Lifting my head and eyes to meet them, I noticed Lynn's tender smile. The children stood staring at me as if they were at a clown show at a travelling circus.

"I'm so glad to see you Jack."

Lynn went on to relate to me how on the day of the accident she was outside hanging laundry when the Med/Stat helicopter circled overhead.

"When I heard the next day what had happened to you I felt so bad. There I was, less than a mile away, enjoying the day, and you were down in the ravine, nearly dead, alone, trying to crawl out. It was like I was so close to you, but I couldn't help you. I didn't know."

I wanted to say thanks and really wanted to relate that there was this turkey in a plastic bag back in the case that needed a lift to my car. But, I couldn't bring myself to say it. Looking at Lynn I couldn't tell if I saw pity or sadness, but I felt a piercing pain inside of me. Something held me tight. I glanced at her children who continued to look at me in disbelief.

When I looked back at Lynn, I simply said, "Thanks for caring." Swallowing, my lips dry, I noticed the luster in Lynn's eyes as tears hovered.

Lynn broke the silence, "I'll call Alice and see if there's anything she needs. Maybe Devin would like to come over and play with Johnny."

Smiling sheepishly I said, "That sounds good."

Reaching out, I pushed the walker ahead, somewhat embarrassed. As I approached the end of the aisle and turned for the exit, the service desk came into view. Working my way over to it, I explained my situation to the woman behind the counter. Sympathetically she reached for the intercom. "Oh no!" I thought.

"Sam, please come to the service counter."

Whew! That was close. I was afraid she was going to announce something along the lines of, "Sam, please help the old crippled guy in the walker retrieve his frozen turkey.

In very short order, Sam arrived. I told him about the sole turkey in a plastic bag and asked to pick it up for me.

Moments later Sam returned, 18 pound bagged frozen turkey in hand.

"Would you like me to take this to your car sir?"

"Sure." I responded.

"If you give me your coupon and receipt, I'll drop it off at the register for you."

"Thank you," I said. At a snail-like pace, I worked my way outdoors, feeling the weight of a dozen eyes watching each of my micro steps.

I reached the car and collapsed into my seat.

"That didn't take long," Dennis said.

A mixed feeling of sadness and embarrassment moved through me.

"I feel like I spent a week in one of Macy's display windows. Thanks for waiting Dennis."

And turkey in hand, we headed home.

CHAPTER 15
Broken Healer

The day after my fall, my two friends and colleagues, Peter and Arnie, had reached out to all of my clients and notified them of my accident. They acted as referral sources as well as on-going sources of information regarding my condition. Based on my initial prognosis, they had informed everyone that it would be many months, perhaps as long as a year, before I'd be back in my office.

While I may have been out of service, my clients and my practice had never been out of my thoughts. On the contrary, my growing awareness of the child within me and the restorative and healing powers of yielding and accepting had shed a new and profound light on my understanding of other people's suffering. It was transforming the very essence of how I listened, interacted and worked with each and every one of them.

That transformation, as had my awareness of how to yield and accept, came in stages.

James
My initial epiphany came in those first few hellish nights in the hospital. I remembered vividly how I had flashed on a client of mine, James, who had been suffering from post-traumatic stress disorder. It was late during a business trip, and he had just put

the key in his hotel door when someone had assaulted him from behind. A man had been hiding in the shadows of the stairwell. He had rushed out while James's back was to him and stabbed him twice. James turned to face his assailant and was stabbed two more times in the chest. As he fell to the floor in his room, the assailant reached into his pocket, took his wallet and ran. That was all James could remember.

As I lay in my own hospital bed, wracked with pain and haunted by the sounds of suffering around me, I thought how similar the next part of James' ordeal was to what had happened to me in the ravine. Somehow James crawled unconsciously down a ninety foot long hallway, around the corner and some forty feet further until he came into the field of vision of the hotel's front desk clerk.

James survived but spent two weeks in the hospital recovering. A friend came to pick him up and take him home, and as the two of them walked to the car, they passed a man who coincidentally resembled the person who had assaulted James. James, on seeing the man, experienced uncontrollable panic, and he collapsed and dropped like a rock to the sidewalk.

He spent that night back in the hospital, and went home only to become agoraphobic. I began seeing him shortly thereafter. And while he recovered significantly from his fears, and eventually returned to work and life, I knew, even in those first nights in the hospital, that in the aftermath of my fall, I would have helped him and listened to him from a very different perspective.

His anxiety and fears had overwhelmed him. He had become agoraphobic because of his intense sense of vulnerability regarding being in the world. From everything I had learned from my fall, I felt confident I would have been able to help him consciously turn into his fears and suffering, not resist them and become their victim.

I didn't know when or if I would see him again or what condition I'd be in when I did, but oh, how much more compassion and understanding I would have for him. His having no memory of how he got from his room to the hotel's front desk had not been something we had spent a lot of time on, but it now carried a great deal of significance for me. Had the Presence engaged a life force within him, "crawling" him as it had crawled me? Did the nearness of death awaken his body's innate intelligence with his own divine instinct? I felt hopeful that in telling him my story, I could show him how "conscious suffering" was an attitude toward oneself that anyone could develop. It was an exploration of oneself in which reflective openness can deepen awareness and allow us a vivid glimpse into our essential nature.

Sally

A couple of weeks later I was in my earliest and most painful stages of rehabilitation with Richard, I lay in my hospital bed early one morning trying to visualize the exercises I would be performing. I was breathing in as deeply as possible, trying to anchor and center myself and allow room for the pain and my fear. As I did, I sensed that someone was in my room.

My eyes began to open, but they involuntarily shut as I was startled to see a client of mine standing there. A mirage? I wasn't ready to see anyone outside of my family or doctors, but there she was. I felt her eyes take in my condition. A sudden sense of vulnerability coursed through my being. Lying there, naked beneath the sheets, so broken and raw, the invisible core of my humanness was now exposed, expressing itself silently. Yet it was the sight of her frightened, wincing, childlike face that burned deep into my mind.

After a moment of awkward silence, I heard my own voice, almost imperceptibly say, "Sally?"

She walked up to the head of the bed, a little too quickly, bent over eagerly, and in an agonizing tone asked, "How are you?"

Struggling with the moment that was saturated with our emotions, I finally responded.

"I'm OK" I said. "I'm just trying to manage the pain."

And then still struggling with the fact that one of my clients was actually standing in my room, I added, "How did you get in?"

As Sally's shaky voice swept over me, I struggled with the experience of having my privacy violated and my own shattered world torn open. But as the moments passed, my reality shifted, and I began to rise up through my sorrow and my sensation of being trapped and exposed.

There was an urgency and vulnerability to Sally's presence that felt suffocating, leaving me exposed to her terrors as well as my own. As awkward as it was for me, I started to find my bearings and find a way to connect. I was yielding to the moment, not resisting it.

"You seem upset. What's going on?" As she spoke, I centered on her frightened and somewhat annoyed tone. Images and memories of her history and our years of working together swept through me. Sally had a major depressive disorder for most of her adult life that was punctuated with bouts of suicidal ideation. It wasn't until I was aware of holding my breath that I realized that a growing sense of alarm and responsibility was gaining momentum within me. The desperateness she was communicating to me did not appear evident to her. Quickly I became more cognizant of the magnitude of her coming here and the far-reaching implications my accident had for her.

Sally had grown up the youngest of three children in a violent, dysfunctional family. By the time her father, whom she contended I not only resembled, but also coincidentally shared a birthday with, abandoned the family, Sally's limited ego strength was depleted. The traumatic childhood had a significant impact on her development and resulted in a lifelong emotional disturbance. Prior to my accident, Sally's condition was stable but precarious. She was fearful of losing Ellen, a friend, who was dying from a very aggressive form of cancer. Her dear friend's heroic but futile struggle had been nearing an end, bringing up very old issues and memories of attachment and loss. As she stood before me, I could feel how terrified Sally was of losing me, and how my accident contributed to the increasingly intensely needy person she had become.

I now saw the full effect of the pain on her face. The experience tortured me while at the same time began to fill me with compassion. She was being pushed well beyond her coping ability. Just as I had finally succeeded in wrestling with my introverted mind, she seemed to compose herself somewhat and asked, "Can I sit with you for a while?"

"Yes." I answered somewhat hesitantly. My pain pulled me in one direction, and hers pulled me in another. My delicate sadness and fiery agony mixed with her fearful vulnerability revealing the frailty and depth of our connection. Breathing deeply, I tried to still the greedy energy within me and open to the state we were both in. I had no reference point for this experience we shared.

Sally reached behind her and took a get well card off the windowsill. "This is the card I sent you."

While reading to me what she had written, tears filled her eyes. Her sincerity dramatized her vulnerability and reached me. She needed to know that she was still alive for me, and once she was assured that I was still alive at all, that I was alive for her as well. My self-consciousness dissolved as I realized I had been her container and had helped hold her brokenness. The brokenness of my own body and the container of our therapy were now both threatened and drew her to me. Sally wanted to be a container for me, attending to me, soothing me, and holding my brokenness as I had held hers.

Haltingly she asked, "Can I touch your arm? Would it hurt?"

The plea in the tone of her voice stirred both empathy and anxiety in me. I wanted to say, "No, please just talk with me," but I didn't have the strength or wits about me to do so. Despite my discomfort with her gesture, I let her touch my arm, and then I began to talk to her about life, change, suffering and what I had learned about the need to be compassionate with ourselves. As I talked, I watched Sally's face begin to relax and her fear subside. I was trying to re-assemble some sense of myself as her therapist, as awkward as it was.

Slowly, I began to feel less and less vulnerable. But given my condition and the anxiety I had worked through at the start of our conversation, it wasn't long before I felt depleted and drained. With nothing left to give and a growing need for privacy, I reassured Sally that we'd talk again soon. As she sensed our time together was over, her fear became palpable again.

"Listen," I said, hoping to alleviate her fear of losing me, "Let's talk again by phone in a few days. I'm not going anywhere."

After Sally left I had felt utterly exhausted. Yet at the same time, I felt in awe of the power of human relationships and the infinite permutations of possibilities that continually reinforce how connected we all are to each other and to the eternal Presence. Even in death, while we may lose our bodies, the Love that connects us lives on.

My encounter with Sally opened my eyes and heart to the possibility that my relationships with my clients would be able to continue, even if, at first, the connections were only by phone. But I could connect and listen and interact with clients in ways more profound than I had ever known. But while thoughts of James and Sally's visit fanned the embers of this idea, the notion didn't fully coalesce until after my dream in which I had been connected to all of humanity through the beating heart of a child. Suffering has a brilliance to it.

For days after that dream, I had remained under the spell of its transformative image. The voice from the timeless sanctuary of my soul continued to vibrate within me. It was as if the sounds of mankind's collective brokenness were speaking with me. Yielding and opening to the dream's invitation, it was at that point that I had earnestly begun to offer phone sessions to clients.

The initial awkwardness in conducting phone therapy gradually diminished as I persevered. My condition had taught me how to give permission to clients to open and surrender more deeply into a humanness that we now both shared. The accident had left me more attentive to my own and others' feelings. This increased sensitivity, when properly managed, allowed me to enter in to another person's world in such a way that their deepest wounds, fears, and vulnerabilities could be heard and responded to. I began noticing it was easier for me to experience and understand what was going on with my clients. With my own pretenses and defensive habits torn away, I seemed to have direct access to their experience. I began to observe how I first felt people through my body; how their emotions, fears and conflicts then bubbled up into my emotional awareness and then intellectual understanding. Learning to trust this process of healing through my brokenness began to feel like a blessing. I was becoming a better therapist.

The process of glimpsing wholeness in my brokenness enabled me to see and experience the wholeness and brokenness of humanity. I had awakened with a new found awareness of both Jackie, that inner child within me, and the Beloved. My capacity to feel had grown deeper.

Perhaps it was more simply my re-discovery of Jackie, his spiritual essence and this deep desire to "reach out" as the dream suggested and once again love and live from that open heart-centered place within. The energies from the spirit world continued at times to lift me from my grounded place within my broken body. It was the pain, I knew, that I needed to consciously suffer if I were to remain in the world as a healer. Learning to continue to receive the pain moment to moment demanded an open-heart, discipline, patience and humility. I could not ask of my clients what I had not learned to do in my own healing.

Becky

One of my most intense phone sessions came just prior to my decision to see patients again in my office. It was with a client named Becky. She was a capable resilient woman whose parents had died tragically in a car accident five years prior to my accident. We had begun working together three years earlier, shortly after her husband, Harold, had developed colon cancer. I had seen the two of them together until Harold died a year ago and then continued my work with Becky. Last summer Laura, Becky's only child, was diagnosed at age 30 with breast cancer.

"Jack, do you remember talking with me the day of your accident?"

"I don't," I said, somewhat surprised by her question.

"I called you about 7:30 that morning before you woke Devin up for school. I had been very upset about Laura's response to chemotherapy."

"Now it's starting to come back to me. Laura had called you during the night because she had been sick and couldn't sleep."

"I just needed to talk with you and get my bearings because I was so upset. Our conversation helped me settle down." She paused, seeming to search for the right words.

"I'm not sure where to start, but when I got the call Monday night that you had a terrible fall, I was sure that my early morning call had distracted you and in some way contributed to your accident. I've felt responsible and guilty ever since. I was afraid to call your home." She took in a deep breath, and I could hear the sadness in her voice.

"After Harold died, I felt the same way. Something bad always seems to happen to people I care about."

I felt Becky's anguish. I knew the sense of responsibility she'd taken on with Harold, in addition to the stress that had worn on them around their marital issues.

"Becky, listen to me very carefully. Your call that morning did not distract me. It had *absolutely* nothing to do with my accident. I was glad you called and happy to have helped." I waited a few beats to let that sink in.

"But I have a question for you. What's it been like for you feeling this way about me and being unable to reach me?"

"Horrible," she answered almost immediately. "I feel like everyone I need or love abandons me; it's just a matter of time."

"Have you ever felt like this before?"

"What do you mean?"

I could hear in her tone she knew what I meant.

"Feeling angry, deserted, abandoned?"

"I felt it when my parents were killed. And sometimes I felt it with Harold, when he was sick and especially after he died."

She started crying, and then there was silence.

"These feelings Becky, you have felt them before. I've felt them since my accident. They're just feelings – normal, understandable feelings. Don't judge yourself by them. Respect the process. Don't turn away from yourself. Let your heart open to yourself."

Her voice broke. "Laura!"

All I could hear over the phone was her sobbing.

"*I'm so afraid of losing her.*"

"Of course you are. You've had so many losses already, and nothing can be more painful than the thought of losing your child."

Becky continued to cry gently.

After a long silence I continued

"Becky, I really am sorry my accident has been such a source of pain and conflict for you. Since my fall, I have gained a much better understanding of what it is to suffer love. I love my family so much, and I can see, hear, and feel their pain, just like you can see and hear Laura's pain."

"We have both been traumatized, and trauma inevitably regresses everyone because it touches us so deeply. We are catapulted into those most tender and gentle places that make us human. It's likely that we haven't touched those places since we were children."

"Your parents' deaths provoked those deep feelings and needs. Harold's death evoked similar feelings. Those losses, like the losses I've suffered, have ripped control away. It has left us wide open to pain, fear and also love if we can find the courage to stay open."

Becky was quiet for a few moments and then responded through her tears.

"Laura was such a beautiful, sensitive child, and I still love her so much. My life with Harold had its challenges, and I know that created stress for Laura. And now I feel so guilty and responsible for her disease."

"Believe me," I responded, "I know all too well about feeling guilty and responsible for the pain I've caused for my family. When I get stuck in my judging mind, I'm miserable. But lately, I've realized that those thoughts not only close my heart but they make it almost impossible for me to need or take in love. They block my understanding of what's going on as well as my ability to grow and heal. In that space nothing reaches me. When I feel that way, I'm tight, anxious, and there is a burning sensation inside of me."

"Me too."

"But when I can be compassionate with myself, accepting, open - I feel better. There is a warmth and spaciousness in my mind and body. Both are helped to heal as my psyche spontaneously flows energy into me and my will is aligned with the moment. I can feel and give love freely.

There was quiet on the other end of the phone, though I could hear her breath trembling and imagined tears in her eyes.

"Becky?"

"Yes."

"I can understand your struggle with Laura's condition and everything it brings up in you in more ways than you can imagine. But, please know, *you are not alone.* I'm going to be ok, and God willing, so will Laura. Try to open your heart and allow all the love you feel for her to meet your grief and fear. Let the pain and fear in. Let it flow through you so you can open yourself to the love that is there. Allow that energy to transform your life."

"I know you're right, Jack," she said through her sobs, "I just don't know if I can do it."

"Becky, you are doing it right now. You're allowing me to experience your grief, love, guilt, anger and need. By doing so, you're identifying less with those feelings. There is some acceptance and space around them. Allow the love that you're feeling right now for Laura to touch that vulnerable self that is now in relationship with me. If you can let my compassion in, you can begin to allow your own compassion to touch those parts of you that are in pain, afraid to love, afraid to lose. Take a few slow, deep breaths."

I redirected Becky's breath deeper into her body. Her critical and judging mind had disengaged somewhat, but there was a lot of "noise" in her. As her diaphragm and her heart began to open more, I had her visualize holding Laura when she was a child, hurt, upset and needy; the love holding the pain. As Becky allowed that connection to occur and the opposites came together I could almost "hear" her body get calmer and calmer, softer and softer.

"Now Becky, can you see in your mind's eye and imagine you as a little girl?"

"Yes."

"Can you pick her up and hold her?"

"She won't let me."

"Just be patient. Let the love that you feel simply flow to her."

"...she's reaching for me. I've got her."

"Let her know that you won't let go of her. Allow her to begin to trust you again."

By the time we ended the session, Becky no longer was stuck in the experience of guilt and responsibility. She also had the tools to understand how those feelings were protecting her from opening to the suffering love she felt for Laura. It was empowering for her to be able to be in and with herself in a softer more connected way.

After I hung up the phone, I lay back in my hospital bed feeling as if I had just birthed a new way of being in life. I had been able to use the lessons learned from my own suffering to help someone else, and that was healing.

James, Sally, a profound dream of holding a child's heart, and a series of remarkable phone sessions had eventually all guided me to the point from which I could actively interact with my clients. And three months from the time I had been rushed into the emergency room, still learning how to "turn into" the sufferings and house the pain, fear and vulnerability, my journey was continuing to move outward and back into life. I had reached the point where I was ready to return to my office, pain, walker and all. I began calling people, relieved and bolstered by their positive responses and good wishes.

Some of the clients had used my fall as a means to initiate changes in their lives and were no longer in need of my services. Others had begun working with someone else. But there were many, some of whom I'd already begun talking with, that scheduled time to see me again in my office.

My transition back to scheduling office hours, even if it was only one day a week, was not without anxiety. I wondered if I could remain in my body, staying open and honoring the suffering without being too distracted by it. I had learned how to do that fairly well when on the phone, but I'd always been in the privacy of my home and hospital bed.

I wondered how upset clients would be with me for the loss, grief or fear my sudden exit from their life may have caused. I didn't know if they would be as honest with me face to face as they had been on the phone.

As the week before my first office session passed, I continued to notice my heightened awareness of my feelings and those of others over the phone. It was as if my body had a new radar system that allowed me to experience and participate in a person's struggles within their bodies. I felt as if both my body and mind had been broken-open, leaving me more receptive and responsive to interpersonal cues and stimuli. For many, their sense that I had compassionately "joined" them seemed to facilitate their surrendering more deeply into their experience. For others, my awareness of the emotion they were feeling and how they held those emotions inside themselves seemed too much for them to take in. Consequently, they would further submerge their experience in some distracting manner. I wasn't sure how best to manage this intuitive bodily awareness, but I did have the realization that although I had lost a lot, I was beginning to gain something essential as a therapist. From being shattered, I was starting to experience a greater wholeness of myself and others.

Going to my office for the first time later in the week brought my recovery to a new level. Peter, a clinical social worker and dear friend of twenty years, had space in the same building and supported me through my first day, driving me there and taking me back home.

That Thursday morning, as Peter opened the door to my office, we both stopped dead in our tracks.

"Wow," I said.

My office was as cold and lifeless as a morgue. Everything looked the same, but the energy had vanished. Slowly I moved across the room on my walker, taking it all in. I looked over at Peter. I could feel his love and support. He brought me a glass of water and closed the door behind him. Very gradually, I sat down and settled into the reality of the experience.

Pushing myself back in my recliner, I took in the African masks, trees, paintings, antiques, and books that surrounded me. They felt like the memories and images of another person, the man I used to be. That man had a physical power and strength. Now I was held together by screws, wires, mesh and plates. Getting from the car to the office with searing pain totally exhausted me. I prayed that I could bring my newfound experience of love and wholeness into the sessions I had scheduled for today.

As the sun's early rays illuminated the office, I closed my eyes and reflected on the timeless Presence that I knew was now with me. I said a short prayer and asked for support and guidance throughout the day. My responsibility for my life had increased immeasurably since confronting death. The encounter had engaged intense emotions which were a powerful growing force in my life. My decision to consciously yield to my suffering and choose to be in the moment with whatever was happening continued to be a challenge. Although the process was redemptive, its pain could both exhaust and terrify. The sense of terror and restlessness that I could feel deep down in my bones was a reminder of how I was still processing a lot of "noise" from the trauma. Yet, alongside this sense of fragility was a growing sense of self-trust that seemed to be linked to being vertical and using a walker.

There had been a "push" from within, urging me to leave the silence and solitude of the forest and my home. I felt committed to emerge from a cocoon-like existence and to re-engage in the world. Professionally and personally, I was grateful for having developed a deeper understanding of how transpersonal energies penetrated my consciousness and rescued me as parts of myself had been torn away. It was really miraculous that while I was overwhelmed mentally, emotionally and physically, my Beloved had remained vigilant. It had continued to organize and store events, out-picture them in dreams, and release selected memories back into my consciousness. Thankfully, these restorative energies had uplifted and sustained me, while down below unconscious defenses were being built to protect those torn away parts of me.

Psychological defenses are both protective and problematic. They are invisible psychic forces that sustain life and also function to hold vulnerable, injured parts of us encapsulated in the unconscious as well as in our bodies. Once there, these parts await their time to be brought back into consciousness and hopefully embraced by us and reintegrated. My challenge, for both myself and the clients I would see that day, would be to consciously help in the opening to and suffering of these tender, painful memories and experiences.

There was a knock on the door, and my first client had arrived.

Jill

"Come in."

Jill opened the door and walked in. I saw her visually flinch as she saw me. In that moment I could see what she saw. There was little resemblance to the man she had last seen in this office. I felt bad for both of us.

"I...I somehow didn't know what to expect in coming here today. I felt very anxious when you said to come in. But I didn't expect this. I'm sorry...Maybe I shouldn't have come."

Jill was trembling. I could hear the emotion in her voice. I thought to myself, "Holy shit, how bad do I really look!"

The realization hit me that my need to be here, in my office, had a whole lot less to do with Jill or anyone else. It was all about me and my will and determination to be here. I hadn't taken in the reality of my condition and how broken I looked to others. I had an intense but momentary desire to hide, but there was nowhere to go.

I took some slow, deep breaths to come into the moment. A wave of sadness washed over me, for what I had lost, and for Jill.

"It's your fragility, Jack. It immediately brought me back into the ICU before Saul died. You were there Jack. You know what I mean."

Saul was Jill's husband, who one afternoon, without any warning, had suffered a massive aneurysm and died. His death had occurred in the early spring before my accident. I had been with Jill when she made the excruciating decision to take Saul off life support. We stood together holding Saul's hand as he took his last breath.

The hospital had sponsored a grief group that had brought Jill great solace. It had also been the venue where she had met a widower named Philip. Over the course of several months, they had begun seeing each other, and throughout the summer, their affection for each other grew. That fall, I had suddenly exited Jill's life, and now for the first time since my accident, I saw what my absence had triggered for her.

"Several times last night I almost called your office to leave a message that I just couldn't come in today. I just wasn't ready."

"I'm sorry Jill. I didn't realize what it would be like for you to see me. I recognize now that I was caught up in my own need to get back into life and be of some value to others. Thank you for being willing to see me."

Slowly and hesitantly, Jill began.

"When I first got the call about you I was in shock. I felt so badly for you, your wife and the boys. But as the weeks went by and you weren't there to talk with, I felt angry and then guilty for feeling that way, knowing how badly hurt you were and the pain you must have been in. You were there with me when Saul died, and I needed you desperately. But suddenly, you too were almost dead, gone. I felt abandoned."

I listened, deeply moved by her honesty.

"I'm sorry Jill. I know how heartbreaking the loss of Saul has been for you. Going through a similar trauma with me couldn't have been an easy follow up. But you've had the strength to turn to Phillip. He's been a real blessing for you."

We talked more about her conflicted feelings about me since the accident, and it slowly flowed into how similar she'd felt with the suddenness of Saul's death. She felt their time together had seemed unfinished and felt great remorse for not making more of their life together.

Our conversation reminded her of a dream she had.

"In this dream, I'm in Europe. I have to get to a meeting, but I discover that I've been traveling in the wrong direction. As I start in the other direction, I come across Phillip who shows me the correct way to go. Phillip and I enter the house I've been looking for, and there in the kitchen is Saul. He's alive but doesn't say a word. I wake up."

"What sense do you make of that dream?"

"I've felt lost and sort of directionless since Saul's death. That was the first time Saul was in a dream of mine that I can remember. When I saw him, I felt a lot of things: happy, confused, guilty...I don't know, but I can still see and feel his presence."

"Go with that. Stay in your body, *breathe*."

"He's reassuring me he's alright. He's reassuring me that it's all right to be with Phillip. If it wasn't for him, I'd still be lost. He helped me get my bearings."

"Why is Saul in the kitchen? What does that mean to you?"

Tears that were held back began to stream down Jill's cheeks. She had obviously been grappling with this question. There was a long silence, filled with her tears and heartache.

"I can't tell what Saul wants to say to me, but I can feel his love and permission, maybe to let myself care about Phillip. There has been such an aching void in my heart. I thought it could never be filled."

Saul's presence was serving as an intercessor from deep within her psyche. Love and grief were truly inextricably woven together.

"Over the last couple of months Jill, I've learned to trust the process of suffering, the daily pain and loss in my life. It tore me wide open. But from moment to moment, I struggled not to deny or avoid the pain but learned to open to it. As I discovered more about myself, I learned that I was blessed from within. The kitchen is such a safe internal space to be in. It's a place of nourishment, where I know you and Saul shared many intimate moments, because we've talked about them. You're now assimilating that love and nurturing, and you are beginning to embody it in your life. It's your life to live now.

"I never realized until this moment," Jill whispers, "that caring about Phillip doesn't mean I loved Saul any less. I love and will always love him."

Our time was up and although I felt drained, there was palpable vitality in the room between the two of us.

"Thanks, Jack. Thank you for coming in today and seeing me."

"I'm glad I did. I'll see you next week."

I saw two more clients that day, and while the encounters were different, the essential themes remained the same. My brokenness had made me more whole as a healer than I had ever been. I was thoroughly drained, but invigorated and grateful in ways I could never have imagined.

Peter returned after my last session, and on our drive home we shared some great laughs reminiscing over some rather "bone-headed" moments in my life. Peter ribbed me for a time I had a deep leg wound from a chainsaw, which he had patched with a bottle of hydrogen peroxide, gauze, and packing tape. I had marched Devin off to a soccer game with that jury-rig. My willfulness had played such a huge role in my life, always turning from and playing through the pain. I had been fighting through everything since as long as I could remember.

"Nothing," Peter said, "has ever stopped you until this accident, my friend."

"And now," I said, "I've come to accept my vulnerability and open myself to all the pain and fear that might come with it. And from that, I have healed – inside and out."

"It never made sense to me before I was broken," I went on, "To allow myself to be broken open. But now I have so much respect for the process of breaking open and choosing to yield my mind into the body that feels like it's causing me the pain."

Peter listened quietly.

"I realize now that my body is a mysterious pattern of movement that I don't understand except to say it is always flowing and changing. I never would have known this if I hadn't fallen."

Peter dropped me off, and as I began the slow trip with the walker to the front door. Devin ran out of the house to greet me. Brendan and Alice waited in the doorway. They were all smiles. I basked in their love and happiness to see me home.

I felt like the most fortunate man on earth.

CHAPTER 16
One Lucky Guy

The first thing I recall after the revision surgery in my elbow and shoulder was the feeling of being rolled along on a gurney. I opened my eyes to the hauntingly familiar sight of green surgical uniforms. An intense and fiery pain assailed me.

"You're in the recovery room. A nurse will be over in a few minutes and shortly take you to your room. Sorry to have to move you," someone told me.

I closed my eyes again, sinking into the pain and helplessness. Someone was talking to me, but as the pain had become unmanageable. My breathing was shallow. It kept getting ensnared by the pain. My right side felt like a whirling continuous circle of fire.

"Hi Jack. I'm Janice, one of the recovery room nurses." Her soft brown eyes and attentive, warm smile helped mitigate the pain.

"How are you feeling after today's surgery?"

Appreciating her presence, I replied, "I'm distracted by the pain. It's so intense right now, but I'm working on it."

We were moving again, and Janice rolled me into the elevator as we spoke.

"I read about your accident in the newspaper. I was on duty that day. And, I've read your whole chart. You sure are one lucky guy. Somebody was certainly watching over you that day."

Although she spoke in a soft voice, every word reached me and reverberated within me.

"I was not only watched over, but taken care of as well."

"I take it your talking about more than the hospital staff." She looked directly into my eyes, and I could tell she wasn't just making small talk. She was engaged and truly interested. I recounted my experience in the ravine, Loraine finding me and being rescued and evacuated. Her eyes never left mine as I detailed the experience.

"I've been a nurse for over twenty years. I've seen it all. The presence of a higher power becomes so apparent at times, and then at other times, it's nowhere to be found."

Her compassion and spiritual sensitivity held my focus.

"You remind me of someone," I murmured. Janice listened while pushing the gurney down the hall.

"The nurse on board the helicopter was an angel of mercy. When people are broken, in pain and fear, the people who attend to them are so important."

Our conversation had softened my awareness and breath, but as we reached the nurses' station, the pain continued to consume me. My elbow and shoulder were on fire. It felt as if some demonic force had risen up from the dark abyss while I was under anesthesia, and attempted to rip my arm right out of the shoulder socket.

It must have been obvious as Janice touched my hand softly and placed in it the morphine pump.

"I'll stop by and check on you at the end of my shift."

I mumbled something and impulsively depressed the button to relieve the pain. Just before my body sailed off into oblivion, I wondered how I'd made that decision so easily

When I awoke later, the persistent pain was still there. I tried to use my breath to move into my body and surrender to it, but I failed. I tried to visualize my shoulder and back where all the scar tissue and adhesions had been torn open. Only seeing it on fire, I tried to imagine cold water gently flowing over it, but I could only hold that image for a short time, and I was consumed again. Suddenly I flashed on the executioner's dream, the man's fear and my compassion for him. I tried again to take a deep breath into the pain and my fear of it, but I failed. The transpersonal energies of the Beloved were nowhere to be found. That relationship I had come to know now replaced by morphine. My consciousness was cloudy. The morphine acted like a powerful vacuum, driving my consciousness into the forgetting room outside of life. The pain in my body eclipsed my will to accept it. I yielded as long as I could. I depressed the button again.

The next time I awoke Alice was sitting beside me. "I feel really disconnected and regressed," I said, looking into her concerned face.

"It will be OK"

"I can't work with the pain or my fear of it."

"Jack, give yourself the day. Tomorrow you may feel differently. You are going to be here two more days anyway, so be patient with yourself."

Alice left when they brought dinner. I wasn't hungry, and I felt agitated and depleted by the pain. I depressed the button and called it a night.

When I awoke on the second day, I felt a little more like myself.

When breakfast arrived, I was surprised to notice I wasn't hungry. I drank some orange juice. I lay back and closed my eyes. The pain was still there, but I felt a bit stronger. I worked on my breathing and then did some self-hypnosis and energy work. That seemed to help me create some softness and space inside my body.

Dr. Passick stopped by during the morning. Everything had gone well in surgery. He described the difficulty he'd had tearing through all the adhesions to rotate my shoulder girdle.

"The revision to your elbow went well. You may not be able to notice the change yet but there should be less pain." He agreed to allow me to switch off the morphine to Tylenol with Codeine.

Gradually, I began to breathe more deeply and open again to the pain. As I did, wet, vulnerable feelings began to interface with it. Once again, I realized how much harder it was to encounter pain after resting in morphine's forgetting room. Although the drug was merciful, it depleted resources I needed to manage suffering. There was a big difference between being in the forgetting room and being in the arms of the Beloved. In both realms my unbearable suffering was temporarily relieved. Returning from the morphine haze found me disoriented and disconnected, but returning to my body from the Beloved, transpersonal energies often sustained me. In opening to my body and trusting the process of suffering they flowed through me and encouraged me back into life.

When Alice came to visit that afternoon, I was in less pain or at least managing it better. We had a good chat and she told me that tomorrow she was taking a personal leave day from work and would be picking me up to take me home as I was to be discharged.

After my dinner that evening, I reflected on the two days following surgery. The assault of the pain following surgery had re-traumatized me, leaving me surprisingly vulnerable to any means of escape. The morphine was necessary but was also a pathetic substitute for the Beloved's energies. All that I'd struggled for over the past few months might have been lost if it wasn't for my persistent knowledge that within my pain and beneath the fear, was a hidden treasure that could only be found by opening to and trusting in my body's innate intelligence.

I eventually began to drift off to sleep, lulled by the distant sounds of murmuring TV's and footsteps moving down the hall as darkness began to displace the day's fading light.

"Struggle," I thought. My nature had been built on struggling and until the accident, deep down inside, I hadn't known any other way. But through my suffering, I had found another way. Rather than simply reacting to what frightened me and trying to overpower or resist it, I'd learned to surrender to it. I had also learned to listen to my pain and people's suffering with my heart. For months the pain had been teaching me about life, truth, and my own nature. Pain and suffering were a natural part of life.

On the edge of sleep, I began slow, deep, diaphragmatic breathing. I directed my breath to the areas of my body still on fire. I noticed my resistance slowly loosening and the tissues, muscles, and ligaments begin to soften. Not trying to change the pain, but just trying to enter it, I fell asleep, and dreamed.

I am up in a space capsule orbiting the earth. It's beautiful, quiet, and very peaceful. Looking at the large console in front of me, I notice a screen. Scrolling along the screen are symbols of ancient hieroglyphics, combined with numbers and signs, resembling formulas from physics.

I'm drawn to the screen. My left hand reaches out to touch it. Immediately the space capsule is falling at a tremendous speed, like an elevator whose cable has been severed. I'm falling, faster and faster. I know I'm going to die. I absolutely know I'm going to die. It's terrifying. Every molecule and cell in my body is saturated with the awareness of imminent death. The capsule is starting to burn up on the outside. It is starting to get extremely hot inside as the capsule continues to fall through space.

Suddenly I hear a voice say, "You touched it. You should not have done that." I am filled with a tremendous amount of grief and regret.

Then, just as I am about to die, the thought occurs to me, "Why, not try to fly this thing?"

I have nothing to lose. I'm going to die, so why not try to live. Reaching out, I put my right hand gently back on the scrolling screen.

Then I woke.

The dream felt like a response to the thoughts and questions I had been mulling over during the day. I felt as if I had been given a diamond, and as I turned it in the light of my mind it reflected information, direction and even a kind of cosmic sense of humor.

The dream felt like a reference to the fall, the instinct to flip around and descend feet first, and my experience in the ravine and the decision to choose life with suffering. It was both terrifying as well as a means to re-experience my Beloved's presence. My rational mind in the ravine had been overwhelmed by fear, pain, and the imminent awareness of death. I didn't remember thinking, "I'm going to die" until after I'd left my body and returned to it. Yet I'm sure on a cellular level my body was saturated with the awareness of imminent death.

I retraced the moments of the dream. The space capsule's terrifying descent was occurring again. My breath caught as I listened, and in that moment came the awareness of my mortality. Chastened and humbled, I chose life, yielding all but love. Life was precious, and I would find the courage to live it fully.

I thought of people I knew who were traumatized and how I had watched their minds implode or explode when disaster struck. So often I had watched as an individual's ego would seize the trauma for its own drama.

I watched how my own mortified ego, with all its early defenses, tried to hook me into the drama of being a victim. But I had witnessed too many people take that bait and unsuspectingly doom their lives to perpetual suffering. I was trying hard not to avoid or exploit my suffering. Only in that neutral state, I felt, could the tragedy bring understanding as well as a release from the old, buried fears, feelings, and judgments that trauma engages.

My shoulder burned. My elbow throbbed. I breathed deeply and slowly, and I counted myself among the truly lucky, the truly blessed.

Life is sacred.

CHAPTER 17
Family Therapy

A Christmas tree with all white lights stood in the middle of the lobby as I was wheeled out of the hospital. I breathed slowly and silently, but in the face of that first glimpse of Christmas, I found no magic in the moment. Any hint of Christmas spirit had been eclipsed by the surgery's pain.

Instead of listening for bells, all I heard was the rain.

"I'll pull the car around to the front entrance. See you in a minute." Alice dashed out into the rain. As an attendant pushed me past the Christmas tree, I reflected on how different this Christmas would be. The excitement of Christmas had always been spontaneously and infectiously powered by the boys. But this year all I felt was pain, indifference, and isolation. I couldn't even find the humor to mutter "Bah. Humbug!" as I was wheeled outside.

As the volunteer pushed me, I greedily inhaled the fresh, cold, wet wind that swept over me. While waiting for Alice, I thought of the dream I had the night before, and how whatever ascent into the heavens I had experienced during my near death experience, I was now certainly in fiery descent back to earth. I closed my eyes and slowly breathed into the pain, choosing it as I had in the dream. I may have glimpsed the beginning of the next world, but like in the ravine, the gravitational pull back into my body was, again, scary and so painful. Fiery nerve pain still merged with surgical pain and that of tender, torn adhesions, and I worked hard to stay in my body and soothe it with my breathing.

Alice and the smiling volunteer helped me into the front seat. I watched Alice in the rearview mirror collapse the wheelchair and put it in the trunk of our Volvo. Seemingly less appreciative of the rejuvenating quality of the weather, she shut the trunk lid with a slam that shook my entire being. Feeling very thin-skinned, I felt my body had just been dammed by the trunk lid. My startle reflex and sensitivity levels were still high.

As Alice started the car and began to drive home, I noticed the rain dripping off her curly hair and onto her jacket. I watched her curls tighten, and her eyes and mouth. Wanting to reach out to her, but feeling too raw and vulnerable, I turned my attention to the road. Watching the wiper blades furiously labor to clear the rain, I tried to attend to a downpour of emotion within me, but failed to find the language necessary to express my experiences to her. This sense of wordlessness is a peculiarity of trauma and had become all too frequent in my life since the accident.

The intensity of the pain that followed this surgery seemed to have combined with the morphine, weakening my mental capacities as well as constricting my ability to experience and use my emotional process. In an odd sort of way, I felt emotionally flooded and numb at the same time. The amplification of the pain and my opening to it seemed to increase my vulnerability, further blurring my capacity for emotional expression.

"Jack, how are you? Are you in a lot of pain?"

Still clouded a bit from the morphine and trauma of the surgery, my mind was working a little erratically. "I'm OK" I started. "I'm in pain, but mostly I'm glad the surgery is behind me."

"Colin is coming tonight," Alice reminded me. "It's not too late to reschedule him if you're not up to it."

I thought for a moment. I was hurting, but not to the exclusion of postponing our family therapy session with Colin. Everyone was hurting, and if the boys, Alice and I didn't talk soon, I didn't see how we would ever truly understand the extent of all of our wounds and how we could start the healing process.

"No, let's keep the appointment. It's important. I'll be OK"

"Are you sure, Jack?" Alice asked.

"It will be good for us."

Once home, I looked out the window from my hospital bed as Alice went to pick up the kids after school. I saw in the rain and fading light outside the grayness of my life. Stripped of my pride and strength, those tender hidden parts of me were once again exposed for all to see. I had hoped that after my surgery more light would be coming into my life. But I couldn't deny the darkness that I was now feeling. I stared into the woods outside the house. It was not even 4:30p.m., but it was nearly dark outside.

"The winter solstice," I thought, December 21st.

Mentally I reminded myself that the darkness was the beginning of light. All living things die, I thought, all dead things decay, and yet from the decay comes life. I struggled to lift my energy up from my pain's dark weight. Perhaps, even here, I could pick up the scent of my Beloved which would lead me back into the light. But where was it? I found myself reflecting on how for months I had been unable to provide for my family financially, or even protect them emotionally from my being a source of pain in their lives. This reality weighed on me heavily and generated a significant amount of anxiety as I anticipated Colin's arrival. I knew if Colin did his job, and I knew he would, that the truth of my family's experiences for the past several months would be expressed.

Alice arrived home with the boys, and they immersed themselves in the evening routine, so much of which I had long taken for granted. Alice began making dinner while helping the boys with their homework. I was still looking out the window, with my head in the forest, unable to lift myself from my gloom.

"Are you hungry? Do you want any dinner?" Alice asked quietly. "Colin will be here fairly soon."

I looked into her calm and serious face concentrating on her eyes. I'd come to know those sad and strained eyes very well. I knew we were both suffering, but we were doing so apart, not together.

"I still feel nauseated from the anesthesia and morphine, but thanks anyway." Alone again, I found myself hoping that this night Colin would be able to light the candle that would reduce our family's darkness by illuminating the humanness of our shared struggle. I formulated a prayer that each of us would find the strength to open within to the suffering which is the path of our Beloved's mercy. The truth of our experiences, I prayed, would touch one another as well as ourselves in a way that would allow us to once again be whole.

I took a deep breath and exhaled knowing that my family would ask of me the strength I had to give. Then they would ask more, and I prayed for the courage to give it.

Colin arrived and everyone sat down around me in the wheelchair. After a few disquieting and somewhat awkward moments, Colin led the way by talking about some of the natural consequences of trauma. As he spoke about how injuries like mine affect not just the injured, but the family around him, the tension dissipated, and he gently, slowly, began to weave together an environment that felt safe and accepting.

But as safe and inviting as the environment became, I became acutely aware of intense but undifferentiated emotion that vibrated throughout my body and threatened to overwhelm me. I found it suddenly very difficult to look at the faces of my family. Each face struck me like a rock thrown through a glass window, shattering my denial and releasing within me intense feelings of sorrow.

"What dad did was stupid." I could see Brendan's mixed feelings as they crossed his face, his love for me conflicting with his desire to be honest and direct. His courage shamed me for having been so self-absorbed, and at the same time, it made me proud.

"The day after the accident," he related, "when Mom and I came to see you in the intensive care unit, you looked like you were on your death bed. It really scared and upset me. You didn't even know I was in the room! It was very, very scary." The intensity and honesty in his voice was riveting.

"I thought about how you could have died in the woods as I looked at you in that hospital bed. And I didn't know how badly you were hurt then. I found out little by little over time. I think it was probably better that I didn't know. Hearing everything all at once would've been way too much for me to handle."

The pain I felt was almost unbearable as I listened to Brendan and heard from his lips the agony my accident had caused him. Yet my empathy and love for him helped me stay in the moment.

Brendan focused on Colin, and continued. "It feels like I haven't had a dad for a long time. He used to be this big, muscular man who didn't depend on me for anything. Now suddenly, he needs me to help him do almost everything. It is difficult, because if I don't help him in the right way, he will be in pain and get upset with me."

Then he turned to me directly.

"You were weaker and more dependent than you are now Dad, and you put me in a hard place. I really tried to be careful and not hurt you, but no matter how I tried to help you, so many times I'd end up hurting you. I felt angry a lot of times, but I didn't want to hurt your feelings because you were already in a lot of pain."

Profoundly moved by his innocent experiences, I heard and saw, in his anger and sorrow, an intense love and need for me. And at that moment, I felt unworthy of his love. I realized, with horror, that despite all the love I felt for my family, I also had the capacity to deeply hurt them. And I had.

There was a part of me that knew how difficult this was for Brendan. He was so sensitive. I silently cheered him on while my insides were quietly bleeding. Devin kept raising his hand, as if he was in school, hoping to get Colin's attention, but Brendan continued.

"I didn't want to see you hurting, so I kept myself busy around the house, helping mom or doing my schoolwork. But it was my job to help you in and out of the wheelchair. Getting you in and out of the car was the hardest for me until you could begin to help.

It was like having a super dad, and then suddenly having no dad, or having a dependent dad but one who had authority over me." He paused. "It was nice to come home from school and have you here, but lots of times I just needed space."

Any remnant illusions I may have had about my son being unscathed by my accident was stripped away. I felt as if I was sitting there naked - a cruel and selfish person exposed before my entire family. I wanted to scream that it was an *accident* and that I was a good father, a loving man. But then I saw the light. This wasn't about me, or who I was or wasn't. It was about Brendan, Devin and Alice, and what it was like inside the world they lived in, that I had inadvertently reshaped.

My heart just burst open inside of me, and I began to listen to Brendan from a place of love for him. It worked for a while, but then my judging mind kicked in. I found myself focusing on Brendan's recollections as memories of incidents from the past several months flooded me. I was accountable for my child's pain and the pain of that guilt was profound. I began taking in Brendan's feelings and turning them into daggers that were piercing me. This I did to myself out of sheer guilt. Inside my head I finally yelled STOP! If I continued to berate myself this way, I would never be able to allow this session with Colin to be a successful vehicle for my family's healing. I mentally redirected and worked on my breathing to neutralize the emotions that were bouncing throughout my head and body. I had to forgive myself.

So with great effort, I pulled myself into the love Brendan and I shared for each other. Immediately the separateness began to dissolve, and I was one with him. I started to really hear him and watch as he took responsibility for the experiences he had with me. He valued himself and demonstrated tremendous courage in being honest and direct. He was, however, unaware how his memories and feelings were helping me learn to become less self-involved. Yes, I had survived this painfully difficult time, but now more than ever, I could see what we had all lost. I was tongue-tied and struggled to find the words to acknowledge Brendan's hurt, anger and sadness and to relate how

I really understood why he had the feelings he did. Apologizing for being the source of so much fear and hurt for him was all the more difficult as I was fighting back the tears of regret and remorse which I feared would uncouple him from his experience.

As Brendan finished speaking, I could see how this boy was becoming an incredible man; a man of integrity, self-respect and honor. I'd watched him defend his second degree black-belt in state and national championships. I'd felt proud of him then as an athlete and martial artist. I felt proud of him now from a spiritual perspective. I saw his soul. His courage honored all of us.

Devin was sitting next to Alice on the sofa. He had his hand raised again. Colin turned to him, and Devin quickly looked at me and then back to Colin.

"I remember being in school, looking out the window and seeing and hearing the police cars and an ambulance go by. After lunch Arnie and Brendan came to school to get me. Brendan looked like he'd been crying. They told me dad had an accident, and that he'd be OK. I knew you were strong, dad, and I'd seen you hurt before; you were always OK"

"I liked the three of us sleeping together in mom and dad's bed the first night or two. A few days later, I remember going to the hospital with mom and Brendan. I brought a picture I drew of me playing soccer for dad. The elevator smelled bad, and I remember walking down different hallways. You looked hurt dad, but I knew you'd be OK. When I looked out the window I saw the same helicopter you rode landing outside. You told me what it was like to hear people screaming at night. I ate the food on the tray beside your bed."

Devin was moving around as he talked, his fear and sadness were tangible and seemed magnified by how young and innocent he was. I wanted to hold him in my arms and tell him how I loved and cared for him. My heart was bursting. I no longer heard my own thinking, only Devin's innocent voice.

"When we left the hospital, we all went to the cafeteria where we ate, and mom bought us candy. I liked it better when you were home. We played chess, and sometimes I'd try to do my homework with you, but I always made mistakes. I goofed up 'cuz I kept paying attention to you. It was hard not to have my dad as my soccer coach, but you came back in the wheelchair and it was better. We all played better when you were there."

As I watched and listened, I thought about how pain and love are interwoven in all of life and especially into the fabric of my loving family. My love for Devin was helping me to stay in my body and suffer the awareness of his painful experiences. Devin's little body emitted an abundance of energy unmatched by a forest fire on a dry windy day. The ache I felt to hold him in my arms and tell him how much I loved him, reassuring him that everything would be OK, was relentless. I wanted to tell him stories about all the wonderful, fun times we had shared over the years. I wanted to console him and tell him that someday this would also be a story that would have its own ending, and that we would absolutely have fun again.

But I just listened.

"My friends would say to me, 'Your dad is going to be OK,' so I wasn't frightened."

I finally couldn't help myself, and I spoke, reassuring Devin that indeed he was right I was hurt, but I would be OK. Soon I would be out of the wheelchair, and we would be back to doing the things we used to do together.

Somehow my reassurance for a return to normal living prompted a confession from Devin. His little lips quivered, appearing to be holding back an ocean of emotion as he said, "A while ago I wanted to run away...but now I don't."

Oh, how that confession struck home.

"I had a dream last night," he said." When I told mom this morning on the way to school, she said I should tell you. It was a scary dream. I was going to tell you, Dad, but I forgot." Devin glanced my way, searching for my support. I smiled and nodded, giving my consent. Dreams were something the boys and I shared with each other since they could talk.

With his eyes on me, Devin began.

"In the dream I had last night, Daddy, you were a robot. You, Brendan and I were in an airplane." Devin sat and now looked to Colin. "Something happened and the plane was going to crash. Brendan and I jumped out and landed in a swamp. The plane crashed with you in it. In the swamp were scary swamp monsters. We were running from them when Walker found us and led us home to where Mom was waiting. I ran in and was telling Mom what happened when Brendan came in with Walker. Then the front door opened and you came in as a robot. That's all I remember."

Like father, like son. We had both had similar dreams, his of a plane, mine of a space capsule. For both of us, our Beloved had expressed itself in an inner symbolic process that was helping us organize and process our own experience. Devin's Beloved was now carrying and caring for wounded, vulnerable parts of him that were once part of his wholeness in the world.

With great warmth Colin asked, "What was it like to have your Dad come home as a robot Devin?"

"Scary I guess. I don't know."

Colin paused just long enough for Devin to blurt out, "Your turn Mom!" We all laughed. Visually relieved that the focus was now directed towards Alice, Devin began to settle down.

Alice began, "I'm really glad you're here Colin. This is something we've all needed for some time." She took a breath before continuing.

"Initially I was numb, just handling all the things that had to be done. I was just putting one foot in front of the other. I didn't get in touch with my fear, hurt or anger for months because I was so busy. Seeing Jack in pain, intense pain, was so difficult. I know he does his best to shield us from it, but we see it or feel it all the same."

"Every day I watch how Jack tries to improve his condition. He always seems to make an effort to have meaningful exchanges with the boys and me. But gradually I've become aware of feeling burdened and resentful. I think deep down that's because Jack didn't take us into account when he climbed the tree that day. Over the years I have asked him not to do things like that when nobody was around. But he did. Somehow, in some way I believe the accident could have been prevented."

Alice's words sent a jolt through my heart. I shut my eyes at the pain. My hands clenched. I wanted to scream, "It was an accident!" But in my sudden anger and pain, I also realized that the place I was listening to Alice from was a different place than I'd been in when the boys were talking. Listening to Alice, my heart had closed. I not only felt judged, but I felt rejected. Yet, as Alice continued to face herself and me in all the pain of this traumatic journey, my respect for her also grew. She knew that to avoid her anger would limit her ability to open to deeper resources and healing energies for both herself and me.

Unfortunately, by that point, I wasn't feeling a lot of healing energy. In fact, I noticed a lot of 'noise' still moving through my body as well as critical judgments in my mind about me and Alice. I struggled to stay open to the pain and the truth I was hearing from my loved ones, but I was starting to sink under the weight of my own critical thinking.

The session continued for almost two hours. At 9:00, we called it a night.

"Colin," said Alice, "Thanks so much for your help. I need to get the boys to bed. There's school tomorrow."

As Alice and the boys left, I sat there relieved and exhausted. Colin and I sat in silence, each of us sorting out and soaking in what had transpired. Colin's empathetic gaze took in my suffering. He finally broke the silence.

"Jack, the inescapable fate of your accident was to make everything you've hidden inside part of your exterior life. I have a tremendous amount of respect for you, I always have. But tonight you were even more of a man for having the courage to face the suffering in your life, hear the painful things your family had to say, and assume responsibility for it. What will emerge from the ashes of your life is the person you have always been and more. Just keep trusting your process."

"Colin, if I hadn't realized in the emergency room that I had to trust the process, I would have been out of my mind by now. For months I've asked myself if I could have done something to avoid the accident. My answer is always the same: I'd have made the same choices. I know that conclusion certainly doesn't exonerate me from the responsibility for the suffering I've created for all of us."

"You, better than anyone, know the pattern of adventure and risk throughout my life. I'm an adventurer who thrives on challenges and the scent of danger. But now, now I'm something else…something tender, vulnerable, something that longs for love and is very sensitive to rejection. Maybe as a child I was this raw and needy but never as an adult. It feels so humiliating. Inside of me there is a constant struggle going on, pulling me in opposing directions. The state I'm in right now pulls me back from being adventurous, but will it always? I pray I'll be able to hold the tension between the two and be accountable to myself and others."

Tears were streaming down my face, and Colin came over to comfort me. He too was choking back tears.

"Jack, I have complete faith in you. What you're doing now in facing all that disowned vulnerability, is the most difficult part of the journey. Remember what Jung said that the only place we can find the 'pearl of great price' is in the shit. Well, you've been sorting through a lot of shit lately. But you've also found the pearl!"

That night after Colin left, and Alice and the boys were in bed, I couldn't sleep at all. My mind was spinning with the words I had heard, the images of each of their faces, the emotions I had seen and felt, and the sorrow and pain that burned within me. I was so proud of the courage and honesty my boys had shown. I honored Alice's honesty and drive to heal. Yet, I also saw all too clearly how this family of mine had descended into a swampy abyss from where we had been haunted by our individual and collective "monsters."

It was the image of the robot that most troubled me. Crashed planes, a swamp, monsters, and me, reimagined as a robot. I couldn't get it out of my mind and heart how alone and scared Devin must have felt at the time of the accident.

I had imposed a terrifying and painful experience on my family, and my awareness of that fact was becoming more and more vivid. It generated tremendous feelings of remorse in me. I knew when normal fight or flight responses to a terrifying situation were thwarted, people instinctively contract or freeze. This freezing response constricts emotions, sensations, energy and memories people would normally express or discharge. These experiences were now bound-up, robot-like, in the nervous system and psyche of not only Devin, but all of us.

Initiating family therapy had provided a safe and receptive place for these memories, feelings and sensations to be experienced and expressed by my family. I knew from the way in which my heart had closed when Alice spoke that at some time, we would have to come to terms with our different views of my "accident."

Now was not that time. My family needed me to hear them, and I needed to let it all in.

I had put them through so much, and the remorse I felt was building inside of me. I thought I had made peace with my guilt months ago, but as the clouds drifted in front of the moon, I realized my sense of resolution was with my own experience, separate from my family's.

I struggled throughout the night to suffer that pain and grief. A couple of hours before dawn, I noticed the sky clearing and glimpsed the full moon. The illumination of the moon, like images in a dream, is an expression of reflected light, revealing the sun which is out of our field of awareness. Almost imperceptibly, I began to accept that I couldn't have known before that day what was happening with my sons. As my Beloved helped me survive, so was everyone's Beloved working and reworking to metabolize and integrate the effects my near death experience had had on them.

As I watched the moon move across the night sky, I prayed. I prayed for healing and my family's wellbeing. I prayed for Alice and me. And from the depth of my soul, I prayed for my sons. "Prayers of gratitude for their love" was my last thought before I finally drifted off to sleep.

CHAPTER 18
Walking Again

Returning to the County Trauma Center was always unnerving. Aside from my own anxiety that came with each visit, being there felt in many ways as if I was living a scene from a macabre nightmare. It wasn't being in the mist of wheelchairs and walkers, but it was the demeanor of so many of the people in them. Everyone seemed to be either staring at the TV or looking blankly out the window. Their eyes seemed torpid, faces colorless, and their bodies listless. Their lethargy spoke volumes about the danger of giving up and the consequence it had for one's personality and life.

For me, my trauma continued to be my wisest doctor, teaching me that healing was as close to me as my own breath. In the face of fear, pain and despair, I had learned to find the will to meet my demons, yielding to them without resistance while trusting my breath to sustain me. Making that choice had created an opening that at times had been filled with grace. A sense of oneness and unconditional acceptance was something that I had discovered existed right inside me, in my own breath.

As I found my way to an empty seat and settled into it, I could see how other patient's defenses had "hardened," separating them from their brokeness. A mix of anxiety and sadness began to flow through me as I contemplated how quickly human beings are transformed by trauma. I too would have become detached from life and isolated from the love around me if I hadn't learned to suffer back into life parts of me that were split off by my fall.

It had taken all the strength and courage I had to choose to suffer the pain of these experiences back into life. For months, my life had fluctuated between pain and relief. I reflected on where my journey had taken me: the dissociation in and out of my body, the re-entry into mental and bodily torment, and a shattered sense of self. Yet it was remaining open to the full impact of the trauma that allowed me to receive my Beloved's mercy. It was the influx of those loving, transpersonal energies that continued to give me hope and relieve the despair I saw in the room around me. I knew as I continued to look around, that vital energies were also orbiting around my fellow patients, attempting to link up with their awareness. But their defenses seemed to insulate them from any stimulation. It scared the hell out of me to think that for many in that room, their traumas were likely life sentences.

I felt someone's gaze. I turned my head to my right to see a lifeless looking man in a wheelchair looking at me. I smiled at him, but he seemed to only glare at me through white, glazed eyes. The way his eyes were directed towards me was so unnerving that I began to feel my spine stiffen as a finger of fear touched me. I turned back, closed my eyes and breathed into the 'noise' moving through my body. It became vividly clear to me at that point that opening to the moment - that moment, was essential. I said a prayer asking for the strength to do exactly that.

"Jack," I heard Dennis say, "They just called your name."

"Thanks, I wasn't paying attention." I grabbed my walker and moved towards the reception room.

"Dr. Asprinio wants a series of x-rays taken of your pelvis. The x-ray department is expecting you." The receptionist spoke mostly to the charts in front of her.

"Can you find your way?" she asked.

"Finding my way isn't a problem, but I could definitely use a wheelchair. It's a long trek."

From the look on her face, you would have thought I had asked her to carry me on her back. After a long pause, and a cold stare, she responded icily, "I'll see what I can do."

"On second thought" I said, "The walk will do me good. Thanks anyway."

As I left the ice queen, I noticed an empty wheelchair just a few feet down the hall.

"Gone in Sixty Seconds," I thought. I looked up and down the hall to ensure I wasn't boosting someone's chair. I placed my walker across the back of it, and wheeled myself to x-ray.

After the usual routine of laying still and having x-rays taken, I was eventually led to an examination room where I was glad to lay down on the table to take the weight off the screws that protruded through the floor of my pelvis.

"Dr. Asprinio is running a bit late." That certainly wasn't a shock, and I was glad to be lying down.

As I lay down, I noticed my breathing was constricted. I was anxious. And with just a little thought, I knew why. I was anticipating, waiting for, hoping for something that might well not happen. Dr. Asprinio had hinted that if all went well, there was a chance I would literally be given my walking papers.

Despite not wanting to set my expectations too high, I began a visualization of walking. I deliberately focused my mind on the muscles I would need and began integrating feelings and sensations. I could "see" myself walking, but I realized I wasn't in my body. I kept "walking" until there was a distinct sense of being in my body and walking. I kept "packing" my breath into my pelvis until my body seemed to vibrate. I felt invigorated. I don't know how much longer I lay there, but I felt close to myself, close to my own body.

Dr. Asprinio walked in and asked me how I was doing. I told him as he put the x-rays up into the viewing box and turned on the light to illuminate them. My breath pinched in for just a moment, and then I let it go. This was the moment of decision. I looked back and forth from the x-rays to the doctor's face.

"The x-rays look good Jack...maybe too good. I can tell you that on the operating table there was no bone fragment larger than one-eighth of an inch. I have never rebuilt a pelvis that was more pulverized than yours. I can also tell you that now – it does look good."

He paused and then turned to me.

"Do you feel up to taking a few steps and seeing how it feels to walk again?"

Just the question was exhilarating.

"Yes," I said, the single word not coming close to the affirmation I felt in my heart.

"Any guidelines?" I said.

"Well, let's start slowly. Step off the table very gently and see if you can walk along the side of it. I'll be standing right beside you."

I stood. My legs trembled, and I experienced a terrifying moment of vulnerability. I took a slow deep breath and reconnected with my intention. I could feel my blood moving and heat coming off my hands. I felt as if I were standing on the very precipice of my life. From up there, I could feel the rumble of fears and energy cascading through my body. Surrendering to the fears, yet somehow managing to stay present, I said, "One breath at a time."

In taking my first step forward, there was a momentary feeling of being unbalanced, but I moved into it and with it, allowing the energy to pull me along. Then raw emotion surged through my body. I used it. My body began vibrating, at times shivering, as I walked beyond the end of the examination table. My steps became automatic, an expression of intention and my body's innate intelligence.

There was a blur of emotion as I began to walk. I cautiously began picking up my pace as I moved out into the hallway. I could feel Dr. Asprinio's presence behind me. A giddy sensation urged me on. Now I was walking into the reception room. I felt a yearning to turn my head to see the doctor's reaction when I heard him shout, "Get the video camera!" The comment launched me. I walked out through the reception room and down the main hall I had visualized walking down previously. The last thing I heard Dr. Asprinio say was, "It's a miracle."

I returned a couple of minutes later, shivering and laughing almost convulsively. He looked at me with an expression of disbelief and wonder.

"In all my years of practice, I have never seen anyone who was bedridden for four months take more than a step or two. It is truly remarkable. I only wished I'd gotten it on video."

I stood silent, stunned and unable to fully comprehend what had just happened. Feeling a tremendous sense of gratitude, I gave thanks for my Beloved's abundant supply of energy and my body's ability to use it.

The session ended with the doctor giving me a cane and suggesting I use it when taking walks with Alice through the forest and around the lake. I walked out into the waiting room with the walker on my shoulder, the cane hanging from it.

Dennis immediately stood up, his eyes wide open. A smile began to move across his face.

"You did it!"

"Yup, I did!" and I handed him my walker. It was only then that I realized other patients were looking at me. I looked out over the sea of faces and my joy and enthusiasm were quickly muffled. Self-consciously I walked out of the waiting room and down the hall using the cane. Once outside I said, "Dennis would you also carry my cane? I don't care how far away the car is, I just want to walk."

"Yes."

"Yes," I said: "Yes, yes, yes! Just say yes."

Each step seemed to release a river of dammed up physiological and psychological energy. As my feet touched the ground the rivers began running together. A vibrating flood of vitality and warmth circulated through my body. The further I walked, the more I noticed my breathing relax. It was as if my breath was linked up with my footsteps in such a way that separate states of helplessness, isolation, and fear seemed to vanish into a sense of oneness within me. Each step knit separate parts of me together.

As I walked, I heard the Med Stat helicopter above me. The sound and image triggered strong feelings and memories, as it always did. I looked toward the helicopter and thought how that patient's Beloved was watching over him or her, as mine had watched and was watching over me. The Beloved carried us when we couldn't carry ourselves. The energy from the Beloved was flowing to me then as I invoked the openness and vulnerability to move out into life.

As Dennis and I got into the car, I asked him if he knew of a poem entitled "Footsteps." He said he did, and recited the last lines for me,"

"…when you see only one set of footprints,
it was then that I carried you."

"Such truth," I said.

The ride home was joyful.

We approached the house just about the time Devin would be getting off the bus. We pulled up and parked behind my friend Dave who was picking up his son Tim. Almost to the minute, the bus pulled up and stopped. I got out of the car and walked to the bus as Devin was getting off. He was talking with Tim and gave me a sideward glance and said, "Hi Dad."

He turned back to finish his conversation.

Suddenly he stopped, snapping his head around towards me, his brown eyes wide in disbelief. "What did the aliens do to you Dad?"

Laughing, we grabbed for each other and held on tight. Our tears flowed. Between Devin, me, Dennis, Dave, his son Tim and the bus driver, there wasn't a dry eye in the house.

CHAPTER 19
The Rehabilitation Journey

"You're lucky to be alive."

I heard that phrase many times that first day and night in the emergency room. At the time, it was an extremely difficult message to hear and only added to the pain and fear I was roiling in.

"You're lucky to be alive." People squinted and slowly shook their heads from side to side.

I hadn't felt lucky. I felt scared. I felt pain. What the doctors were essentially saying was just a slightly more user-friendly version of, "you should be dead." When they looked at me in disbelief, amazed I was still breathing after such a fall, it was as if they were really trying to figure out what they had missed that had kept me alive. If I had died, I'm sure a fair number of the staff would have said something to the effect of, "yes, that makes more sense…he *should* be dead."

"You're lucky to be walking."

I also heard that phrase a lot. I heard it when I started using the walker and when I started walking on my own in December. I knew I was lucky. I was grateful to have made it to the wheelchair. I was grateful for being able to move around with the walker. And the joy I felt taking my first steps on my own was more than I could put into words. By the grace of the Beloved, I was not only walking, but becoming more whole than I had ever been. I was nurturing the little boy within me, Jackie, and had experienced the miracle of being immersed in and supported by the intoxicating presence of the Beloved.

"You're a lucky man."

But as grateful as I was, it took walking through the doors of the rehabilitation center that January to crystalize for me just how lucky I really was.

The landscape of the rehab center was in itself surreal, a self-sustaining rehabilitative Disneyland of sorts, complete with a café, a grocery store, and home interiors with a kitchen, bedroom, dining room, and living room. There was even an actual car and bus that had been cut in half lengthwise, all tools of the trade to help people rework themselves into the day-to-day of life.

Within this landscape, however, it was the sudden exposure to so many broken people that sent me reeling. In the first room I saw, my eyes took in more than my heart could bear: so many broken people. On a raised, padded platform a man lay motionless while a therapist manipulated his leg. Near them, a woman with disheveled hair struggled to walk on a prosthetic leg while supporting herself on parallel bars. On another platform, lay a man whose arm (which ended at his elbow) was held and rotated by his therapist. A woman sitting at a table worked with a therapist who patiently attempted to get her to use her hand. The right side of the woman's face, shoulder and arm sagged.

The more I looked, the more brokenness I saw – twisted or missing limbs, the aftermath of horrific burns, and scarring and disfigurement that were testaments to accidents or illnesses that I couldn't even imagine.

As the images burned into my mind, they brought pain. Real pain that was emotional and psychic. They triggered vivid memories of the last several months in the form of fragmented frames of pain and panic. Falling. Looking up, broken from the rocks. The medevac helicopter. Entering the emergency room. Choking on my meal. A night without morphine. Gary manipulating my limbs. My father tripping and falling on me.

I saw myself looking out through pain-filled traumatized eyes at Brendan a few days after the accident. I wondered if I had looked as shell-shocked as these patients did, and if he too had wanted to run.

A tempest of emotion coursed through my body and a single word ran through my mind. Dissociation. I could feel the split opening as it had for me in the ravine; that split between the observing self and the experiencing self. As I stood there and looked more closely into these patients' shell-shocked eyes, it was evident that for so many of them, nobody was home. They had distanced themselves from the pain and the trauma. They were accommodating it, shrinking before it.

Fragmented frames of speechless terror continued to tear through me. As vivid moments of my months of trauma flashed through my mind, I felt a sudden sense of protective detachment come over me. I felt overwhelmed and was too helpless or powerless to prevent it. My deliverance was through the doorway of dissociation.

As the images grew brighter and sharper in my mind, I could feel my heart pounding in my ears. I found myself holding my breath.

"Breathe," I said to myself.

I shifted my awareness into my body, only to find fear coiled around it like a snake. Threatened and vulnerable, I wrestled the fear to create some space within.

"Focus. It's just fear," I heard myself say. The voice within continued: "Trust yourself. Open to the present. Holding back anything will only undermine the recovery process."

"But, but," I argued with myself, "This is just too overwhelming."

The voice within responded, "All those feelings, all the pain, are the stepping-stones of your recovery. Move with it. Flow with it like a river, allowing and letting go as you move along. As you do, you'll release the Beloved's dynamic energy within you."

"Jack, are you OK?" David asked. "Jack?"

I felt disoriented and it took me a moment to respond.

"Yeah, I guess so. It's a lot to take in. This experience is provoking a lot of memories and feelings."

As I began to talk with David the shock wave moved through me.

"Most people," David said, "have a strong initial response on their first visit. But generally as patients settle in they do very well."

"There must be a talented group of therapists that work here," I said.

"We like to think so. Come with me."

We passed out of that room and into the treatment room where I met Maggie. I would be working with Maggie, who seemed quite likeable, and David, who had escorted me through the center. Both of them wanted to know how I could have shattered as much of my body as I did and be standing there that day.

"You're a lucky man," they echoed.

"So let's start at the neck and work our way down," said Maggie.

And so over the course of the next hour and a half, we delved deep into my body and all its broken, severed or frozen parts. There was damage I hadn't been aware of, and as they took their inventory, I listened. I heard them underscore "undiagnosed thoracic, suprascapular, clavicle and shoulder damage." I heard them discuss how my spinal injuries had resulted in my pelvis being locked in a "twisted, corkscrewed manner."

I repeated to myself, "Focus! Breathe! Relax!"

I may have been "a very lucky man," but the more we talked, the more I could tell how overwhelmed they were at the task of rehabilitating me. The journey ahead seemed endless. But if there was any hope, I knew I had to move in the direction of what was frozen and heat it up through movement.

I flashed on the space capsule dream. I was living it. The inescapable terrifying descent into my body was going to happen here. These people were going to open me up. Powerful innate forces within my nervous system were certainly going to be unleashed. At the same time, residual energy that was locked within frozen joints and swollen constricted muscles and tissues would be released. Oh boy! I knew what was coming. Would God be merciful? Could I open to being assaulted by fear and fiery pain with compassion? Would I allow it to guide me back into my body? Only if I could consciously yield to the inevitable avalanche of sensation was there hope to once again live life fully.

"Jack, Jack! Are you OK?"

I had drifted off again in my thoughts. "I'm back," I said. "Sorry about that."

"Jack, we need to establish some goals for three and six months from now. How do you see yourself functioning three months from now?"

"I'd like to be walking without a limp. I'd like to shake hands using my right hand. Oh, and I'd like to raise my right hand above my head."

"That may be a bit ambitions," cautioned David. "The neurologist reports suggest it will take eighteen to twenty-four months for those nerves to establish new pathways, if at all."

"I know," I said. "But Maggie asked what my goals are, not the neurologist's." We all laughed.

"What do you expect to be doing six months from now, in June?" Maggie continued.

"June," I thought to myself. All at once I flashed on issues of autonomy, boundaries, personal responsibilities, assertion, surrender and balance that were part of my own professional therapeutic map with people I treated. I knew that if I was going to find my way along these scary stepping-stones that I had to take responsibility for my progress. Then out of the blue I associated June with doing triathlons. All I had to do was hear the word June.

"For the past several years I've always participated in a Memorial Day triathlon," I blurted. "I want to do it again this year."

David looked at me, trying to keep a poker face. Then he smiled. Maggie nodded her head and wrote down my six-month goal with a straight face.

For me the goal wasn't so much about achieving something, but about having a focus. The memory and knowledge of what I needed to do to train for the triathlon would help me move along the stepping stones and give the pain and fear purpose and direction. But I couldn't kid myself. The vividness of what I saw outside this room terrified me. I also needed the triathlon as a goal to protect myself from dissolving into dissociation. The prospect of being trapped in this traumatized population provoked fear of the potential loss of hope. That prospect far outweighed the inevitable confrontation with the inherent fear and pain in the rehabilitative process.

"That's it for us today," David said. He showed me around the center and explained that my neurological symptoms were similar to those of stroke patients and would be treated in a comparable manner.

As we walked, the truth about the rehabilitative process continued to become clearer: Only I could determine my recovery. The rehabilitation team could provide expertise, but I had to drive the process. The quality of my participation would define my future. Yet, my fragile sense of self was all I had to sustain myself out in the world. My new sense of self, joyfully enlarged from having embraced Jackie and the Beloved now needed me to bring Jack back. The urge to abort the tension between Jack and Jackie was very strong. Yet I knew bearing the tension would enable me to sustain the greater sense of wholeness that dealing with the accident had birthed.

Arriving at the fitness center, I followed David over to a cross-cable machine where a man was standing beside someone in a wheelchair, his back to me. What I noticed was his total concentration on his exercise.

"Jack, I would like you to meet Paul. Paul will be another one of your therapists."

"Jack, I'll be with you in just a moment." He continued his work with the man in the wheelchair.

I was six feet away, and his intensity struck me. Then I noticed his two prosthetic legs. I realized in that moment that all the patients were crawling through the bloody ravines of their own losses, struggling to emerge more whole. As I watched this man, I could see how he did not allow his disability to define him. I could feel how tightly wrapped he was inside himself. He pushed beyond his limits. The more I observed him, the more I liked him. There was a powerful resonance matched by equally buoyant hope. He had learned to survive and perhaps even more. His struggle shaped and defined the texture and meaning of his life.

Paul called out my name, and just as he did, the man I had been studying backed his wheelchair out of the cable machine and faced me. I held my breath. His beard poorly disguised a wiggling mass of pink scar tissue that crisscrossed his face like some primitive face painting. But it was the fire in his eyes that I responded to. I stuck out my left hand.

"Jack," I said, introducing myself. "I'm glad I got a chance to watch you work out. I hope I can find some of that energy and intensity inside of me." He took my hand and looked at me.

"If you can't," he said, "Paul will help you find it. By the way, I'm Tim. See you around."

"OK," Paul said. "Let me walk you through some of the exercises you'll be doing. Some will build strength, all of them will get your circulation going and improve your range of motion." He got me started on some free weights.

"Let's try a few things and get our bearings on what we need to focus on."

I was shocked to see how much strength I had lost and how my muscles had atrophied. But as that thought went through my mind, I thought of Tim who I had just met. I imagined he probably would give anything to have weak and atrophied legs.

I was "lucky to be walking." I smiled in spite of myself.

After an hour of hard-fought failures with few triumphant moments, I left Paul and entered the locker room. As I changed into my bathing suit, I began to feel as if the past month's blurred horizons were beginning to come into focus. This environment was forcing me to define again who I was and where I was. Although the process was painful, I knew I needed this pain to move across the bridge. It was then that I realized that my Beloved's energy which had buoyed me up in the past months, however capriciously, was less noticeable today. Perhaps, I thought, it had sustained my life and soothed me during the darkest and most tormenting part of this journey and maybe its present absence was created for me to find the will I needed to more deeply re-engage in life. The inflow of those vital energies from my psyche had been beautiful and their power awesome. I had glimpsed a fuller experience of my deepest potential, one that I would try to honor for the rest of my life.

Two more therapists greeted me as I walked out to the pool, Vickie and Ron. They handed me a pair of non-slip socks, which I knew was a good idea, but still made me feel like I had just entered my 90's.

Into the pool I went, and once there, they put me through a series of therapeutic exercises, then began working on my gait. The warm water combined with a sense of buoyancy not only relieved my tension, but provided freedom from some of the pain. When my individual instruction was over and before I participated in a class, I floated. After lying on my back or being stuck in a wheelchair for months, the sense of weightlessness was exhilarating. I didn't want it to stop.

A group of four women and two men joined me in the pool. The youngest of them was at least 20 years older than I was. They were all recovering from either hip replacements or back surgery, and I found their good spirits and lively mood oddly annoying. First no-skid socks, and then I was struggling to keep up with the eighty year olds.

"Shit," I thought. The water suddenly felt colder.

The cold reality of the neurophysiological limitations of my body assaulted me from a direction I never expected. The enforced inactivity and powerlessness of the past several months had not only stripped my body of its strength and conditioning, but it had ruptured my self-image and self-esteem, leaving me feeling as if old age had taken over. Skepticism began to swim through my consciousness...a triathlon? It was no wonder Maggie and David looked at me and then at each other as if I were psychotic.

I could feel a bitter rebellion taking place within me as I struggled to maintain the pace of my fellow geriatric patients. My hope and triumphant moments of an hour ago were now silenced. Although I was fifty years old, I had never had the confrontation with aging that I was now experiencing.

I remember thinking to myself that my injuries had sped up the aging process. The clock was now ticking faster for me than anyone else. I had identified with Tim not only because he was in his 30's, but because of his athletic "intensity." And then, with the intensity of a bolt of lightning, came the awareness once again of that loss of the powerful swimmer-athlete I once was. It suddenly felt unbearable to be restricted to the level of functioning I was experiencing. I wasn't swimming, I was bobbing - up and down, knees bending, legs kicking, arms reaching,

"NO!" I screamed out.

That got everyone's attention. They all stopped and looked at me. We all stopped bobbing, until I rather feebly muttered, "Sorry."

The class continued, and as I tried to get my bearings, something in me shifted.

"No," I repeated in my head. The second time I said it, it reverberated within in me with less shock and more resolve.

No. I wasn't going to be subjected to an accelerated aging process or fall victim to self-pity. I would consciously direct as much physical and psychic energy as I could find to facilitate my healing and recovery. There was nothing to cling to here. My center of experience had to shift from the inner world of my Beloved back to my ego if I was going to recover. Jack, not Jackie had to reemerge if I was going to live in this world. The shift had happened, and the choice was made. Jack was coming back.

While I was changing in the locker room, and had discarded my no-slip socks, Tim rolled in. We began to talk and almost instantly found an easy place between us of mutual respect and warmth. His condition was the result of a motorcycle accident that happened a year ago. He had been riding through an intersection when a car ran a red light and changed his life forever. The bitterness in his story was palpable and understandable. Yet as I listened to him, there was a dignity, even a beauty in how he had responded to his fate. I could see clearly how the magnitude of his loss and pain had necessarily engaged a warrior component within him to offset the depth of his depression and despair. He actively allowed and used the pain in his recovery process to connect him to desires to live and make the most of his life. There was no security in his life either, only his choice to be led forward by courageously confronting what life now asked of him.

I would need to resurrect the weary warrior within me. Depression and hopelessness could clearly dominate my vulnerable being without the warrior. I thought of Tim's drive, and I realized that if I could centralize the process in my heart, perhaps the warrior in me could open to the pain and unlock the supercharged energy that lay trapped within my nervous system. Without the warrior, I would be lost.

Tim and I said goodbye.

I limped back toward my car, cane in hand and very aware that Tim and so many other people in the center behind me might never walk anywhere again.

I was lucky to be walking.

I was lucky to be alive.

CHAPTER 20
A Tearful World, With Willful People

The greatest barrier in my rehabilitative quest, I realized, was not physical but psychological.

Pain and suffering can be symptoms of psychological conflict and decline on one hand or of developmental transition and growth on the other. The outcome depends in part on whether they are appropriately diagnosed and treated. With the help of all my various physical therapists, I learned the difference between good pain and bad pain. Generally, all the pain, and there was a lot of it, was the good kind.

I continued to find that the most successful way to navigate the pain was by opening to it. Muscle awareness, breath work, stilling the mind and visualization were techniques I used continually to manage pain. My will was gathering force. Being able to walk and DO anything enhanced my sense of mastery and self-esteem. Slowly and grudgingly this feeble body was being coaxed into movement and expansion as glacial areas, seemingly frozen forever, began to heat up. With my mind free of thought, and focused on my breathing, I could be fully absorbed in the exercises that were tearing through adhesions and straining scar tissue. In each movement, there was a generative void, not the vegetative blankness of PTSD that frightened me so much.

It was the pool that now became my salvation. Hidden resources, which had been dormant for months, began to nourish me as I saturated myself in the warm, wet, pleasurable water. A sense of buoyancy not only relieved my tension, but provided me freedom from some of the pain. When my individual instruction was over, and before I participated in class, I floated. The cold reality of the physical limitations of my body no longer assaulted me, but instead challenged me. I progressed quickly and both of my therapists were supportive of my scheduling more pool time.

Wearing a life vest in the deep end of the pool, I began simply running in place. Running in eight feet of water began to awaken my slumbering cardiovascular system. At the same time, running improved the flexibility and range of motion in my muscles and joints. Months of grievous knowledge that I could never run again on land turned to joy as I thrashed about in the water. Ten minutes soon became twenty, as I found my rhythm and a synthesis of body, mind and spirit began to develop. As the running took over, I began to feel completely synchronized within it. All that mattered was what I was doing. All outside distractions just faded away. The awareness of my breath was all that was left. I knew this place, and in this place my Beloved knew me.

Memories from the ravine floated into my mind as I began to feel reconnected to the Beloved's inherent existence within me. I had crossed over to the other side, glimpsed the psyche's unfathomable depths, and been met there by the Beloved. It was in the ravine that my spirit had sustained me while my ego collapsed. That vast, interconnected expanse had sustained and encompassed Jack and Jackie's worlds. The release of this dynamic energy had sustained and uplifted me while never overwhelming my conscious personality.

In the first few weeks, I seemed to receive the merciful blessings when I needed them. But as time went on, I had felt abandoned, forced to reluctantly fend for myself and struggle with not only the assaulting pain but also frequent eruptions of unresolved, early psychological issues. I wondered if it had been the Beloved's intent all along for me to learn how personal suffering can serve as an instrument to open the heart. Perhaps it was up to me alone to find and sustain hope. Had I not been broken-open, I would never have penetrated the primitive defenses that not only made up my personality but also protected it. I felt blessed that Jackie and the Beloved's intangible, yet integral dynamic energy had found its way into my life. Yet the process of reconnecting both body and mind and re-making Jack as a unified whole was daunting.

As arduous a task as physical therapy was, it at least was tangible. The process was clearly defined, the goals concrete. Most of my effort was directed towards getting my body back and creating the semblance of health and functioning. My mind was lagging behind. The clue, I realized, was the anxiety I experienced when I looked into the eyes of many fellow patients and saw that scary vegetative void; so many of the patients seemed to have had their individual lights put out by their respective traumatic experiences. I imagined that I was in a better mental state than they were, but was I?

I began again to think about how the psyche intervenes in the traumatic moment. I thought about the ravine, how my consciousness had been displaced, insulating me from the unbearable experiences. How I slid back and forth on a sort of ligament between the emerald leaves in the light and my broken body. Much of the ravine's terror and pain, I knew, had been banished to my body or relegated to discreet psychical fragments. My normally unified awareness, emotions, thoughts, imagery and sensations had been separated, not allowed to integrate. This was not under the control of my will, it manifested itself independent of "me". My job now, I knew, was to unite those dismembered parts of myself.

Yet I knew there were primitive, archaic forces within me whose job it was to continue to protect me and not allow these connections to take place. This psychic process of defense suspends parts of ourselves in order to assure the survival of the human person. The patients around me had survived their traumas, but, I thought, their own unique light was clearly suspended, lost in what appeared to be that vegetative void. My fear of becoming like them made me run that much harder in the pool. I sought solace in the sharp tears that stung my eyes and the sweet scent and warmth of the Beloved as it flowed into me.

The best thing I found I could do with this anxiety was to direct it into my physical rehabilitation. The process was painful and scary, but I felt some measure of control there. I knew I should give Colin a call and talk with him about my concerns, but at the time I just felt too thin-skinned. I decided that before I saw Colin, I needed to gain a greater sense of mastery over my body and my use of it. In talking with Paul, I realized how important it was to organize my rehabilitation around the athlete in me. The equipment at the rehab center was limited compared to what I was used to at my prior gym. I knew the level of conditioning a triathlon was going to demand of me in five months and with Paul's support and confidence in me I returned.

So, four days a week, in addition to rehab, I went to the gym and did a split routine of two times a week for each muscle group. The triathlon was giving my life direction.

Alone and clinging to my cane, I reentered the gym a very different man than the one before the accident. Nevertheless, I hobbled up the steps, my right side hanging limp, and walked into the gym with a dream, desire and a sense of discipline. Everything I did took an enormous amount of time, but because I did it by myself and for myself, I was thrilled. The months of being humiliatingly dependent were over.

Because I could use only my left arm, it would take me a few minutes to adjust the seat and the machine's poundage. Previously, the same adjustment took a few mindless seconds. I learned I could be patient, very patient. Using the equipment required me to pick up my useless right arm and put that hand on the handgrip. A series of tests showed that I had only thirty percent neurological functioning in my right shoulder and arm. The muscles there were largely deaf to my commands, but I directed those that still responded. Together my arms would pull or push while I felt the scar tissue grind or the burning flash of jumping electrical activity. I did very light weights and tried to extend my repetitions to muscular exhaustion. As I worked, I tried to visualize the nerve-muscle pathways rebuilding. Blood began circulating through the damaged areas of my right side. I focused moment-to-moment on my changing physical state.

In the gym, muscular power was king, and men and women yearned for beauty and vitality. In the locker room, I felt self-conscious and deformed in comparison to them and to the man I had once been. Yet in the rehabilitation center's locker room, I was surrounded by men who would instantly trade their lack of arm or leg for my neurologically impaired limb or shattered pelvis.

At the gym, my condition elicited curious questions or supportive comments. I learned to give a limited report of my accident and the extent of damage. Often I'd watch men become overwhelmed as I answered their questions. Frequently, they did not know what to say, except something like, "I've been complaining for weeks since I had my shoulder surgery. I can't do the things I used to and the pain keeps me up at night. But after watching and listening to you, I feel better already, I've got nothing to complain about."

I began and ended every workout at the gym with a dip in the whirlpool. The heat and the pulsating pressure of the water soothed my pain, temporarily. One day when I limped over to the whirlpool after my workout, I saw a man at the far end, his face strangely immobile. I carefully and slowly moved down the stairs into the pool.

As I slipped into the water up to my neck, I heard the man beside me ask rather abruptly, "What happened to you?"

I started to give him the abbreviated version, but something in the way he listened, his sad absorption of my narration, urged me to be more disclosing. I told him about the ravine, my near death experience, being sustained by the Beloved, my rescue, hospitalization and my early attempts at rehabilitation.

The sorrow in his eyes turned to words as he said solemnly, "My son died just two weeks ago in a car accident. I just returned here today to try to live, to be normal, but I just didn't feel like working out. I decided to sit in the whirlpool before I went home. When I saw you struggling over here, I thought of my son."

He stopped talking.

Tears began to roll down his cheeks. I waited. Other men who approached the whirlpool turned and walked away. I talked with him about my own experience of not being able to protect the ones I love and what I had learned in opening to the grief and loss in my life. Tears were now running down my cheeks as I told him love never dies, that he was being held in loving arms as we spoke, and that it was the love in his heart that united him with his son.

"It's just so hard to be without him" he said. "I keep seeing him in others, you know, but it's not him."

I told him about how I learned to surrender to the pain and how, as it touched me, it led me. I related how I had learned to forgive myself, and he talked about his love for his son.

By the time we got out of the tub we both felt our lives had been enriched by this fated or chance encounter. His openhearted "thank you" touched me in a way a "thank you" never had before. I never learned his name. He doesn't know mine. But the moments we spent together were profound.

I drove home. I noticed that my body, which was normally tightened around the pain, was relaxed. The flesh, muscles, ligaments, tissues – everything had softened.

They had been led by my heart.

CHAPTER 21
I Once Had a Dad

"Thank You."

I started each morning with those words, silently reciting a prayer of gratitude. It varied from day-to-day, but my thanks was constant.

Thank You for the miracle of walking. Thank You for my family. Thank You for my life, my friends, the rehabilitation, or sometimes something as simple as gratitude for an early morning cup of coffee while watching the snow blanket the trees outside our home.

Sometimes I grimaced through the "thank you's" because pain remained a chronic companion. It ebbed and flowed at different levels from day to day and was the most consistent challenge I had in staying open and remaining hopeful. But for the most part, I was managing it.

Although slowly, I was also recovering. Alice and the kids were better too. I was walking, less reliant on everyone around me and was making progress at rehab.

As Devin might say, the Aliens were doing a good job with me.

But through the gratitude and the rehabilitation, I was not blind to the fact that there was still a post traumatic undertow that was capturing parts of our family in different ways. We were still struggling to understand the process we were working through. Making bearable the "unbearable" was not an easy task for any of us. Each of us still showed signs of stress. We were all in the throes of healing.

Devin's teacher had reported that he was a bit restless in class and somewhat needy, but it was manageable. He was keeping up with his work. Brendan's schoolwork was on track and he was having a very successful wrestling season as an eighth grader. He was undefeated with only two matches remaining in the season. I got a more detailed and piercing glimpse of his thoughts one evening after Alice and I had put the kids to bed.

"Brendan brought home a school assignment he'd gotten back in English class today," Alice mentioned. "He shared it with me after I picked him up from wrestling. It was a poem he wrote about your accident." She hesitated.

"Do you want to read it?"

"Of course I do."

I Once

I once had a dad who could run and play.
I once had a dad who I could chase away.
I once had a dad who could play all day.
I once had a dad who could stay at home.
I once had a dad who could sleep in his own bed.

Now I have a dad who rolls around.
Now I have a dad who can't run around.
Now I have a dad who can barely feel from the neck down.
Now I have a dad who is in constant pain.
Now I have a dad who is not vain.

My dad was in the hospital because he forgot he can't fly.
My dad was in the hospital because he almost died.
My dad was in the hospital because he fell fifty feet onto a ledge.

I hate my dad for that, but there is nothing I can do.

When I finished reading the poem, everything seemed to have stopped. I had even stopped breathing.

"He loves you a lot." Alice said.

"I know," I responded, almost in a whisper. "But the truth hurts."

"We all have our own way of working out the aftermath of your fall."

"I'm thankful for that," I said through my tears. I was once again overwhelmed with guilt.

"The more he can admit and experience his feelings," I said, "The wiser and stronger he'll become."

As I said, the pain came in waves, and it wasn't just the physical pain. The guilt I felt for what I had done to Alice and the boys was never far from the surface, and it bore a pain and weight all of its own. In that emotional pain was also the barrier that was keeping Alice and me from re-establishing a deeper relationship. We viewed my accident differently, and we would need to reconcile our different views and feelings about it before we could be truly close again. It was a tough rift to bridge.

What led to a more honest exchange about our personal impressions of my fall was actually initiated with my mentioning my growing uneasiness of being out in public. In the course of a discussion about my level of distractedness in social settings, Alice suggested I look into something called Eye Movement Desensitization and Reprocessing, or EMDR.

"It's working for me, Jack. Maybe you should give it a try."

I listened and was certainly open to it. In theory it sounded like something we could all use. To oversimplify, the theory was to visit a scene from my accident while tracking the therapist's moving finger. The sequence is repeated until the patient no longer reports anxiety. A more positive thought is then paired with the traumatic memory while continuing the eye movements. The technique, as well as Alice's positive experiences with it, made me curious.

I agreed to go with Alice and made every effort to approach the session with an open heart and an open mind. But it went poorly, to say the least. My anxiety level had skyrocketed on the way to the session, and I was anxious about being late to Brendan's last wrestling match of the season. I was feeling fragile, "loosely stitched together," as I had told Alice. I remember during the drive how Alice's sensitivity to my overtly present anxiety helped and strengthened my desire to reconnect with her in a much deeper way. I was relieved that Alice and the boys were not denying their struggle and pain. Each of them had gathered people around them who could see them and affirm their experience.

But fear, shame, and a hyper vigilance bubbled up in me the moment I entered the room. And it was a combination of the therapist's tone and her first question that put me on the defensive and shut me down.

"Tell me Jack," she began, "why are you here?"

I tried to breathe, and went on to answer that I wanted to support Alice, and that I was curious. But I ended the thought by saying that personally I didn't want any help, and that I had my own therapist.

I backtracked a bit at that point and tried to amend my comment to appease the therapist who I had obviously offended. But there was no salvaging the session. Fear and distrust had cast a shadow over me, and once the words "I don't need this" found their way into my head, I had disengaged.

At one point the therapist looked at me and said, "I feel like I've lost you Jack. Where are you?"

I had been staring out the window. "Do you see that tree out there?" As she turned to look out the window, I continued. "I'm out there, in the tree. I just don't feel safe here."

Not too long after that, Alice and I walked to the car in silence. We sat in the car a few moments before either of us spoke.

"I'm sorry that seemed so painful for you," Alice began softly. "I only wanted to try to retrieve some of the closeness we'd lost since the accident. I just wanted some of the old 'you' and 'us' back."

Hearing Alice's words added to the shaking in my body. Intense energy and feelings that had been suffocated in the office began to surface.

"I want that too, but I immediately felt judged by her. I felt as if she never saw me. She never really looked. All she saw was her view of me. There was no way I could open into the intense realities of the last six months. If I had, my shame and guilt would have been compounded, because she never saw me."

"Most importantly," I continued, "I'm devastated that I couldn't reach deep enough to heal what's separating us from each other. I want and need the old 'us' back too."

I told her that I was glad she'd been helped, but I couldn't do the work necessary if I didn't feel safe or seen. I spaced out like I'd done at other times; a breaker switch in my nervous system got flipped by some invisible, psychic force inside me. There was a fundamental disconnection from my body. I really felt like I was outside in that tree. I didn't want to turn away, it just happened. That force that set off the breaker switch was a protective impulse, but now I saw how problematic that had become. Just walking into that office I had become hyper. Perhaps it was my sense that painful, traumatic experiences or sensations were going to get provoked.

"When the therapist started asking questions, I just got triggered inside out. It feels like it's something I can't control, but I will promise you I'll increase my awareness of it and try to get a handle on it."

As we drove up to the middle school gym, I was quiet. I thought I understood Post Traumatic Stress Disorders and how insidiously the forces of trauma could extend inward throughout the body and mind. Yet after becoming unglued, I realized my greatest adversary was my own personality. I had foolishly thought that I alone could modify the psychological forces of the trauma by simply wrestling with my personality's need to compulsively control and protect me.

Humbly, with cane in hand and Alice at my side, I walked into the gym on a cold day in February.

As we sat down on the bleachers, Brendan and his teammates ran out onto the mat and began warming up. Thank God, I thought, for Alice and the boys. Without them I certainly wouldn't have the passion for life that I enjoyed. Without them, I am sure that my life would most likely have ended in the ravine.

Brendan faced a tough opponent that day. He had lost to him last season. We watched what was an incredibly intense match, I don't think Alice or I exhaled once. But towards the end of the third period, Brendan put his opponent in a move called a cradle, pinning him in the final moments. The referee raised Brendan's arm into the air, and Alice and I began to breathe normally again.

I could not perceive, nor could I foresee how Brendan's compressed and expressed suffering of the last few months was shaping his future life. But I was certain that it was. The echo of his poem still reverberated within me. The gnawing sense of guilt I felt was worse than any physical pain that tormented me.

His win buoyed us that evening, and all of our spirits were high. Brendan masqueraded as an adolescent, but through the eyes of our souls, Alice and I saw his timeless beauty and perfection. Still, as our evening wore down, I couldn't shake the agitation I had felt from the day's therapy session.

"I'm out there, in the tree. I just don't feel safe here." I thought for a moment of my comment and of the irony that of all places, I would feel safe in a tree. Then I pondered the intensity of the anger and disassociation I had felt that day. I picked up the phone.

"Arnie? You have time for a walk Saturday? I need to talk."

CHAPTER 22

Inside Out and Upside Down

It was a sunny but frigid Sunday in March when Arnie and I began our walk through the forest. We covered a lot of the day-to-day small talk, and then I brought up the session with Alice and her therapist.

"You told her you were out there in the tree?"

"…and that I didn't feel safe and didn't need her help." I finished for him.

"I just dissociated. On some level I'm still so fragile that when my defense system gets activated, I freeze despite the heat. I've felt so humiliated for so many months I simply couldn't go through it again. It felt unbearable to be invisible to her. I just couldn't get past the judgment, the therapist's, Alice's, my own – all of them, I guess."

Arnie nodded his head as we walked down to the lake.

"I was anxious going in, but I thought I could manage it. But from the moment I walked in, I didn't feel like the therapist's humanity was there for me. I felt judged. The tension level kept rising. I wanted to leave, but I couldn't. I felt nothing except a tremendous tension in my body. I wasn't able to concentrate; then suddenly I was gone. It was like I was sucked out through a black hole. The next thing I knew, I was spaced out in a tree. I felt safe. Time stood still. It's like I was in the hub of a wheel; everything was moving around me while I was in a quiet, empty space."

"Has that happened before?" Arnie asked.

"A few times," I answered. "Sometimes when it happens, it feels like a defect that generates a judgment within me and at other times, it's more of a fertile void. In the session, when I came back into the room from being outside, all I felt was angry – angry at the therapist and at myself."

Arnie's expression was sad. "And, what about Alice?"

"I don't know," I said. "I could see her anxiety and pain and knew she was hoping for a good experience. Maybe I was also angry at her because it brought up for me her view that what happened was not an accident. If that's the case, I'm the cruelest person on earth to impose this kind of pain on my family."

We stopped walking, and Arnie's eyes locked on mine. "Is that how you feel?"

I stood, as if rooted to the ground, staring over the rock wall to the lake beyond. I shrugged.

"I can take responsibility for the pain I've put myself through. But no way did I climb that tree that day to shatter everyone's life. To me, it was just an accident. I've come to accept it as my fate, though the fact that it's also their fate brings me an entirely different dimension of pain."

Arnie was quiet for a few moments. "I don't have any way of knowing whether it was an accident, fate, or just the result of your being a risk-oriented man. But I can understand how much you're hurting right now."

We began walking back toward the lake again. Arnie continued.

"You probably know this already Jack, but once you started walking again, I immediately noticed aspects of the old Jack re-emerge. Until about a month ago, your pain and despair were obvious but so was your love. There were times when you were zoned out and we talked about and worked on helping you get back into your body. What you used to refer to as Jackie was a state that was around a lot. I don't see Jackie so much anymore."

"Really? Say more."

"The lone warrior, athlete, receded in the face of your overwhelming injuries. A softer, more vulnerable and open you became more present. Jackie was in life. But once you got mobile and began walking again, I began to see old Jack come back to life. My hope is that we don't lose Jackie."

"Me too, Arnie, but I don't know how to get back into life with all the pain and vulnerability I feel and stay really open with people. It's exhausting to do everything I am doing and try to appear normal. Something really big shifted inside of me after that fall. A lot about it is good. Yet, there are moments when some tender membrane inside my mind ruptures, and I'm gone or I explode. Either way, what follows is a dark, persecutory period. It's as if some part of me intervenes to save me from an experience of humiliation in the world only to persecute and humiliate me within my own mind."

Empathically Arnie held my gaze. "I didn't mean that as a criticism Jack. I really admire you for getting up and taking everything back on your shoulders. I guess what I'm really saying is that I just miss the way we were together when you were not yet walking."

"I know what you mean," I said, "and let's try to keep that quality of relatedness in our friendship. But honestly, what I need most from you is your support and understanding. Since I started walking, I feel like I've been given a new lease on life. I'm so grateful that I can walk and that I'm no longer a source of pain or suffering for my family. I want to appear like I'm the old Jack and Dad, not the vulnerable, dependent man, father that I had become. I need the control and I need to regain a sense of mastery over my body and life. My sense of self as a man depends on it."

As we sat down on a rock and looked out over the lake, Arnie asked, "How can I be of help?"

"This new level of honesty and openness is what feels best to me right now."

"You got it. Anything else?"

"I guess I just need you or someone to know how hard it is for me even if I don't show it. I have a sense that you would understand this better than anyone."

Arnie took a deep breath. "I've watched from the outside; been sort of a witness to this whole thing. But only you really know what's going on inside of you." He paused. I could see he was making a decision about what, if anything, to say next.

"It's been really intense for me. Honestly, it's scared the hell out of me at times and at other times, I felt really high after being with you. There were few, if any, moments between those two extremes. It meant a lot to me that you reached out to me and let me in."

I started to squirm as tears filled my eyes. The lake began to blur, and I looked down, trying to contain the dam that already had burst inside of me. I opened my mouth and began to say something but it was drowned out by my sobs. My body heaved.

Arnie put his arm on my shoulder. There was no way I could stop the sobs that tore through my body. I just went with it.

Barely able to speak, I said, "It felt humiliating and wonderful at the same time to need you."

As I looked over at Arnie, I saw in his wet eyes various shades of emotion; love, compassion and respect. His gaze shifted from me to the lake, and he said, "You're more of a man than any man I know. Thanks for allowing me to be your friend."

Looking at Arnie I thought to myself, this is what love looks and feels like.

At that moment, it felt as if all I needed to heal me was love. I found myself wanting to tell Arnie all that I had been keeping to myself. I knew in that moment that if my life was ever going to resemble what it looked like before the accident, I needed to trust somebody with the truth I was struggling with. The fear of opening more rattled around inside me. A knot of fear formed in my diaphragm. It pulled steadily tighter as I pondered Arnie's possible responses.

I leaned into the fear and hope and let go.

"I look a lot better outwardly than I feel inwardly," I began.

"The trauma is kicking my ass. I can accept that the accident was a life-shattering event that has changed the meaning of my life and that I'll never be the same. And In some ways, that's for the better. Months of being helpless and dependent constantly reengaged moments and issues from my childhood and allowed the boy in me to come back into life. That's the good part."

I stopped briefly to get my thoughts aligned.

"But right now, letting Jackie dominate my life just doesn't feel safe. Something switched inside of me once I began walking and for some reason I now only feel safe when I'm alone. It's like I have a startle response dial in me that is set at its most sensitive setting, especially in social situations. The slightest thing sets me off."

I took some slow, deep breaths

"I'm getting a little better at dealing with being so thin-skinned, but it's exhausting at times. What really scares me is if I'm wounded or feel wounded, there erupts from within me this primitive, aggressive, irrational rage. Two weeks ago there was an incident with Alice, and I blew. A blind rage came through me that turned me inside-out and upside-down. I felt terrible. I also felt disoriented afterwards. I couldn't regulate the intensity, and I couldn't articulate how I was feeling. It scared the hell out of me. Alice, too.

"Sometimes it's so intense that when I get home, I go out into the forest alone. I get the biggest tree limb I can find on the ground and just smash it against a tree until it shatters. Very intense sounds come out of me, as well as powerful bodily sensations. I'm getting better at dealing with it, but I'm not sure what this force is, its source, or if it wants to protect or destroy me. It must have its conception in the ravine. It's like those dream tigers that were going to devour me when I was in the crib the first night in the hospital. But now it's no dream, and I've become the tiger. Thank God I can keep my family safe from me in this forest sanctuary."

Arnie sat there, just looking at me, for what seemed like a long time; waiting, I think, to make sure I had said everything I needed to say. Glancing out over the lake and then back at me, a "Wow!" emerged from his smile.

"What better place to let the wild animal out of you than in this forest." We both started laughing.

"Just let me know," he said, "before you let it out and I'll make sure I'm home. The doors and windows will be locked."

We laughed some more and then Arnie said, "Jack, you were faced with an inescapable threat, life or death. The instinctual portions of your brain and nervous system took over to protect you. You also had a profound spiritual experience. Remember a couple of months ago when I came over and put my hands beneath your broken back, and you released all that pain?"

"Yea."

"Well, I'll never forget it. You told me that Mike said you were out of your body and needed to be in it to heal."

"Yeah."

"That day we triggered some of the residual energy from the accident. Your body discharged it, and to your credit, you went with it. Mike told you that there was a lot of this trapped energy inside your body and nervous system."

"That's a moment I'll never forget. There was pain, then fear and vulnerability, followed by a moment of darkness and then just this enormous flash of red. It got brighter and hotter until it eclipsed me." I took a deep breath.

There are things about the accident that I remember and other things I'm blank about. I must have more than a dozen cassettes filled with my dictations about my experiences over the past six months. I have no interest in listening to them. I just want to move on. I feel haunted enough by memories of months on my back and in a wheelchair."

"You have every right to be haunted, Jack. You have been through so much." He placed his arm on my shoulder.

"Lean on me when you need to, and I'm glad you've scheduled an appointment with Colin. And don't forget to call me before you go rampaging through the forest again."

We laughed and talked as we slowly walked back to the house. That night I had a dream.

I am climbing a snow-covered mountain. In front of me is a woman. Without any warning, she falls into a really deep crevasse.

I try to help her, but I only have one good arm. I attach a rope I have with me to a rock outcropping, and then wrap it around my good arm. Slowly I begin repelling down the snowy, icy crevasse. I drop maybe thirty or forty feet and land in snow. I see only her feet sticking out of the snow nearby. She is totally embedded.

I begin trying to dig her out with my good arm. At some point I am aware that I'm outside of my body watching myself dig. Suddenly I'm back inside my body reaching for her, but now I too am upside-down. Her eyes are wide open, and she is looking at me as I try to pull and lift her out. But I can't get her free and now we're both stuck. I don't know how long we are both stuck upside-down looking at each other, but it's a while.

Unexpectedly I call out for help. Then I hear voices above us. I call out again. Slowly, gradually we are both pulled out.

My good arm is tightly wrapped around her.

CHAPTER 23
The Great Light

As much as I knew seeing Colin was the right thing to do, I was feeling very anxious. It had been several days since my afternoon with Arnie, and as I drove to Colin's that evening, I couldn't help but think back to the last time I saw him. It had been the winter solstice at my home, the night I spent listening to the pain and suffering that I had caused Alice and the boys. It was a long, dark night for me.

"Good to see you walking Jack." His hand closed on mine. "Come in. I was so glad to hear from you. How have you been doing?"

"Coming along," I said. "Lord knows, I'm glad to be walking."

The sincerity and obvious caringness of his words and demeanor were calming, and I could feel my anxiety begin to subside. I took a breath and paused before I started to fill Colin in on the last two months. .

"Do you remember when I saw you last, I told you about a dream I had the first night in the hospital? I was in a crib, surrounded by tigers who were about to devour me, when an elephant charged in and carried me to safety."

Colin nodded.

"At the time, the dream infused me with hope that I would survive the terror of my situation. But now when I think of that dream, I have a different view. I realize that these tigers are a part of me; an instinctual, terrifying part of me, and not just in my dreams."

Colin looked at me intently, and I continued.

"I went to a therapy session with Alice. Almost as soon as I sat down with them, I picked up the scent of judgment. I tried to manage my anxiety, which seemed to pounce on me, but the scent filled my nostrils, dried out my mouth and set off an electric charge that went twisting through my body. It flashed DANGER! Fear and anger seemed to overwhelm me, and then I just spaced out. I stared out at a tree outside her window, and dissociated from the therapist and my fear and anger."

"The danger I felt is the same kind of danger I sense when I am out in public, but bigger and closer. When it looms, It makes me feel like an animal at the total mercy of its rage."

I paused a moment, vividly remembering the feelings of rage and fear and anger. In just relating the story at the therapist's office I could sense the tigers beneath the surface.

"I did not sleep well that night, and the next day I was still so agitated I couldn't sit still. I took a walk in the woods and tried to discharge the intense energy that had mobilized to defend me. Like I told Arnie, the rage surged through me as I smashed one branch after another against a tree. I realized afterwards that I was venting the rage surge outwardly in a harmless way. It could just as easily be inwardly directed self-destructively. For some reason, once I started walking I seem to have come full circle back into that initial wild, savage jungle that I found myself in the first day. The very thought of that primordial state of existence brings up terrifying images and memories, mostly of being in the hospital. I know that only in remembering, reliving and resolving these experiences can my life ever get back to normal, not that I am at all sure of what being "normal" is any more.

Colin's eyes had widened slightly as he looked at me, clearly taking in my concern and anxiety.

"Sounds like that therapy session was another trauma experience," Colin said. "And, it seems like you feared shame or humiliation. Do you remember what you were feeling when you went in there?"

"Like the identified patient," I replied. "Like the wild man who's done something stupid and brought pain to the people he loves."

"Like that learning-disabled, troubled kid who was always picked on and struggled not to be a disappointment to his family?" Colin asked.

"Yes exactly."

"It's really the old wound, Jack," Colin said, "and you must be revisiting that shame place everywhere you go. Those old angry places that defended you in the past will start to growl and either attack you or cut you off from feeling. But don't forget, the elephant's a part of you too, along with the tigers. That elephant is a powerful inner ally and one that all our previous work together has strengthened in you."

As he said this, Colin reached down and patted a large carved wooden elephant that supported his chair-side table. I laughed and realized that wise old elephant's ears had heard my whole story, and I remembered all the other elephants that came up in my dreams and what a powerful healing presence their initial images had been.

Colin's perspective made sense and relieved some of my anxiety.

"In just talking about this," I mentioned, "I'm feeling a hot twitchy energy that seems to charge out of my hands and feet."

"I know," Colin said. "I can almost feel your anxiety that boiled up as you were speaking."

"That day in the ravine," I continued, "my nervous system had swung between fear and courage. I had lost all ability to self-regulate. My mind and body had expanded as it shattered and then it contracted as I crawled in terror and pain. Those tigers were integral to my survival. But now it seems they have to be tamed, digested and re-assimilated with other aspects of my trauma."

"I don't understand," I said, "how something that was so funda-mental to my survival has become so problematic and so persecu-tory, now that I'm walking and again back in the world."

"Well, it's the lifelong problem that's been with you and a lot of others with a trauma history." Colin replied.

"It's the split between love and rage, the division between vul-nerable expression on the one hand and archetypal aggression on the other. That rage becomes a protection, but also the persecutor of that vulnerable core, causing ever more shame within. When you were flat on your back healing, those defenses were out of commission. You had an 'excuse' to be your lovable, vulnerable childhood self. You were like a magical boy – completely open. Arnie and others just wanted to be around you. But when you got on your feet again, the old 'superman' defenses kicked in. That was your old adaptation. Clearly now you need a new, more flex-ible way to be in the world – a new adaptation. That's what seems to be happening already and something we can work on together."

I nodded my head. "That makes a lot of sense Colin. The body and mind really are one. I didn't have any surges until I began walk-ing and started physical therapy. Once there, I was forced to deal with the frozen, numb, glacial areas in my body and begin coaxing them into movement and communication with each other."

"I had a dream last night," I said, as I pulled out my recording. "I want you to hear the tape I made of last night's dream."

As the tape played I concentrated on Colin's expression. His eyes flicked from the tape deck to me and back again as he lis-tened to me relate the dream of climbing the snow covered moun-tain and the woman who had fallen upside down into the deep crevasse.

When the narration ended, he asked, "So what are your asso-ciations to that dream?"

"It's a perfect self-portrait reflecting what we're talking about," I began. "The intense physical pain of the rehabilitation process I am now in has certainly driven me inward after the feeling that's been isolated from my daily reality. That feeling has been trapped beneath scar tissue and adhesions since the accident. This feminine-feeling dimension of me is engulfed within a crevasse that was created when my body-mind was split open. Now frozen upside down, she needs me to make a connection with her.

With no thought for my own safety, I'm committed to her rescue. With limited ability and a rope, I made a connection between my conscious personality and my psyche. But in doing so, I too got buried in the snow upside down. Only my feet were sticking out. The immediate associations I have with my feet are the memories of my father and Alycia massaging them when I was hospitalized, and their tenderness, love and compassion that was mingled with my gratitude and tearful suffering. I guess my feet are the sensitive, feeling dimension of me that if I were upright, which I'm not, would be grounded on the earth and supporting me.

If my suffering has taught me anything, it's taught me humility and a sense of gratitude for those people who I've reached out to and who have been there for me. I guess that's why I'm hypersensitive to the people who are helping me now. I need them, feet first, feeling first, to help me. I think of all my different physical therapists trying to help retrieve those frozen parts of me from within their protective cocoons. And of course you, Arnie and other friends whose love and caring is helping me to redeem the suffering parts of me."

While I was talking, I noticed Colin had opened his mouth a couple of times to say something but had changed his mind. When I had finished, he just looked at me smiling.

"I just asked you for an association. That sounded more like you were giving a paper at the Jung institute."

We both laughed.

"I guess I'm feeling reinvigorated."

I had laughed with Arnie, and was laughing with Colin. I was finding the sense of hope that I was looking for. I was feeling a tremendous sense of gratitude for Colin's unconditional acceptance of me in the state I was in. As Colin began responding to me, I saw a bright flash of respect and hope in his eyes.

"Listen." Colin said. "That's a wonderful dream! A 'working through' dream and you had it exactly right after that tearful session with Arnie, right? Was your heart opened?"

"Yeah," I said.

"It's as if the dream repeats your fall into the ravine, but with a big difference. This time it's a woman who falls 30 or 40 feet, and this time you descend that same distance on a rope – not in a free fall with a smoking chainsaw in your hand. And, this time, it's to save her – to save your feminine-feeling self. And remember the in-and-out dissociation you described to me while you were crawling for your life through the rocks with your one good arm?"

"Yeah," I said, "with the leaves going from green to silver and back again."

"Right," Colin replied. "Well it's here in this image too – even the call for help which is a really important new element. And here, when you're lifted up, you have that feminine self tightly held in your good arm. You lost her for a while after you started walking. You got cold and angry and 'stony' again, but you've pulled her out now, and I'm sure it's because of all that warm feeling that you recovered yesterday."

The threat that hung before me regarding returning to therapy dissolved in that hour. More than once hope surged within me as I listened to Colin.

"I know we only have a few minutes left, but I have a question. In driving here and thinking about the dream, the associations came to me quickly. What about the mountain? The mountain is a part of something larger, like a mountain range.

The association I had was from a long time ago, when I was traveling from a border town in India to Katmandu, Nepal on the top of a logging truck. At dawn, while lying on top of the logs, in my sleeping bag with only my head sticking out, we crested the first range. The light was just striking Everest. The experience was one of the most profound spiritual moments in my life. The mountain, the mountain range, the light and sky were all one in the most profound way. Everest stood out but it was clearly a part of something greater, the mountain range. In an interesting way the sky around Everest stood out. Everest reached the highest, uniting earth and sky.

Since the accident I've continued to feel like I'm part of something larger. That "something," what I call the Beloved, sustained me in the ravine and for a while afterward. The Beloved silently came, asking for nothing, yet giving everything. Its quietness, like the sky's, seemed to encompass the world. Colin, don't you think we all are part of a vast mountain range, united in our humanness yet as ourselves separate mountains? And is not my drama in the dream simply the story of humanity; sacrifice, redemption and unity? Consciously or unconsciously don't we all at times get gripped by the workings of the psyche and swept up to serve a cause greater than ourselves? My act of selflessness in the dream may have been driven by love, compassion, or simply the transpersonal energies of the psyche.

When I die and pass beyond the glittering treetops will I just be waking up and discover it was all a dream?"

Colin smiled, "Well, that's exactly the view of Hindu mythology, where the great God Vishnu dreams up the entire world. It's a powerful archetypal image – that our lives are extensions or out-picturing of a great numinous reality that stands behind 'this' world and realizes 'its' life through the struggles of 'our' lives. Every once in a while we get a glimpse into that great light, gleaming behind the veil of our time-and-space bound existence. It sounds like your openness to all the suffering in your recovery has given you such a glimpse."

CHAPTER 24
Leap of Faith

Pain.

Fear it. Mask it. Mute it.

Whether it's psychological or physical, shut it out.

A host of industries in our culture have made multiple billions of dollars with variations on those themes. They proselytize keeping pain at bay and have convinced us that any brush with it is the antithesis to healing. If it doesn't hurt, it isn't broken. If it hurts, block it out.

They have left us with a much distorted view of healing.

In my two months of rehabilitation, I had learned time and time again just how essential it was to be centered in my body and to meet my challenges head on and fully aware. Masking and muting, I had learned, would not only minimize my ability to heal, but prevent me from opening more deeply to life and the purpose of suffering. I had witnessed it in so many others. I had seen just how trauma can paralyze any of us if we try to avoid whatever is causing us pain. Fear and aversion to pain end up compounding it. Ironically, it seems, that what we generally try to avoid is exactly what we have to experience to heal. Only by doing that, do we understand its purpose in life.

It upset me a great deal to see so many of my fellow patients become resigned to their losses with bitterness and self-reproach.

The experience was teaching me a great deal about how complex the resolution of grief is when we lose a part of ourselves on a physical and psychological level. Forward movement demands some form of inner realignment and reappraisal of self that is inevitably gut-wrenching and painful. To resist it is to be trapped by it. To open myself to it and trust in the Beloved was my path to recovery and to love and happiness.

My ability to adjust and cope with losses was rooted in a psychological and spiritual framework. I had found that by opening to the pain, sorrow and fear that was now a part of my life, I was able to access deeper resources and healing energies.

My therapists were both confused and inspired by my work ethic. Frequently they would caution me, thinking I was overextending myself in an effort to regain some sense of mastery in my life. The risk, we all knew, was that having a goal of participating in a triathlon could, in and of itself, create a crisis. But for me, the goal pulled me forward and gave the pain meaning. The power and control that I found came from making the choice to say "Yes," yielding to whatever the moment held, and thereby allowing it to pull me forward and teach me whatever I needed to learn on whatever level I needed to learn it.

As I pulled into the rehab center on a chilly March afternoon, I realized once again that I had underestimated the magnitude of the forces that were unleashed in the ravine. I sat in my car for a moment and watched people in wheelchairs and others with walkers or canes slowly enter the front door. The view humbled and saddened me. For twenty-five years, I had envisioned myself as a change agent for people. Helping people heal had given my life purpose, direction and meaning. My accident had changed all that. Now I was facing the most difficult client and the most challenging case of my life - myself.

Trauma, I was now discovering from a very different perspective, was remembered in the body and by the body. It was bound to my core and possessed me like a secret, desperate lover. As mindful as I tried to be, this lover generally lived outside of my awareness. It had buried itself within my body in various physical ailments, constricted emotional states, private sensory experiences and different biological processes. I had come to accept that the body had an intelligence of its own, one that was as mysterious as it was obvious.

Looking out through my windshield, I watched a slow parade of traumatized human beings make their way into the rehabilitative facility. The sight brought tears to my eyes and the memory of something Victor Frankl once said, "Suffering can be endured with dignity." Everything can be taken from a man but one thing, that last of the human freedoms – to choose one's attitude in any given set of circumstances, to choose one's own way."

As the clatter of freezing rain assaulted the windshield, I opened the car door and limped towards the entrance. Zipping up my jacket and pulling down my hat, I joined the parade with a sense of humility that was interwoven with a perspective of gratitude that held mine and others' suffering.

I stopped by the fitness center to give Paul an update on my progress at the gym. In front of me Tim sat in his wheelchair intent and focused, his face and shirt covered with perspiration. I watched as he finished off a set of barbell presses with about sixty pounds on the bar. His mental concentration and courage defined him, not his disability. When he finished, I said hello to Paul and then to Tim.

"You've got quite a pump going in those shoulders today. I hope one day to be able to do the same."

Tim shrugged, inching forward in his wheelchair as a smile moved across the crisscrossed scars on his face.

"It's taken me nearly a year to get to this level," he said. "You'll be there before you know it."

As his voice trailed off, Paul said, "We'll see what you can do in an hour or so, after you see David."

"He's such a sadist" I said. "He's not happy unless he "hears" the adhesions tear."

We all laughed.

"But I do have more range of motion. I'll show you what I'm able to do when I see you."

Both Maggie and David were free when I got to them.

"No waiting today for my two favorite physical therapists."

"I had a cancellation, and Maggie just finished up. We got a good night's rest. We're ready for you. We got a stronger electrical stimulation machine just for you. Let's see if we can get a little deeper in your glutes and break up some of that chronic muscle spasm."

"I'm ready."

I laid down on the table and they began working on me. It wasn't long before my breath came in gushes as I struggled to stay open to the pain, to choose it, not mask or mute it.

"Stay with it Jack. We're getting more range of motion and the scar tissue is starting to become more pliable."

I stayed with it. I let it in. In accepting it and giving myself over to it, I knew I was healing. The alternative was to resist and tighten up, the by-products of which would be more pain, more psychological trauma, and all around less healing. I breathed. I tried to relax. I let the energy flow through me.

Half way through the session Paul offered a progress report, which helped me even more to stay open to the process.

"You're getting stronger in every area of your body," he said.

"I can see muscle mass developing. You still have some neurological limitations and the hardware is still restricting you, but I'm impressed. The extra workout days at your gym are starting to pay off."

"Thanks," I said. "It's slow but steady. Some days are easier than others."

After an hour with Paul, I found my way out of the fitness center, into the locker room and on my way to the pool, towel in hand.

Vickie greeted me, "Nobody but the three of us today."

Ron quickly added, "The class was cancelled because so many people were out with the flu."

I glanced around, not believing my good fortune. I searched my memory trying to conjure up if I'd ever had the pool to myself. Never. Cardio conditioning had been limited both because the pool was busy and because I could only bike for thirty minutes due to the screws protruding from the bottom of my pelvis.

Ron moved toward the pool saying, "Let's start with the standard exercises and then we'll work on your walking."

My energy pulsed. In a second, I was in the water doing exercises with Ron's help. Vickie occasionally interjected a comment from her chair.

The three of us had gotten to know each other fairly well in the past few months because I was always pressing them to let me work out in the pool after class. After about a month, we jointly devised a system that would keep me safe yet allow me a cardio workout. We attached one end of a long bungee cord to the ladder in the deep end of the pool and the other end to a floatation vest that I wore for work in the deep end. I would slip into the pool, put on the vest and move out into the water until the cord was snug and then begin to "swim". It was an odd sight.

Most of my kick came from my right leg, while most of my pull came from my left arm. My right arm could get out of the water but would flop back down with a sagging motion before I'd pull it back and attempt to stretch it forward once again.

Flop. Pull. Lift. Repeat. It wasn't Olympic form, but it was recovery.

Vickie and Ron would watch me as I splashed and thrashed about, outward directed but inward bound. I would surge forward only to have the cord tighten and pull me back, continuously seeking but never gaining much distance. I struggled against the adhesions and scar tissue that always seemed to hold me back. Spasms and jolts of pain tested my commitment.

I stared at the empty pool thinking how I had never had the opportunity to "swim" for more than twenty minutes. I smiled at the empty water. In a short twenty minute session, I found I could slip into a "zone" that was almost trance-like. Once in that "trance," I was able to move beyond the pain and the fear. I experienced being run rather than running or being swum rather than swimming. There was "noise" from the pain, but it existed within the spaciousness of that trance. Sometimes in this state I'd have flashes of insight, memory fragments, mental images or simply surges of energy.

If that could happen in the short span of twenty minutes, I wondered what 40 could bring in an empty pool with no other distractions.

After Ron and I finished the therapeutic exercises and worked on my gait, I was free to get into the floatation vest and "swim". Ron attached the bungee cord to the ladder, and off I went. There was something very integrative about swimming. I felt as if all my body parts were forced to "talk" with each other. As I began swimming, energy came to me, and as I opened to it more followed.

I thrashed. My right arm lifted, flopped and pulled. I slowly found my zone. And after what must have been 30 minutes, a sudden memory flashed through my mind of a near-drowning experience I had survived off the Outer Banks. I was aware of it entering my mind and allowed it to pass while remaining with my breath in the expansive laboring movement. Towards the end of my time in the water, when my breath was fiery and my body exhausted, there were several more flashes from the same incident. Then my nervous system went into overdrive, provoked by a powerful drive from deep within, I turned my body over to the water and allowed the residual energy that was triggered to be discharged. As I swam, my heart raced, and my mind was flooded with memories and images of that day at the Outer Banks.

It was early August, a little more than a month before my accident. We were preparing to evacuate from the oceanfront house we were vacationing in on the northern Outer Banks of the Carolinas. A hurricane was bearing down on us, and the surf had been building for days. We had spent hours hooting and howling it up as we surfed and boogie boarded the waves when they were four or six feet, but they had built to well over 12 feet high, and we gave no thought to getting into the explosive surf. As if to accentuate that sentiment, a rescue helicopter thundered up and down the shoreline.

I started to swim a little harder in the pool as my adrenaline started to surge as images and emotions of that day moved through me.

I had packed the car in my bathing suit as massive waves twelve to sixteen feet high were smacking into the bulkhead, carrying spray over the house and onto the street. I dried off and sat down to eat breakfast in the dining room overlooking the angry ocean. As I watched the storm, I noticed two teenage boys with surfboards attempting to get out past the shore break. A bit of a riptide had formed there. One boy got under a wave and was quickly pulled out. I ran to the window to see the other boy driven back by the wave and deposited on the road. Turning my attention back to the ocean I couldn't see the other surfer. Speechless, I stood there and helplessly looked for the other boy. Then I saw him, several waves out, still on his surfboard, being pulled further from shore. Suddenly, an immense wave collapsed onto him. The board shot straight up out of the wave and was quickly swept away. The force of the wave had torn off the leash that had attached the board to the boy. There was no sign of him. After several long seconds, he popped up and I saw a head with arms thrashing at the crest of another wave.

I yelled for Alice as I ran for the boogie boards on the deck, the last thing to be packed. I grabbed the smallest board, leashed it tight to my wrist and as I was running across the deck wrapped it a couple of times around my hand. Not a thought about my own safety or the potential impact on my family crossed my mind as I sprinted toward the ocean. The wave intervals were horrendously brief before these monsters exploded onto the bulkhead that protected our house. Without pausing I continued running and dove through a wall of water as it burst against the bulkhead. It was as if God's breath paused for a moment as I dropped into a mad cauldron of backwash. Immediately, I knew I would die if caught by the next savage wave and hurled against the bulkhead. The ocean's kamikaze impulse seemed to cease for a few seconds as I furiously kicked and swam, the boogie board flapping around. I began to feel myself being caught between the onslaught of the next massive wave and the sucking pull of the previous wave's backwash. I intensified my kick while my strokes became harder and deeper.

As the next wave curled above me, I dove beneath it, emerging at the base of the next wave. I sucked in a deep breath as this wave began to lift me. Again, I dove as deep as I could. Instantly I was shot ten feet in the air as I exited the backside of the collapsing wave. I came down hard with both hands holding onto the leash. The board, thankfully, remained attached.

It's one thing to look for signs of someone in the surf from above the raging sea, stationary behind a glass window. It's quite another thing to be in the cauldron, with your eyes just inches above the surface, trying to find another head that's rising and falling in different rhythms in the wind, current, and 16 foot seas. I plunged through the waves and kicked with everything I had. The power and speed of those waves was on a scale far beyond anything I'd ever encountered before. My body was on fire from my efforts. There were less than 10 seconds between each wave, and as I rose to the crest of each mountainous wall of water, I looked around desperately for the boy.

He appeared finally about 100 feet to my left. The current was racing parallel to the beach, and I moved with it towards him. I called to him but the wind and sound of the exploding surf was too loud for him to hear me. He appeared and reappeared as the waves relentlessly surged over us. With my pulse pounding and with renewed intention, I kicked towards him. Now, maybe twenty feet away, he appeared to see me. He disappeared and bobbed back up to the surface with each wave. I watched him disappear beneath the next wave, and to my horror, he stayed under.

From somewhere within me, there came still another surge of adrenaline as I closed the distance between us. Reaching for him beneath the water, I grabbed his hair and arm and yanked. He came up. Initially expressionless, his eyes began to focus on me. He gave a shout and started clawing at me for the board. I tried to get the board under him. Terrified, he began pushing me down and kicking, as he tried to get on top of me. He pummeled me and thrashed about like a wild man. Too exhausted to struggle, I slowly began to sink beneath him suddenly surrounded by a complete quiet and calm beneath the wind and waves.

With one strong stroke, I pulled myself further down and away from him and bobbed up behind him and out of reach.

As I moved toward him cautiously, he began to scream, "I'm going to die, I'm going to die!"

"STOP!" I shouted. I grabbed his arm and leashed the board to it. I moved out of his reach, and we just drifted for a moment, up and then down the backside of several waves. The current was sweeping parallel to the beach at a furious pace, but no longer did it seem to be taking us deeper into the Atlantic. As his panic subsided his eyes came into focus. I asked him his name.

"Paul," he told me.

"Paul, we have to do this <u>together</u> if we're going to make it back," I told him. His eyes now wide open, he nodded. "We both have to use the boogie board. You keep it. It's leashed to you. <u>Never</u> let go of the board. We have to work our way in with the current." I could see I was finally reaching him. I kept talking as I got up beside him.

"Paul, we're going to make it," I told him

He held the board, with both hands. I worked my right arm around his waist and paddled with my left.

"KICK!" I shouted. We both kicked, and my left arm pulled as we slid up and down the backside of those enormous waves. We moved closer toward the shore but were also racing down the beach in the current. In between massive waves, I could see a section of beach and yelled in Paul's' ear.

"We have to get to the beach before we're swept north and slam into the bulkhead." He nodded. The waves were hitting the shore with a deafening sound, and after two or three waves somehow failed to launch us toward the beach, I looked back just in time to see a tremendous wall of water begin to peak behind us.

"HOLD ON!!" I screamed. Paul's eyes bulged wide. I grabbed the board's tail with my left hand and grasped Paul tightly around his waist with my right arm. The wave hurled us forward with indescribable force and speed. The board, mostly submerged except for its nose, provided us just enough flotation to move quickly up the shoulder of the wave. We rocketed down its face, and then the wave curled and collapsed over our heads. In the next moment we were held powerless in the wave's seething, sucking tube. I took a deep breath an instant before tons of water collapsed on us and viciously yanked me off Paul. I was cartwheeling and spinning up, down and sideways all at once. It couldn't have been more than a few seconds underwater but it felt like an eternity.

The next thing I knew I was like a stone skipping across a calm lake as I bounced up the beach and skidded to a stop on my hands and knees. Wiping the salt from my eyes I noticed the surge had deposited Paul, lying on the board, some twenty feet in front of me. My heart still racing and close to exhaustion, I stumbled forward on trembling legs. My chest, abdomen, arms slowly released the tension as my ears roared still with the sound of the ocean behind me. I started to yell to Paul, but I stopped as I noticed a woman and two others running towards him.

The woman, apparently his mother, was screaming at Paul with a ferocity that matched the raging sea. The man, who must have been his father, glared at Paul, not being able to get a word in. The other boy must have been Paul's younger brother. I recognized him as the other kid that had not made it past the breakwater. I wondered if I would have to rescue Paul from the relentless shouts of his mother.

The board lay on the beach. I bent down, picked it up and saw Alice and the boys running towards me with expressions of relief on their faces. By then, Paul's family, still furious with him, were half way down the street.

The memory slowly dissipated as I felt myself pulling hard against the chord that anchored me to the side of the pool. I was breathing hard, and I slowly returned to the moment. I stopped and floated for a few moments, calming down and letting the surge of adrenaline recede slowly.

As I got out of the pool Vickie said, "That was some swim!"

"You have no idea," I said, and wondered aloud how long I had been in the water.

"You were swimming for a little over 40 minutes. You certainly found your rhythm."

I thanked Ron and Vickie for their support, and I turned and walked back to the locker room. As I sat down on the bench my whole body was still trembling.

Was this the energetic discharge from an intense experience I'd had last summer, or something else? Was it my brain's attempt to resolve or discharge from my central nervous system a knotted memory or was it more of a symbol of the Beloved in action, in life, directing me or any of us to experience not so much what we want but more what It wants for us.

As I dressed I couldn't stop thinking about the moment I saw Paul in trouble in those waves. Something transcended that moment and engaged me, carried me into the surf without me thinking about myself or my family. It was an action and force beyond thought, and one that plays itself out in firemen, soldiers, parents, policemen, housewives, many times a day, throughout the world.

"I don't know," is the common refrain from uncommon heroes, "I just did it."

As I walked out to the car there was an inch of beautiful snow on the ground that silenced my footsteps. There was something, I thought, in a human being that was receptive to being seized and possessed by this force. It was not a passive receptivity that occurs when one holds oneself open, but rather receptivity to allowing oneself to be the vehicle for whatever movement may emerge. As far as I could tell there was no willpower involved. Our egos were survival oriented first; each man for himself. My first awareness of being separate from the boy, no longer fully possessed by the force, was when in reaching him he tried to push me down and get on top of me. Then and not until then did I realize there was a real possibility of drowning and never returning to my family. Yet, very quickly, the force took possession of me again, binding me to the boy once more in some living process that was independent of me.

And then it struck me. That which transcended me in that moment, the force that possessed and sustained me then, was the same force that sustained me in the ravine in that moment of death; that Beloved that continues on and carries us when the body dies; that which is the very source and mystery of life.

As I drove up the driveway to my home, I thought again about how spirit is hidden in illness, trauma, and life and death dramas. People throughout the world are pulled into these exceptional and extreme conditions and states not only to help or heal, but also as vehicles of spirit in a living process of life, independent of our conceptions of identity and reality.

Pain.

Mute it. Mask it. And when you do, you will become a prisoner of it.

Today, as I had done for so many days at the rehabilitation center, I had opened myself to the moment and didn't resist the pain of the physical therapy or the acute discomfort of swimming against the bungee cord in the pool. I didn't resist, and in being connected to my body and accepting of its painful messages, compressed energy had poured out of me.

I parked the car in the garage and as I walked up to the house I could hear Walker barking and see Alice and the boys inside. I was relieved that my family was at home when I got there.

"I had an amazing experience in the pool," I began. "I let my body speak its mind, and out poured all this compressed energy and emotion from the summer."

As I recounted my swim in the pool and the transcendent energies that made the memories of the day in the surf so vivid, I noticed tears on Devin's cheeks. I hadn't seen many tears since my accident. I picked him up and held him close.

"What's the matter pal?" I could feel Devin's chest pounding against mine. What burst out of him was the flood of emotion that he'd been holding onto for months.

"I thought you were going to drown, daddy!"

With that statement out, he buried his face into my neck and sobbed. His emotions brought all of us to tears. With open hearts and minds, accepting of the love, pain and everything in between, there was a reconnection taking place not just between my mind, body and soul but with my entire family.

CHAPTER 25

Spring Arrives – With a Smack!

Coaching the boys' soccer team was as much a part of my recovery as my days at rehab and the seemingly endless hours at the gym. While the physical therapy was healing my body, coaching Devin and the boys had been a personal and symbolic ligament connecting me in my traumatized state with the community and world at large.

In early spring, Devin and I walked into the gym for our last indoor winter soccer practice. The boys' vitality was electric. I felt myself lean into the experience and onto my cane as I invited into my being the team's liveliness. That innocent, untamed energy and aliveness lying behind the personalities of pre-adolescent boys uplifted me, moved me forward, and helped me soften my social-self-consciousness. It was in this wonderful forest of vitality and unbridled enthusiasm that I gathered and directed the boys' wild energy. Harnessing it was not always easy, but it was then that they experienced the power of the athlete within.

We began practicing. I shouted out encouragement, reminded them to focus, not to be afraid to shoot with either foot, and all the guidance I could muster in preparation of our upcoming tournament, And they played their hearts out, racing up and down the court with the energy, effort and joy that buoyed us all.

We were about half way through a practice game, the part of practice the boys enjoyed most. They had to execute the skills and strategy we would need for the indoor tournament on Saturday.

"Look around guys. See who's open. Remember we are a team. Pass the ball and move to an open space," I encouraged.

"Focus guys!"

No sooner had I said the word "focus," then a shot on goal went wide and "smack!" hit me right in the face.

The gym went absolutely silent. As my vision cleared I looked around and the boys were frozen, staring at me with a mixture of anxiety and curiosity. It was as if they were waiting to see if I would crumble, fall and break into 1000 little pieces.

I started laughing, and the entire gym breathed a huge sigh of relief.

"I guess it's me who needs to pay closer attention to what's going on." And then they were back at it.

"Breathe." I thought, as I reoriented back into the moment with my adrenaline surging. I took a couple of steps to land back in my body and tried to restore control by focusing on the boys. I felt like I was still partly knocked out of my body. Centering myself in my body was my first priority as I now moved up and down the sidelines, cane in hand, taking slow deep breaths. That familiar, undifferentiated adrenaline rush that I felt in the ravine as well as at times throughout my life was present. As I hobbled along watching practice another part of me was engaged with memories of being blind-sided, 'sucker-punched' in the face. Being caught unaware and being slapped or hit in the face was an old childhood experience. I couldn't "feel it through" right now, but the congealed emotions were certainly a part of the agitation that coursed through my body.

As I watched and directed practice I found myself preoccupied with what had happened. I quickly realized that I had seen the ball coming in the last second but was transfixed, like a deer frozen in the headlights of an oncoming car. A kind of reflex paralysis had occurred which never would have happened before the accident. The significance of the event was what was missing. It wasn't just my enervated arm's failure to block the shot, it was more than that. It was almost as if in a split second I went into a trance state where there was a loss of, or suspension of, initiative and critical judgment.

This narrowing of consciousness was a reminder to me that although I "looked great" (at least to others), the trauma's psychic scars were evident at least to me. This schism in my mind would take longer to heal than the "incredible" recovery that my body was going through.

Life was such a contradiction. A part of me was enmeshed in this trauma trap, while another part was enjoying the aliveness of this vanishing moment with the boys. I thought back to my swim the previous week, my recollection of my rescue swim. and how great I felt after my central nervous system had cleared out some of its 'noise'. Still trembling all I could do was move, breathe and stay grounded. A critical voice in my head also added to the mix, saying, "You jerk. Had you been paying attention you might not have gotten smacked with the ball."

I let that voice quickly pass, shifted back to my breath, into a place of acceptance for myself, and rejoined the boys in the energy and passion for the game.

Throughout the rest of practice the energy continued to move through my body as I moved along with it. Thank God for Jack, the doer and mover, I thought, who despite this 'noise' was willing to be 'out there' with it, suffering the energy, fear and feelings back into life. This process, I knew, was part of a larger process that allowed me to expose Jackie and carry him carefully back into the world, a world I once protected him from.

On our way home from soccer, Devin and I talked about the evening, and agreed that the team was ready for Saturday's tournament. He asked if we'd have time in the evening to draw. "My homework is all done. I only have to practice the violin."

Since my return home from the hospital, Devin and I would spend time before bedtime drawing. Drawing allowed us to expose and share "stuff" that was going on for both of us. It was a fun time as we got absorbed into the moment and were free to be.

As I listened to Devin talk, I could feel how the trauma had bound our lives together in a mysterious manner, both bitter and sweet. I sensed that the robot of his earlier dream was becoming more humanized again. More and more the old dad he had lost was coming back into his life. We got out of the car and walked into the house.

"Dad spaced out and got smacked in the face with a soccer ball," he announced to Alice and Brendan. It seemed the practice hadn't tapped an ounce of his energy or enthusiasm. But Alice and Brendan's responses were unusually subdued.

"What's wrong?" I asked.

"We just got a call from a friend of Grandpa's, Barbara . He seems to have had a heart attack. He's stable, but is still undergoing more tests at the hospital to determine how much damage was done."

I stood there in shock, smacked now with an emotional blow that seemed to stop time the way the errant soccer ball had in the gym. Everyone looked at me so lovingly. My eyes filled with tears. I wanted to escape the torment of the present moment, but I knew there was no place to go. I took a deep breath and allowed the 'wet' entangled feelings to rumble through me. I let my heart open to the painfulness of the news and tried to stay present. My head was jumping into the past, "…my accident was probably the cause," and to the future, "maybe I should fly down to Florida to assess the situation…"

"Did Barbara leave a number where she can be reached?" Alice handed me a notepaper with all the information and I went into another room to make the call. Barbara told me that for the past week, not only wasn't Dad playing golf, but he was lethargic, sleeping twelve hours at night and napping during the day. He became exhausted just going out to dinner. This was not the behavior of the dad I knew, but symptoms of a body in trouble.

By the time I was off the phone, the boys were in bed. I stopped by to give them a kiss and reassure them that grandpa would be all right. I came back upstairs and Alice and I talked for a while, but my chest was still tight and my breathing shallow.

Again, I was circling through a familiar situation. Whether I liked it or not, I was moving towards another experience of death. Not my death, but rather the fear of my father's. That fear had me in its grip just as surely as my body was seized when struck by the soccer ball. Alice was great. She was understanding and support-ive, but it didn't take my edge off.

"I think I need to go for a walk, I won't be long."

Somehow, being outside in the night allowed me to relax more. The darkness helped dissolve the sharp pain in my heart. What's my dad's response to his condition? What does this experience want with him? With me? I didn't want to let it in. I didn't want to suffer any more, nor did my father want the pain and fear. Yet, in the darkness, I could see my father and I were being drawn together again to experience and express our humanness. But fear had me in its grip, and my immediate emotional response to the truth of the experience was blunted. Jackie was nowhere to be found.

Over the course of the next few days, I spoke with Dad in the hospital several times as well as the doctors. His condition was serious, but not life-threatening. It was decided he would return to Boston within the week to be seen by his own cardiologist. I planned to go up and visit him on his return home.

I found relief in writing or dictating my experience while walk-ing. Because my body could hold no more, I continued to feel the need for an external container so as to not repress the surging emotional process that was moving through my mind and body. There seemed, nevertheless, to be a powerful dissociating current that was uncoupling my father's situation from my own internal process. Somewhere in my mind or body there was a fear of experi-encing the pain inherent in the situation. My mind felt at war with itself. It was apparent that one part was instinctively attempting to bury or repress the experience and adjunctive emotions while another part of my mind was attempting to retrieve and integrate the experience.

The split within me stayed until gradually it dawned on me that my mind was willing but not my body. The visceral experience of being 'smacked' at soccer practice coupled with walking into the house and again being blind-sided by my dad's condition and the energy and emotion it carried had gotten stuck inside of me. The intention of the bodily emotional experience got trapped in the body. I thought, as I realized this, if I were a gazelle and didn't 'move' or 'be moved' by the sight of a predator, I'd be dead by now. The distance between the trapped emotional experience in my body and it being registered in my mind seemed unbridgeable. After three sleepless nights, I had a dream.

> I'm with my dad, and we're having a great time. We return home and go to bed. When I wake up in the morning, he's dead. Tearfully I lay beside him. He is still warm. I take his hand in mine and gently hold it as I feel rigor mortis begin to set in.
>
> The dream transitions, and I'm in a restaurant. A woman comes up to me. She appears to recognize me. Her voice is one of tenderness and compassion as she asks me, "How are you doing?"
>
> She shows such love that I want to tell her my dad just died but I can't manage the magnitude and intensity of emotions within me.

And there it was! The duality of my mind/body split was embraced by a higher unity. I woke sobbing. My inner architect came through again with the images I needed to feel through the experience. Initially, I thought the dream had to do with my dad, my concern for him, and the intensity of the feelings bound up within our shared lives. And it might, but as the day passed and I continued to reflect on the dream. It felt like it was also some-

Spring Arrives – With a Smack!

thing more. My accident had brought my father and me into a deeper relationship. The tears occurred as I laid beside him, hand in hand and felt the rigor mortis set in. The body was still warm, but he was not there, just as I wasn't when I got the news, and my body stiffened.

Then the feminine appeared in a nurturing environment. It could have been Alice, Jackie or the Beloved compassionately asking for my response. But my emotions were trapped, frozen within a state of rigor mortis, caught again like a deer, frozen in the bright intense light of the moment.

Through my fall and the intense process of my recovery, I knew in my mind that death was not the cessation of everything we have known. There is love. And love goes on, and into it we dissolve and become a part of that which animates life. At some point, my father would die. And when he did, his love and our love would survive him. I knew this truth in my mind, but feeling this truth in my body would take time.

CHAPTER 26
Dad

It was early morning as I drove back to New York from a two day visit with my father at his home in Massachusetts. Although I was looking forward to Devin's soccer game at noon, my thoughts kept returning to Dad. The time spent with him after his heart attack in Florida had been initially shocking and emotionally painful but had slowly evolved into something tender and intimate.

Nothing could have prepared me for how much he had aged in a few short months. My father had always maintained the presence and bearing of a decorated World War II infantry officer, proud, rational and independent. Now, his identity had collapsed into that of a frail, frightened and utterly human old man. The sight of him had broken my heart, leaving me feeling so much sorrow and compassion for him. As I looked at him, I wondered about the way he had looked at me in the hospital that first week following the accident.

His mantra, "Life is hard. Be a rock," had been shattered by the blow of the cardiologist's cold hammer. "Unless you undergo open-heart surgery very soon, it's unlikely that you will live for more than three months."

Dad's warrior armor had been stripped away by the pain of his physical condition and an intense state of emotional upheaval.

I knew well the "place" he was in. This military man's traumatic experiences have buried themselves deep in his body, bound to his core. Buried within but outside of his awareness, his heart was asking one last time to be allowed to open and confess its secrets so that forgiveness and acceptance could be found. This crisis had broken him open as my fall had opened me, and now old, latent conflicts raged in his body and mind.

Being with him and watching him that first day, had rekindled so many memories of my accident. His crisis, like mine, had a powerful regressive pull to it. He watched my breakdown become a breakthrough for me on many levels. I hoped he could do the same. This might be his last chance to open to his psyche's facilitation of a more inclusive personality. Dad's confused, fearful and disoriented state of mind was indicative that he was already undergoing a therapeutic process from within that was far superior to anything I or anyone else could administer from the outside. Would he discover who his internal teacher-therapist was, as I had? Could he bow his proud head and say "yes," consciously suffering what was before him?

A lifetime of habitually repressing his emotional "wetness" now threatened to overwhelm him. Yet only if he could slow-down and open to this "wetness" would it carry with it the healing energies his body-mind needed at this time. Unfortunately, Dad was not aware of his mind's healing powers. Nevertheless, I prayed he could shift the fear and noise in his head into neutral, open his heart, and trust a terrifying process to lead him to a better place. I assured him that God would support his willingness to adapt to both the internal and external realities before him. I told him that in fact, there was a safety net that would catch and hold him as it had for me.

The first day, we talked about his condition and how he'd witnessed pain and terror open me up and teach me about letting go; about love, forgiveness, and the wisdom of my body. He truly tried to listen, but it was apparent that he was trapped within a whirlwind of fears. Watching him provoked a lot of compassion, as I understood how deep his patterns of resisting and repressing were. Our roles had switched, and I could only give back to him the same loving kindness he'd given to me.

On the second day of my visit, Dad began to talk about how letting go seemed so irrational and weak. In the midst of that conversation, we began to talk about Genevieve, my mother, and more poignantly just how vivid and painful her death had been for each of us, though in different ways. My father, who had never missed a day of work in forty years, took to his bed, devastated by her death. That was only the second time in my life I had ever seen him cry and not heroically push on. As we spoke by his bedside, and the fear of his condition gripped him, for the first time I could see and hear the elusive little boy behind my father's militaristic bearing.

I felt much closer to him as I watched this scared, alone, vulnerable boy-man. Being fully aware of him, without judgment, was extraordinary. Instantly my grasping at being helpful shifted into being aware of sensations and feelings about this unmasked man before me. It was a powerful healing moment for me. In that instant, something new was born between us. Emerging from beneath the heavy armor of the soldier was a boy, just as my fall had released Jackie. There was a sense of breathless wonder in the moment.

Although time had healed the worst of the pain associated with my mother, my father's condition now inflamed it for us both. I watched my dad soften as I began to recall the last two times I saw my mother.

"Dad, remember when mom was in the hospital? We were all there on the death watch as she wasn't expected to last through the night?"

"Yes," he said, his eyes looking far off into the distance, yet locking onto something very close to his heart.

"Remember how she was so agitated she had to be restrained, and how we took turns alone with her throughout the night?"

In her agitation she had pulled all the tubes out of her body. Later she was tied down and her rasping breathing came in unison with the respirator's hiss. The tubes ran into her arms and to or from other parts of her body beneath the sheet that covered her. I remember sitting on the edge of the bed, stroking her hair and shoulder.

She was always so full of pride, I remembered. She said, "don't want to die here…not like this." I remember smelling her essence as she lay there soaked in sweat, the heart monitor erratically reflecting her will to live. A lifetime of love, unexpressed, moved through my hands. We were both fighters who knew better how to struggle than to yield.

"We talked a lot that night," I told dad. "Then I watched her sleep. She was right. She didn't want to die that way or that day in the hospital. In the morning her vital signs were miraculously stable, and a week later you took her home."

There was a far off look in my father's tear-filled eyes. He simply nodded.

"Three months later the two of you stopped by to see me in Rye, on your way back from a weekend visiting friends in Philadelphia. I remember the thrill of us going out to dinner." I paused, asking my next question as gently as I could.

"What happened after you and mom got home from that trip?"

I sat in silence. I had always wanted to hear this story but had never before asked. Dad worked his way back into that moment and looked back at me.

"We had only been home a short while, but it was late. I went into the bedroom to unpack and change. Your mother said she'd join me in a moment and sat down in the kitchen to have a glass of milk and a cookie. I heard a loud crash and ran into the kitchen. Your mother lay dead on the floor…right here…where I'm sitting. There wasn't anything I could do."

He started to cry and I just sat with him, loving the vulnerable man in front of me. Muffled fears and sorrows moved out of his body. He no longer held in his feelings.

By the time we made dinner, ate it, and I cleaned up, it was late. We decided to go to bed. Dad hadn't taken a nap and he looked exhausted. I had just gotten out of the shower when he knocked on the door.

"What's up?" I asked.

He looked at me for a moment and then handed me an envelope with *Jack* written across it and beneath, *Dad XO.*

"Since I got back from Florida, I've been putting my house together. I had put this letter with my will and other things for after I passed on, but I just thought I should give it to you now."

I opened the envelope and pulled out a letter on official stationary. Across the top of it read "Office of the Chief of Police, Pittsburgh, Pa.

```
                              November 9, 1965
    Reverend Paul Gallagher
    Sacred Heart Rectory 376 Hancock Street

                        Re: Jack Weafer
    Dear Reverend Gallagher:
        Your letter of October 26, 1965 has been
    received, and it was with great joy that I
    learned Jack Weafer was endeavoring to "pick up
    the pieces" and that his endeavor was bearing the
    fruit of his labor. It is not every youngster
    that tries to undo the harm he has done himself.
        This particular youngster was handled on a
    local basis, as all restitution had been made
    by the parents with arrangements for parental
    supervision due to the fact the family was moving
    out of State. Therefore there is no official Court
    Record, only the Department file copies.
        I am sure Jack has benefited from your
    interest and concern, and you are to be commended
    for your efforts.
                        Sincerely,

                        Clarence W. Smith
                        Sergeant, Juvenile Unit
```

Here was a letter referring to the most painful, turbulent years of my upbringing – years when my rebellious acting-out had caused everyone a lot of pain and humiliation. My father had never spoken to me about the felonies I had been arrested for. This letter was clearly his awkward effort to do so.

As I read the letter my hands began to shake. As I thought back in time, I could once again hear the sound of the gun shot ringing in my ears. I must have been out of my mind. At 15, I had stolen a car on a very snowy night with some friends. I attempted to outdrive and literally outrun the police. When I tried to run, my coat had gotten caught on the car door handle. As the police were ushering me into their car, I kicked one of them in the shins and took off again.

"Stop or I will shoot," an officer shouted. I kept running. I heard his gun fire and turned down a driveway, leapt over a fence, and took off down a side street. I saw a car surrounded by snow berms and quickly dug through one and hid under the car. I remember vividly how my head pounded in the darkness beneath the car's chassis. The police cars circled the neighborhood for hours. When I finally snuck back home at around 2:00a.m., mom was waiting for me and pummeled me with a broom.

I reached out and hugged my father and he held me to him. Something passed silently between us during that vulnerable moment. Whatever it was, I only glimpsed it fleetingly, and then it dissolved. Perhaps it was not just me at this time who saw an inconsolable little boy, and loved him without judgment.

Later, with a deep sense of gratitude, I kissed my father goodnight. "I love you Dad. I'll stop in for a second first thing in the morning before I leave"

"I love you too Jack."

I went to bed that night thinking about the past two days and all that had transpired. I thought about growing up in my family, my adolescence, and my mother telling me she had only seen my father cry twice in her life; once when his mother died and the other time after my arrest.

I had chosen to go to Norwich University because it was a military college, and I had hoped to redeem myself for so deeply wounding my father. He had often said, "Your years at Norwich

University were the best years of our lives together." I wasn't much of a scholar then, but my being a good athlete and my three years of being elected to the Corps of Cadets Honor Committee had meant the world to him. I lay in bed for a long time that night, reverently pondering the wonder of my life and how mysteriously things happen.

CHAPTER 27
Judgment Day

"Dad, phone's for you," Brendan called.

It was Sunday evening after I had returned from Dad's and coached Devin's game. I thought it might be dad and was surprised to hear Jones's voice, the vice-president of the soccer club.

"Jack, I need you to attend a special board meeting Tuesday night. There have been some concerns about your coaching."

"Whose concerns?" I asked.

The silence at the other end of the call was palpable.

He had no answers and asked again of I would come.

"The only people who might have any concerns would be the parents of the kids. If there are "concerns," I would like to ask them to the meeting. Any objections?"

After another prolonged silence, he responded.

"No objections"

"I'll be there then," I told him.

As I hung up, I began to shake with pain and anger I could not comprehend. My conversation had led me violently backwards. I was falling again, but this time into a psychic ravine of chaos. Emotional shock waves were set loose and a rush of adrenaline and tumultuous energy swept through me, tearing apart my delicate sense of reality as time circled back. Feeling bushwhacked

and faced with the inescapable threat of a mortifying public hearing, and the potential loss of the team, deep traumatic residue was
re-stimulated. I just stood there "shell shocked" as I clutched the
phone in my hand.

In retrospect I realize it was another full-blown PTSD response.
I remember hearing what sounded like Alice's far off and faint
voice saying, "What's the matter?"

Slowly, as I reentered my body, I noticed my breath was held
and chest constricted. Breathing deeply, I tried to go with the
energy and sensations coursing through my mind and body. But I
was frozen.

"Jack. What's the matter?" Alice's alarm further complicated
my situation.

Tongue-tied, I gestured for her to wait a moment as I tried to
let more of the intensity of the moment and my irritation move
through me unobstructed. Jones had hung up with his usual haste.
Struggling with the reactivated traumatic effects of the phone call,
I awkwardly explained to Alice the nature of the call and the scheduled hearing in two days.

As I talked with Alice, feelings of incredible rage and helplessness surged through me. While for months I had felt engulfed by
a process that seemed capable of destroying me, I for the first time
since my accident, felt equally capable of destroying others. It was
then that I noticed my hands, both clamped tight into vibrating
fists. Even my withered, broken right hands' knuckles were white,
ready to defend and protect what I cherished. Supercharged energy
surged through this warrior's traumatized body from unconscious
depths.

Alice's words sailed past me as I was made deaf by the noise
of the battle inside. Struggling, I tried to focus in on Alice, as the
boys now stood beside us. I heard her last sentence. "…these petty
people's lives are only concerned about power and control. Your
life is about courage and change."

"That petty coward," I thought to myself. He has already executed me and is hiding behind a couple of parents' concerns.

I tried to be objective and reassuring for Devin, containing as best I could my deep feelings of being upset. But my perceptive son saw right through me.

"Does this mean you won't be able to coach the team, Dad?" The question pierced my heart.

"I don't know what it means, Devin, but I assure you most of the parents support me and I'm sure it will work out. The team is coming back, and we will have a great spring season."

For the first time since the phone call, I became aware of someone, and something more important than myself. Something beyond my ego had been engaged, and it asked that I take into account not only my son, but all the boys on the team. As the immediate crisis settled down and my boys went back to preparing for the next school day, I told Alice I couldn't sit still and needed to take a walk.

The moon that April night was nearly full. Hanging low in the sky it illuminated the driveway and forest, permitting me to walk, cane in hand, without a flashlight. Jones' tone and words cycled repeatedly through my mind, inciting a righteous rage that left me in a mental fog. Hoping to clear my head and anchor myself in my body, I walked along focusing on my breathing. But my energy was up in the fog, leaving me feeling disconnected from the earth. Halfway down the driveway I turned up a logging trail.

Walking along beneath the moon, dark shadows surrounded me. The wind seemed to shift direction tormenting me with failure. I didn't want to open to this experience. I wanted to vomit it back on Jones. Let him taste the humiliated bile from my gut. I instinctively resisted and refused to digest this moment. The shadows, I imagined, were taking delight in my suffering. Following an impulse I bent down and grabbed a limb I was about to step over. Swinging violently at the nearest shadow I swung it against a tree in a convulsive fit of rage. Agitated energy drove me on as I continually picked up limbs and smashed them against trees and the imagined perpetrators of my pain.

Gradually, with hands trembling, diaphragm vibrating, and heart pounding, my body began to release some of what circulated through my nervous system and mind. With the ghosts temporarily subdued and once again in my body, a sense of aliveness slowly began to emerge from the numbness and fog that had swept over me. Picking up my cane, I began walking up the mountain again. With feet that felt the earth below, my focus shifted to my heart that was twisted with grief.

"Why? Why now?" I wrestled with these bitter questions in the darkness. "How could anyone who has watched me climb back from the grave and onto the field not know how much this team and the boys mean to me." Tears began to fall at my feet as I realized how coaching felt like both a redemptive act for my broken body and an atonement for the "sin" of the accident.

When I arrived at the top of the mountain I looked out at the valley below and then to the star studded sky. Sorrow mixing with despair began to spill over and run down my cheeks. I felt trapped in a situation that I didn't understand, and a fierce need to relieve it.

"How could my will to live and my love for Devin and the other boys on the team have produced such a crisis?" The stars were silent. A cool breeze came along and soothed my hot tears. My back and hip were hurting so I sat down on a log and gave in to the gravitational pull from deep inside of me. Feeling alone and weak I just couldn't believe I was being asked to suffer more. I had said "Yes" for months to unrelenting pain and suffering, and I wanted it to be over. There was tremendous internal pressure to avoid this crisis, but I knew it wasn't possible. The rage I felt due to feeling humiliated was like a weight on my heart that I knew only I could relieve.

I stood with my back in spasm. Leaning more heavily on the cane, I began walking down the logging trail. I thought I would find my Beloved in the forest, but all had been silent except for the noise within me.

"OK," I thought to myself. "I'll do this alone." I know what it's like to be attacked, shamed and devalued. I'd spent my childhood learning to defend and protect myself from those experiences. As

I continued down the mountain I could feel the old heroic armor being laid down over my heart and body. I could feel the old conditioning return from years of growing up as the son of a military officer and my own military training. The military psychology of reducing the enemy to an 'it', and being an object myself, was useful once again. I was enveloped within a tapestry of memories of "me" versus "them". I had wanted to feel my Beloved's presence but instead found the warrior's will to live and bear the pain of my brokenness beneath the armor that was now forming over me. Through my recovery, I had come back to the world carrying my humanness, having left the dying warrior in the ravine. But now I recognized that without the warrior, the lions of the world would surely devour me as well as those I loved.

I had always been fiercely protective, but as I walked along sharpening my spears, I thought of a friend of mine. Harry was a lawyer; not just any lawyer, but a brilliant, nationally renowned litigator who once shared with me a dream in which he saw himself licking the flesh off of live lambs. Just what I need, I thought, a friend whose legal tongue could lick the flesh off the predators that threatened me. As I neared the house, I felt relieved and focused. I had begun to formulate a plan.

"Better?" Alice asked as I entered the house.

"A little," I said. "I'm going to call Harry and see if he's free Tuesday. He dreams about slaughtering lambs. That's the type of help I can use."

Alice looked at me intently for a moment pondering what I'd said. I went to say goodnight to the boys and assure them I was OK and back safely from the mountain top.

I lay in bed reading for hours that night. When I finally turned off the light, I looked up at the stars through the skylight and softly asked for help. Thoughts and emotions shot by like blazing stars until suddenly I had the thought: "Did my recovery somehow mask my fragileness and vulnerability? Were people unaware of the state I was in and the sensitivity I required from them? Did they somehow see strength where I only felt broken? Or was it my brokenness that they saw and despised? Had my recovery's single-mindedness, aroused by my guilt, willfulness or sense of responsibility, been perceived as resilience and challenged them? Or was it confirmation of who I was and how different my definition of coaching was from theirs?

The last thing I wanted in my life was some kind of power-control conflict, but it felt like it was the soccer board's issue, not mine. This was not a fight I started, nor was it one I would lay down for. I'd been down long enough.

Monday morning I awoke remembering a dream fragment. I trusted the messages hidden in my dreams. I took comfort from what they revealed within the deepest dimensions of myself I not only wasn't alone, but another was there recording each moment of my life, holding it for me while supporting and guiding me through life.

My next door neighbor is building a wall. I stop by to chat with him and notice his unusual wall construction. After he digs the trench he carefully places cardboard and empty egg crates in the trench before setting his rock and mortar mix.

Upon reflection, I realized that within me, walls were being built over the discarded containers for something fragile – eggs, life's potential...my vulnerable feelings perhaps. If I felt the need, and I certainly did, to protect myself from an external threat, I needed to be able to contain and process the underlying feelings and fears also. The dream stayed with me on my way to work, and I made a conscious note to remain as aware as possible of my own affective experiences throughout the day.

The dream had given me a blueprint to look at what was going on within me, allowing me an understanding of the innate defenses being built, and also questioning their purpose and going deeper into my process. By the time I got to the office, a certain degree of frenetic thinking and ruminating from the night before had subsided. When my mind was clouded with the noise of my own thoughts and anxieties, it limited not only what

I heard a client say but also how I heard it. I had some time before my first client, so I meditated and shifted my mind into neutral, allowing for a free flowing process with an attitude of compassion towards myself.

My preparation for the day allowed me to be touched by my clients suffering. There was a softness and firmness that moved through me as I helped people open to their struggles and torments. It was reaffirming for me to help them understand the existence of their suffering and find a perspective or meaning for it.

At different times of the day, I could see and feel how some clients had worked through painful issues or complexes and found some measure of peace in their lives. At moments I felt inspired, and at other times, ashamed of my own fear and weakness in turning away from my own suffering the previous night. During certain moments of the day, intrusive thoughts and memories reentered my consciousness. I not only saw how emotionally flooded I had been, but that I had only perceived the stress as external and beyond my control, making it much more frightening. I saw now how the experience reconstructed painful childhood experiences which I thought had been finally fully resolved in the past several months by my re-experiencing Jackie.

I realized that I had done that rather privately with family and friends, but not out in public. Why did a public process, which engaged feelings of failure and shame, need to be enacted and suffered? I knew how childhood complexes like this one could function independent of my personality and have their own thoughts and beliefs associated around an emotional nucleus. I knew they could force themselves upon a person's consciousness; Whether it was externally stimulated or internally engaged, I recognized I was responsible for my team and myself and was free to choose my attitude and response to the situation.

The Warrior and Wildman in me had heard the battle cry and were ready for war, but the healer now heard the cry of Jackie. I felt torn between protecting my still fragile self-image and pride or the deeper more vulnerable child of the past who had become so special to me over the past few months.

As the day went along, I felt I should be paying my clients for the insights I was getting into my problem as I guided them along in their own search and discovery process. I saw through one client's process how the grandiosity, inflation, and power that surged through my wild man and warrior last night was healthy and protected my vulnerable interior as long as I stayed in relationship to that vulnerability.

Something Arnie said to me a month or so before came back to me. He had said that once I'd started walking I'd changed and there was no longer the "high" in being with me. I'd told him it couldn't be sustained because my recovery demanded that I gain dominion over my body, just as my ego had to prevail over my psyche. But deep down, I too missed the high from being wide open, needing, loving and being given to. It was in those moments when the transpersonal energy flowed within me and between us. But my family, clients and team needed me back, and I had been totally focused on my come-back, perhaps to the exclusion of my own deeper self and Jackie. This crisis seemed like an inordinately excessive process to undergo because I felt so fragile. I didn't know if I was strong enough to contain the powerful affect or if I ran the risk of fragmenting or falling apart under the weight of it all.

That evening, when Alice and I arrived at the middle school where the soccer meeting was being held, we were warmly greeted by nearly all of the team parents, both fathers and mothers. The parents were very supportive of me and were extremely upset that anyone would make a decision that affected their sons without consulting them. Standing there in a kind of dry calmness, I quickly became uncomfortable with both their praise of me as well as their anger at the situation. Excusing myself, I made my way to the gym where the soccer meeting was in process. Although I felt flight-fight instincts engaging in me the moment, I opened the door. Looking out over the crowd I immediately caught Jones's eye and saw him stiffen. As his eyes slowly blinked, I watched as if a steel door had been tightly closed.

The atmosphere was tense. I was perhaps fifteen minutes earlier than my appointed time and had walked into ongoing club business.

"A bunch of political bullshit," a man responded when I asked him what was up. "Some parent is pissed at Coach Fred for not including their slacker, rarely-show kid on the travel team."

I looked over at Fred sitting on a bench looking like he was going to explode while the club president, Mr. Zealot, conducted proceedings. Suddenly Fred's dam burst.

"That's a damn lie," he screamed, and walked out of the gym.

The disorderly meeting became chaotic as Zealot, who'd lost his sacrosanct posture, pleaded for order. The incident had set off my adrenaline and set my hormones racing. Turning, I walked out of the gym and down the empty hallway, passing blissfully quiet, empty classrooms, wishing I could somehow extract the quiet spaciousness and inject it into my own mind and body. I thought of my dream from the previous night and the purpose and functions of walls.

As I walked, I reaffirmed to myself that the real threat was not a few ignorant people, but rather becoming alienated from my life within and the boys outside. I was caught in a process that was bigger than I was and one that would directly affect those I loved.

Hearing a lot of commotion back towards the gym, I turned around and walked back down the long corridor. Entering the gym, I walked over and stood by the bleachers in front of Jones and Zealot. Alice and the rest of the parents collected and stood off to the side.

Jones and Zealot, who had been quietly talking, now stopped and turned to face not me, but my team's parents. "Wrong choice" I thought to myself. Zealot spoke.

"This hearing is not about Jack's competency as a coach, it's about the club's policy regarding substitution."

His disregard of me and engagement of the parents was an obvious tactical error as the parents glared at him resentfully. His banal and insipid statements went unanswered until his closing remarks.

"And so, in closing, the 50% rule is simply what we feel is best for the team."

The statement ignited a firestorm. Parents shouted at the same time, all mirroring each other's thoughts.

"Don't tell me what's best for my son or the team."

"My son went out to play travel soccer. If my son just wanted to have fun and kick the ball around he would have stayed in the in-house program or left back in Division 2 or 3. But this is Division 1 soccer and he loves it. He enjoys playing competitively, and he's grown in more ways than you could ever understand by having Jack as a coach. He sees himself as a soccer player. His grades are improved. He believes in himself."

"You mean to tell me if my son isn't paying attention to the game, is up in the trees playing, it's up to Jack to go find him and put him in the game? What's the point? So he can play in a game he's not interested in? That's just stupid."

And on it went.

I stood there watching Jones' and Zealot's hearts harden. Whatever their motive might have been, it certainly was not benign in its consequences. Having power and being responsible for its consequences was not anything these men knew anything about.

I flashed back to the image of Fred exploding and wondered if I would be able to contain and absorb much more of this when I heard Jones say, "This is not Jack's team, it's the club's team."

So the truth slipped out, and I could feel it burning through me like acid. Pain in life comes from denying truth and today there was no denying that my fate had already been sealed behind closed doors. This would be the last season I would coach these boys.

The parents equally felt the weight of the statement as one said, "I'll take my son to another town where he can play competitively, and grow and develop as a soccer player."

As the parents continued to vocalize their opposition to the club's dictatorial use of its authority and unilateral decision making, I raised my hand. Instinctively and intuitively I knew my son and the rest of the boys had already been taken from me. A bitter grief began to build within me and something snapped. The boys had been a personal and symbolic ligament connecting me in my traumatized state with the community. That ligament snapped in that moment as I realized what a fool I was to think that the club would safeguard my position as a coach while I was recovering. Something essential within me that had been part of my drive to recover began to pour out of me.

I remained standing there for some time, hand raised, eating my pride and anger.

I could feel the walls within me thicken, both containing me and isolating me from a process from which I couldn't be protected. My commitment to myself and the team kept me in check, but the warrior and wild-man which stood on either side of me were beating their drums. I stood there, granting Jones and the soccer board the power to acknowledge or deny me, knowing they would always be threatened by men like me.

But my dignity was found in the freedom to choose to consciously suffer this process, one which felt unbearable in the moment. The one thing that sustained me was the love and affection that I felt from the parents as they affirmed my humanness and value. As the moral universe seemed to spin out of control, I waved my hand, gritted my teeth as a wave of helpless rage exploded in my body, and whispered over and over, "breathe," "stay present."

Jones looked at me and nodded as Zealot raised his hand to silence the parents.

"Let me make sure I understand what you are saying" I said. "You're not saying that I'm an unfit coach. You are saying that the parents' presence here tonight to acknowledge my competency as well as affirm their support of how I'm coaching the team is entirely irrelevant. The problem quite simply is this club has a fifty percent playing rule which applies to everyone regardless of their behavior or attendance. The fact that I know several coaches in this club who do not adhere to this rule is also irrelevant. Let me remind you that the league stipulates the fifty percent rule only applies to Divisions two and three. I've never met, nor have I seen a coach in Division 1 adhere to this rule. There is a league meeting next week and I would like to raise the issue with them. Whatever decision they make I'll adhere to as long as it applies to all teams and coaches in Division 1."

Zealot and Jones looked at each other, nodded, and then said, "Meeting adjourned."

Several of the parents, still very upset, continued to challenge the policy. I walked out of the gym knowing the meeting had nothing to do with the substitution policy but rather the removal of me. As I walked down the corridor and to the front doors, I heard my team's parents behind me. Some parents were arguing with board members, some with each other and some like me, silent. The impact of the charade ricocheted around and within all of us.

I was waiting in the car when Alice arrived, having walked out talking with several people. Alice was livid but as we drove home, and she talked, I became increasingly sadder. Alice was great in seeing, understanding and accepting me. We realized in hindsight that we had both seen it coming since the fall, when I came back and began coaching from my wheelchair. I said to Alice, "That's why they call hindsight the cruelest sight of all."

I could so easily have died in that ravine, but life was given back to me. I remember saying to Alice, "There just has to be a purpose to what's happening beyond what anyone can see in the moment."

"You know," I said "My responsibility and duty as a coach was an extension of my sense of myself as a father. I've worked so hard to come back, but I feel something is dying, and I don't know how to sustain its life."

After two nights that were mostly sleepless, I finally fell into a fast and deep sleep that Friday. But I awoke with a start around 2am. My heart was pounding, as I vividly recalled the end of a dream.

Someone's going to be executed in the morning, and the Royal Decree is that anyone who opposes it will also be executed. Everyone comes out to witness it and see if anyone opposes it. I come out also. Three children have come out to oppose the execution. They're linked arm in arm at a big old iron gate. It appears to be two girls, about 12 and 8 and a boy about 6. I go up to them. They all become very excited, thinking that I also am opposing the execution. But I only want to understand what it is that they are willing to sacrifice their lives for.

Their innocence touches me deeply. I kneel down by the gate. The oldest girl whispers something to me. She says that she lied about being dead before, and that she's now alive. I feel like I'm back in a confessional; she's relieved to have told me the truth. As she begins to weep, I weep with her.

Then I'm in a big church standing by the organ. As I touch items of the kids, which people have given me, people begin cutting off chunks of my hair. Then I start to cry, aware now that I'm the "someone" who will die with the children. Apparently I'm the only one who is going to die with them. I don't want to die, but I don't want the children to die alone. I'm weak in the legs, and people hold me as I walk to the iron gate where the children are.

I stand with them. The night is beginning to lift and dawn is coming. I see something in the distance but it is not yet clear to me. I am afraid to die. The children don't seem afraid. I'm glad we have each other.

I wake up as the pre-dawn sky becomes a mix of purple, gold and red.

261

CHAPTER 28
Bearing Witness

Resonating deep beneath the turbulence of my life, the dream percolated within me for days. It rekindled a vision that had nearly been extinguished by the latest trauma in my life. The messages and symbols from the inner realm were alive, nourishing my fragile sense of self, and reminding me that I was not alone. After months of being engulfed by the trauma's aftermath, and having major portions of my life stripped away, I just couldn't imagine tolerating more pain, grief or loss. Now the source of the pain wasn't nerve damage or scar tissue but my community, which I thought I'd been serving!

Injustice had always been a rallying point around which my drum-beating, sword-wielding inner allies had gathered power. It had always been a powerful stimulant which engaged the hero and heightened the meaning of my life. My warrior energies could taste blood with the soccer board. Right now it was my own, but I wanted nothing better than to spill the blood of these little big men and the passive members whose silence supported them. Not only had they never talked with me, but now they sought to take away what was so precious to me, my opportunity to coach these boys.

I didn't want to give up my quest to help illuminate for these kids their amazing potential. Now was a profound, poignant time in coaching them. My wounds and love for my players were not secret, but obvious for all to see. How could the board judge me without ever talking with me or the majority of the parents? My whole body shuddered with the masculine imperative to destroy the source of the injustice. At the same time, the psychotherapist in me knew that causing others pain in an effort to relieve my own pain would only add layers of suffering onto the children and myself. I didn't know if I had the ego-strength to contain the intensity that was surging through my traumatized body and mind. My Beloved had sent me a dream, almost a summons, asking me to turn inward to find my way, but I didn't like this dream.

I wanted a dream about strong ego coping, flexing and developing those ego muscles. I didn't want to turn inward, and I sure as hell didn't want to die. I'd just clawed my way back from death's doorway. I wanted to expose the soccer club's petty and naïve power politics and initiate a more integrative definition and experience of sport in my community. I certainly didn't want to sacrifice what I'd struggled so hard to achieve! I stood at a crossroads.

Would I turn in the direction of psychological freedom, or would the sound of the drums, the taste for blood, my love for the boys or my righteous rage have its way? I felt too weak for the task and the forces of resistance within my ego were so powerful. Could I deny what I experienced in the ravine or the gifts I'd received from consciously suffering over the past several months? What was my responsibility as a coach or a father? What did the dream show me about how a man finds his purpose in life or how a man suffers? Recovering my physiological functioning now seemed much easier than reestablishing a state of psychological health. The dream had unearthed the psychological dynamics beneath my personality, and it moved me deeply away from the material world. I wanted a life that had value, not so much in a material way, but in a deeper more meaningful direction.

It was the dream's depiction of awaiting an execution that resonated perfectly with the crises taking place around the threat of losing my coaching job. The treasure of the dream, however, summoned me to go beneath my fear, hurt and doubt and join the children at the gate. This ancient gate was like a navel, an axis that connects the realm of the ego with the unfathomable depths of the psyche. I might be awaiting an execution of attachment in my external life, but the dream's execution was by royal decree.

The sacred, with its inevitable sense of profound mystery, had organized an execution within my psyche, and by the end of the dream, it turns out the person to be executed was none other than me. Everyone comes out to witness this execution and to see if anyone is going to oppose it. The only opposition is by children who have a reverence for life and are willing to answer to life by sacrificing themselves.

In the darkness I felt an instinctive movement towards these children. A feeling of compassion drew me toward them with a desire to understand why. The gravitational pull towards the children's heroic opposition to the execution became the source of the drama. Was the gate a reference to the orphanage gate I knew as a boy? No longer a boy, I now experienced myself as a father drawn by a sense of responsibility I couldn't flee. The fatherly feelings reminded me of how I felt towards the boys on my soccer team, but there were inner children and something about a complete surrender to their loving energies was being required of me.

In the dream, the children's openness and innocence touched me deeply. Action and awareness merge as I kneel down beside the girl. A bond is forming between us that is rooted in sacrifice, compassion and death. Powerful, inexplicable feelings move through the girl and me at the gate. This love that I feel is so intense, perhaps because it exists within a context of death, the total surrender of ego. The girl whispers to me that she lied before about being dead. In that moment, I came full circle back to a dream I had nearly ten years ago of a little girl sacrificing herself to protect the life of a boy. Now the girl has returned from the land of the undead, and our tears express the truth of the experience and the joy of our reunion.

It was an expression of love and suffering not only intra-psychically, but between the ego and the psyche's inner representative which now showed me an imaginable response to the execution. The children would die with the executed so that he wouldn't suffer alone. The executed was me.

Summoned to the church, I stood beside the organ, feeling, touching and remembering the experiences of childhood. The objects of the children that I hold are imbued with tremendous energy as I allow this energy to flow through me as my hair is cut off like Samson's, and in the process, I remember and reconnect with the strength and virility that had been the cornerstone of my self-concept soon to be sacrificed. This process of renunciation is not a passive or fatalistic resignation to suffering, but rather a conscious choice to suffer the process of becoming whole.

I go to join the children and they me, but the experience left me weak. With the loss of my self-concept and ego strength behind me, I walk toward the children supported by the earth and affirming hands. Joining the children of the night, we stood together, willing to suffer the process and discover its meaning. By accepting that I couldn't prevent the execution or the children's sacrifice, I joined them in a process that clarified who I am. The courage to meet the new dawn is met with compassion and a renunciation of my separateness and heroic strivings. The unknown "someone" to be executed became me. Clearly what was ending in this sacrifice was my identification with being a hero protecting the innocent. The heroic warrior, my inner Samson, was dying along with the innocents he had always protected.

We stood together, locked arm in arm, as we became fully attentive to the sounds and experiences of joy and suffering in the universe. We were no longer separate in the experience of life. We became one with life as death approached.

As I thought about the dream, I realized that my old heroic posture had been intimately connected to my innocence. Years ago, my own innocence had been traumatically ruptured, but it had never disappeared – leading a secret life inside as "Jackie", my own pre-traumatic inner child-self. I saw this innocence again in my boys. The warrior in me would do anything to protect it.

The dream seemed to require that the innocent (child) parts of me had to enter a process of suffering, mortality, and death. And along with them, my heroic ego-stance would also have to be sacrificed. This was the hardest, most difficult thing in the world for me to do, to let innocence suffer pain. And I felt so innocent of the soccer Bozos' accusations!

Yet the dream's message was clear. This wasn't just about an injustice to a soccer coach. It was about my own transformation. But whether or not I could show up for this execution, I didn't know.

The air was clean and filled with light as I walked in the woods on Friday. The forest seemed gently touched by spring, as new life awaited its birth day. The nagging noise in my head and body from Tuesday's meeting still lingered but so did the dream. As I came to a stream, I sat down on a rock which was being warmed by sunshine. Breathing deeply, I settled into the moment and the sound of the stream beside me. The stream seemed to hum its own wet song that had an eternal rhythm echoing all around me. Leaves floated in the foam of the rocky pool below my feet. The stream's songs began to weave a spell over me. For a moment I thought I could hear the voice of the little girl from the night world whimpering in my ear: "I love you. Thank you." It was she who had saved a part of me when I was a young boy. Now she offered me, as a man, a way to heroically face, rather than heroically fix, this wound, torn open by life.

Sitting at this gateway in nature, I felt the movement between the inner and outer worlds. The inevitable merging of personal and transpersonal themes in life seemed natural here. Looking around, my eye was drawn to a skunk cabbage, emerging from nature's understructure. Reaching down, I touched its green leaves and attempted to dislodge it from its hidden seat. But the cabbage roots were too firmly fixed in their dark, wet home. A home that I couldn't see but was nevertheless nourishing. A life that generates leaves that reach out for the light. I thought about my own roots, deep within the psyche, where compassionate love for the children seemed to connect the inner and outer realms. Was that man a reflection of me, or was I a reflection of him? I didn't have that answer, but the surging energy in my body told me my inner Samson may have been shorn within a church, but today he was as hairy as ever and still sought relief in the crimson joy of battle.

Unexpectedly in the valley below, two deer began to wander out from within the Mountain Laurel. First one, then the other, cautiously moved towards the stream. I watched them meander about for a few minutes. All at once I heard a snort, and then I saw a rustle in the Mountain Laurel. It was a buck who must have picked up my scent. The two deer, with heads up and ears rotating in an effort to hear the approach, quietly but swiftly bounced off into the forest.

The experience re-engaged a memory of the first and only time I had killed an animal.

It was autumn, in these woods, not far from where I now sat. I had walked up on a buck I was upwind from. Standing there for some time, I watched this beautiful animal and wondered how long he had wandered this forest. As the wind around me began to moan, I silently asked permission to take his life. "Send a sign," I whispered under my breath. Not two seconds later he lifted his head, his rack held high with eyes that stared into the bowels of me. The depths of his mystic eyes were as expansive as the sky. He held my gaze. My heart pounded as I raised my bow. He never took his eyes off me until my arrow dropped him to the ground. It wasn't until I'd taken two steps towards him that I felt fully back in my body and emotions. Kneeling beside him, I stroked his neck and long back, and felt his last breath – shudder. It was then that I realized the dead space in the warrior inside me. I had felt connected with the deer until right before I released the arrow and then not again for a few seconds. It felt to me that we both left our bodies during that dead space when each of us participated in a ritual as old as man. It was that mystic look in his eyes, his willingness to die, to sacrifice his life so that his body could feed my family and friends that reminded me of the dream and the timeless story of love and sacrifice.

The dream, like the kill, was a living process that I could heed or deny, like my latest hearing with the soccer authorities. The response I chose would engage aspects of me which could generate a greater sense of wholeness, or, if denied, a source of painful fragmentation in my life. I had to take this responsibility seriously, and I had to do it consciously. I wanted to make the choice, remain in my body and avoid creating a dead space in the painful march into my unrelenting fate.

CHAPTER 29
A Boy Becomes a
Man and Vice Versa

Sunday morning was game day, and it was blustery, cold, and wet. I awoke early, with a body and heart that ached. Lying in bed and listening to the rainfall, I reflected over the past week, as well as the eight months since the accident.

"Eight months," I said quietly to myself.

It was hard to comprehend all that had gone on. I had transitioned from a man who "shouldn't be alive," and a patient who "will probably never walk again," to a man rehabilitating, physically training to make it through an annual Sprint Triathlon, and now psychologically trying to balance an evolving and recovering personality. I could see how my being broken-open, with my personality destabilized, had retired my faithful warrior and left me open to unconscious experiences of myself reentering my life.

Jackie, who had always been alive, albeit hidden, within the psychic realm, had existed in the outside world through my identification with my sons and the team. Prior to my being able to walk, I had suffered Jackie back into existence in my life, only to have him recede as I began my "heroic" rehabilitative journey. But the team, I now realized from the dream, had become a sort of touchstone for me to both redeem myself as well as become aware of the separateness of my own inner life with Jackie. In my rehabilitative drive, my own ego boundaries, which were still very fluid, had incorporated the team, making my suffering meaningful. Yet the dream "asked" that I withdraw the projection of Jackie from the boys and allow the heroic ideal to be cut away. Then the boys might find their own heros within themselves, and I could turn inward to my psychic realm and there companion Jackie.

As I lay there listening to the rain, it was the power of the psyche, which had become woven inside Jackie with outside Jack, that amazed me. The dream had sobered me, but I still felt intoxicated by the power of the projected little boy onto the team. I wondered if that dead zone in the warrior that I'd thought about in the ravine on Friday was the place where Jackie slept all these years. Had this compulsive heroic ideal driven me all my life? Had it been set up in childhood by love for my decorated wartime father? Was I carrying his projected hero? Had I always sought to prove myself equal to those ideals? Was it the mutual loss of both my father's and my heroic ideal that allowed the tenderness to flow unimpeded for the first time between us? But without that heroic ideal and the reintegrating of the warrior in my life, how could I maintain the rehabilitative drive and participate in the triathlon next month and deal with cruel and destructive people? I needed the warrior to help me manage the physical pain in my life and recover more of my functioning.

Slowly I got out of bed, limped into the kitchen, and put some coffee on. In darkness I sat there, looking out the window towards the east, sipping coffee. The sound of rain mixed with a view of the muted sunrise that barely illuminated the dark green forest which held my attention. It wasn't until my second cup of coffee that I realized the state of psychological paralysis I was in.

Inside of me a battle of wills was taking place. One moment there would be a powerful compulsive urge to identify with the heroic warrior and the need to protect the children and my own position. In the next, I would be swept up by a longing for Jackie and the children who stood by the sacred gate. In the midst of this battle, I began to notice that my own increased awareness of this struggle was both heightening and soothing my pain at the same time.

It was raining heavily when we arrived at the Raiders' sports complex. Parents surrounded the field, huddled together beneath an assortment of colorful umbrellas, while boys and girls splashed back and forth. Glancing over to where the Raiders were warming up, I could see that we Scorpions, as a team, were out-skilled, and that I would probably be out-coached. But hey, judging from the sound of delight coming from our boys who were already soaked, we'd have more fun.

One of the messages I'd been giving the boys all spring was how to absorb their limitations without submitting to them, while at the same time reaching beyond and aligning with that force that lies within each of us. I reminded them frequently how that force had the ability to carry each of us to our potential. We are seldom aware of that force, I would explain, until the moment we open to it and allow it to flow through us. In every game in Division 1 soccer we were reaching for the stars, sometimes surprising ourselves with moments of greatness when that force flowed through us. But as often, we weren't successful, the reaching and failing process shaping our experience of ourselves.

My game time pep talk carried with it my respect and belief in each of them and the team as a whole. Looking into their eyes, I saw excitement and their belief in me and maybe even in themselves.

"You guys have worked hard to be here, and you have certainly earned the right to be here. I believe in everyone one of you, and all of you as a team. Believe in yourselves. Play hard. Play smart. Have fun."

The day was truly epic. With the exception of the fact we were in the throes of a soccer match, I felt the tone of the afternoon was straight out of Shakespeare's tempest. I felt a natural nervousness for our team, while internally I also wrestled with the emotion that swirled inside of me regarding the upcoming hearing of my status as a coach and the fact this might be the last game I was allowed to coach. And the boys played with a fervor that exceeded the intensity of the day's storm.

The two teams were well matched through the first half. Both teams learned to compensate for the wind and rain, and by the end of the first quarter it was tied at 1-1. In the second quarter, the rhythm of the game picked up. The Raiders adapted more quickly than we did, earning them an early 2-1 lead. But that deficit led quickly to a catalytic moment for me, the team, and Devin.

Devin's response to dropping behind by a goal seemed to transform him. He and his teammates Nick and Logan in particular, seemed to suddenly develop an intensity I had never before seen in them. They began to play with a fury that transcended simply playing for pleasure. There was an unprecedented resolve and purpose to their game, and it was exhilarating to see.

Devin had dropped back numerous times from his forward position to talk with his midfielders, and after a great exchange between him and Logan, Devin began charging downfield carving Z's as he wove the ball between defenders toward the opposing goalie. Devin took advantage of the size of the net and fired a shot into the upper right corner.

The goal seemed to ignite both teams as I heard the Raiders coach yell, "Mark number 1 and stay on him!"

It was at that point that I made my substitutions. They included one for Devin. He came off the field annoyed and with tears in his eyes. His sense of responsibility for scoring and keeping the team in the game was clearly apparent to me. He had always taken a leadership position among his teammates, but today I sensed something deeper, more urgent and fiery coming from him.

"Dad, put me back in," he pleaded as he gulped down some water.

As I looked into his eyes, I saw and felt the burden of his sense of responsibility for the team and something else. I'd seen and heard this urgency come from Devin before, but today something deeper quivered inside of him. It was reminiscent of something he had said on the ride home from practice on Friday.

"Dad, I don't want to play soccer just for fun. Why is the stupid soccer club making us lose just to have fun? Nobody else in Division 1 is playing for fun. Nickie, Mike, Kyle and me were talking and we want to play better and win more games."

I had tried to give Devin a different perspective, one that included playing for fun, but I could see how it was affecting him and the other boys self-image and self-esteem. He had talked about how he had wanted to decide what playing soccer meant to him and not have someone else impose their meaning on something that was important to him. Maybe it was that determination I saw and heard in him as the rain poured over us. Devin's passion to excel had always been his hallmark and now, more than ever, it appeared to conflict with the club's adherence to mediocrity.

As the half came to close, the Raiders scored and took the lead 3-2. As the cheers from their team died down, Devin shouted at me.

"See what happens. The team needs me!"

Looking at him I watched the tears flow from his eyes, mingling with the rain streaking down his face. The rain seemed to magnify the tears, both falling together toward the earth. His eyes pleaded with me. I realized in that moment he needed that sense of responsibility for the team and for a win that I felt was a burden for him and wanted to remove. To protect him from that responsibility was to deny him something vital in his own development. Normally I restrained his natural passion, but the vividness of the fiery process taking place deep within him was larger than the moment. I knew my son, and I knew this was a moment to step aside, as I'd done at other times with other players when I saw their inside merging with an event or moment in the outside world.

As he stood beside me, I realized it was moments like these that the club wanted to protect children from. Well-intentioned, perhaps, but as Devin stood by me agitated, I knew I was compounding his suffering by resisting his will.

The Raiders' coach had not yet made one substitution, keeping his most skilled players on the field. Who was I protecting or sacrificing? Devin's sense of responsibility lent dignity to his life and gave it meaning.

In that last minute of play before the half I made my decision.

At half time, as the boys sucked on oranges and drank their sport drink beneath their parent's umbrellas, I was overcome by feelings of deep love and appreciation for these boys who I now realized were also playing to save their coach from execution. As the wind and rain blew, I felt the boys again as an external ligament which connected my inner self to the external world in such a deep and meaningful way. A wave of grief united with hope as I saw the child within me in each one of them. I knew in that moment that even without me as a coach these boys were now well on their way to becoming fine young men.

It was then that I stopped caring what the outcome of the next day's league meeting would be. All the boys' eyes were riveted on me except Devin, whose eyes remained fixed on the field. Feeling a psychic inter-nervousness with the boys, like a father for his sons, I knew I had a responsibility to be myself here and stand for what I knew to be true, that we were all more, much more, than our fears, doubts, and conditioning defined.

"We can win this game," I affirmed. "Each one of you has what it takes to come together as a team today and win."

I had watched the boys reach for the stars before and sometimes surprise themselves with moments of greatness. As halftime came to a close, I assured the boys once again that they were capable of responding to the challenge before them. We were all worthy of the tests that came our way, whatever they might be.

The second half started with renewed and untiring intensity from both teams. And relatively early on, Devin again worked in amazing synchronicity with his teammates and stormed down the field for his third goal of the game, impressing even the referee, who shook his head in amazement after he signaled Devin's shot as a goal. The opposing goalie picked himself up out of the mud and yelled at his defenders while Devin was being mobbed by his teammates.

Although the game was tied, it was a long way from over. The Raiders were now more upset than ever and played with a vengeance. But we were up to the test, and each ball was hard fought for and won. Near the end of the third quarter, the Raiders scored and went up 4-3. When the whistle blew to end the quarter, I told the boys that we'd win with honor or lose nobly because everyone was playing up to or beyond their ability.

The last quarter built to a level of intensity that almost defied description. Both teams rallied while, as if driven by the energy on the field, the storm itself was reaching a peak. But in the back and forth of the two teams, and all the combined drive and resolve of the players on the field, it was Devin who seemed to transcend the moment above all others.

At one point, he raced back to help his midfielders and despite warnings of "Man ON," was able to steal the ball from the Raider offense and drive it back down the field. Parents and players alike shouted in unison.

"Go Devin, Go!"

As I watched Devin, I was acutely aware of my own separateness from him. A slow withdrawal of my own psychic energy from him began to occur. The more I let go, the more he seemed to find his own source of energy and motivation. He had now moved through five Raiders and was one on one with the keeper. He pretended to go left, then cut right, faked the shot with his right but instead took the shot with his left and put the ball in the left corner of the net. Everyone went wild, Scorpions cheering, Raiders reeling from the blow.

Tears blurred my vision, because I knew from the bottom of my feet to the hair on my head, that his triumph was my loss. Could I endure it consciously, and allow Devin and his team's freedom to emerge? It felt so painful to love with an open hand, but I knew I would. The whistle blew. The referee walked back to the middle of the field and suddenly looked at me, his lips in a slight smile.

We both knew we were watching this young player birth himself on the field. Devin didn't need to become a hero to be a man. This was not a desire for glory, but rather his facing his fears and opening deeply into himself. He was drawn down into and through a labyrinth, following something within himself through a process of sacrifice into the very center of his own existence, and there he found what was beyond his personal self.

In the final minutes, with the game tied, Devin's body quivered with a living fire; there was a raw visceral energy coming from him. His feelings had become the guide to choices he was making. I could see he was conscious of turning himself over to the process.

Devin seemed to fill and saturate himself with energy that connected him with his teammates; a dynamic energy of passion. His play inspired them and nourished a strength and desire within them as well. He seemed to physically and emotionally traverse the Raiders' territory, stripping away their strengths and revealing vulnerabilities and gaps I couldn't see. I watched him continue to transform as the result of his experience of the game. There was a kind of abandonment to himself, birthed out of his own joy and total enthusiasm for the game.

The Raiders weren't surrendering, but Devin out dribbled them or threw them off with hip feints. With lightening changes in rhythm and high speed dribbling that seemed to defy gravity, he remained disciplined and under control until there was only one last defender between him and the goalie. My stomach tightened; my heart beat so fast I thought it would explode. I had withdrawn the projection of my own boy, Jackie. This now was Devin, and he had fully embraced himself. With a spectacular piece of footwork, he broke free into that sacred green space inside the box. There was no denying Devin now. He was clearly infused with an energy that was otherworldly. He seemed to dance with the ball as he pulled the goalie towards him and in the last moment chipped it over his head.

Goal.

We held on the last two minutes and won 5-4. Devin had successfully not only exorcised his own personal demons, but mine as well by opening up to his own psychic life and bringing forth a hero that inspired all who watched him that day. The boys were still in a pile on the field with Devin on the bottom. As everyone got up, still hugging each other, and especially Devin, I looked deeply into each of their faces. In the past I could see a touch of envy in some of the other boys when Devin played well, but not today. Each boy seemed to rejoice in the victory that perhaps engaged in each of them more of their own ability and potential then they had ever previously realized. Devin represented them all, the best of them all.

It wasn't Devin who had been too much for the Raiders today it was boys becoming men that had been too much. As I went out on the field, and we all lined up to shake the other team's hands, I thought of how often men feel as if they are never enough of a man to get their father's love, respect and approval to be anointed into manhood. There had been a process of initiation and transformation during that game, and one I knew Devin would never forget. I hugged him on the field to the cheers of the crowd, cheers that still echo in my mind to this day.

I grieved the loss of him as my little boy, but I knew Jackie awaited me at the gate. The love and respect I felt for Devin and all the boys was the space where I could begin to negotiate their freedom. The renunciation of them as <u>my</u> boys, <u>my</u> team was the first step. So I guess Jones was right, they weren't MY team but they also weren't the club's possession either. They, like all children, needed a loving hand to guide them, an open hand, one that could guide but not possess. I saw them that day for what they were, boys being baptized into the waters of masculine ritual, waters that nurture their minds and bodies and illuminate their souls.

CHAPTER 30
The Verdict

The day following the match my thoughts were churning. The rain had ceased, but the storm in my mind had abated only slightly. I was filled with pride and joy for Devin, the team's incredible performance and the win. And at the same time, I was almost overcome with a fiery yet frozen quality about that evening's league meeting. I knew that these symptoms reflected the amount of life energy trapped in both my mind and body. At the nexus of those conflicting emotions I struggled to find my center. A whirlwind of thoughts spanning all the way to my first moments in the ravine consumed me.

Devin's day at the match had been momentous. Courageously, he had opened to the suffering of my accident that had haunted his existence for months. Trusting to his deepest self, he had yielded to something much larger than his little ego. As he opened to this force, all of his sorrows and joys found an outlet in one incredible performance. He was a vehicle for something much larger than himself that day, something that also galvanized the entire team. I had stood there in awe watching what appeared to be the hand of God reaching up through his brokenness, carrying forth into the world an experience of himself that gave dignity and meaning to his life and the team.

On the ride home from the game the day before Devin asked, "Dad, do you think when the league gets the score they'll know you're a good coach? We beat the number 2 team in our division!"

I paused before answering, knowing that Devin wanted not only to relieve his suffering and the team's, but mine as well.

"Devin," I said, "You made mom and me so very proud today. You played so well, and felt good about yourself and so did the team. But truthfully Pal, you know how it goes. We won today, but maybe next week we'll lose. What's important is not simply winning or losing but allowing yourself, as you did today, to be all you can be. It's that commitment to excellence that counts and ultimately shapes your life."

I wasn't satisfied with my answer. Although Devin took it in and seemed to ponder it, I continued to ponder his question. Who did winning serve? Obviously, Devin had played his little heart out for me. He had wanted to be the hero for everyone, for himself, for the team, for his coach, and for his Dad.

It was all part of developing a heroic identity, but it also served to redeem him and alleviate his helplessness and sense of himself and his team as losers. It was not the time now to explain to him the lessons I had learned over the last several months that the most difficult part of being a winner was the reconciliation with the loser within us. I knew now more clearly than ever that we aren't winners or losers, good or bad, right or wrong. We are all elements of both. We are winners and losers, good and bad, right and wrong. Most people, it seemed, didn't struggle with this paradox very much. The struggle was difficult and illogical. When I felt wounded, as I now did with the soccer club, it became painfully difficult to hold both the dark and the light – both right and wrong. I knew I had limitations as a coach. I just wished someone had talked with me about their concerns rather than creating a bogus issue like the substitution rule.

Devin, I knew, had also begun the long and arduous journey toward manhood, a journey in which his psyche would increasingly ask him to suffer whatever he found unbearable in life. He too would discover that he was a winner and loser, and his struggle with paradoxical nature would shape him. But for now, his 'loser' had been redeemed by a self-transcendence that made the unbearable bearable, and through its agency, he had opened to the potential person within.

I realized that Devin, Brendan, and I all stood at a crossroad, one common to fathers and sons. Our paths were now taking us in different directions. My sons' paths were leading them toward the heroic masculine ideal. This high road was narrow, restrictive and consequently necessitated a leaving behind or splitting off of parts of themselves that were incongruent with the ideal. I knew this path only too well. I had left Jackie behind many years prior, and I had only now begun to reintegrate him into my life. The boys were separating from Alice and me and were transitioning from male childhood to manhood. At the same time, I was reviving the child within me, drawn down back into the valley, having already traveled the high road to the pinnacle of many mountains.

As I sat in my office with clients the day after the match, my thoughts distracted me. Mental and physical "noise" continued to erupt within me unbidden. The anxiety about the coming night's league meeting continued to boot my nervous system into high gear, and my internal conflict interrupted my clients' processes.

The first time I had a break between clients I lay down and did a relaxation exercise followed by a self-hypnosis process. As I did, an insight came to me. My childhood traumas predisposed me to feeling an intense sense of vulnerability, especially around public exposure. My helplessness within the soccer crisis and the public forum I would be exposed to was now compounding the post-traumatic stress I was already experiencing in my recovery. Residual feelings of helplessness as well as my physical and emotional memories of my experience in the ravine and at the hospital were traumatically encoded on a cellular level. They were being set off, released, and amplified throughout my body by the soccer crisis. I was opening and submitting to the affect as well as the physical cellular memory as best I could. I would then reaffirm it or discharge it. All told, the process was overwhelming.

I thought back to the ravine. My fall had broken open my mind and body and I had become part of nature, immersed into something greater, floating in it, taken up by its current. In that trauma, "I" was no more. My mind and the energy were yielded, and the Beloved had taken hold and possessed me

In the hours, days, and months that followed my fall, I had suffered the loss and celebrated the return of my Beloved many times, and I had learned how to open to, suffer, and accept pain in my body and life. There, under the surface of the pain and in the life of my being, roamed the Beloved. The awareness I'd gained in opening to my own bodily processes and their underlying affective experience had allowed me to see and feel the tender thorns in the psyches of not just myself, but of my clients. My broken body and my process of recovery had made me more receptive to not only the presence of my Beloved, but to the Beloved's all-pervading spirit shining through others.

That Spirit is, for the most part, unseen. Yet I know when I'm touched by the power of its love, a love which so often moves in my heart and allows me to see, really see, the essence of a client. Through my sense and understanding of the Beloved, a doorway frequently opens into my clients' hearts, and the invisible becomes visible. When this revelation is experienced, it seems to respond to an individual's deepest needs to be seen and understood. His or her fears and suffering are then seen from a different perspective, and our rapport deepens. Most people come into therapy wanting relief from their suffering, longing to be pain free. It is only with love that I've found I can turn people back into their suffering through which they then find relief. As I learned in the hospital and repeatedly learned throughout my recovery, it is often the very pain we are trying to avoid that can unlock the key to our healing.

I know I am not alone in my "out-of-body" experience in the ravine. Traumatized people everywhere have been cut lose from their anchors in the ego world and set adrift in a completely spiritual realm. The journey back into this world and the resetting of anchors can be a very physically, emotionally and psychically entangling process.

The spirit realm can have an undertow which leaves us restless at heart, yearning to taste again the transpersonal, invisible energies. But that transpersonal elevation and expansion of the ego occurs at a time when our defenses are shattered. When that transpersonal energy retreats, and our defenses reform, we are frequently left longing for the "not-me" transpersonal energy. It is at that point we are most vulnerable to becoming inflated with grandiosity or perhaps we turn to drugs or alcohol to recapture the transpersonal high. So many of the traumatized people I have seen as clients have been caught in this tormented process for years.

The only way out is down; down into the suffering, into the midst of the torn open cry where omnipresent love awaits – love that we cannot see, for which we have no image. But its presence and grace heals us from within the darkness.

As I left my office and began driving to the league meeting, I thought back to words I had heard from so many people, and a thought Alice in particular had reminded me of more than once.

"It's a miracle you weren't killed or suffered severe brain damage."

In the parking lot of the meeting, I closed my eyes and focused on my breathing. I felt a kind of "wet" irritability infused with adrenaline. As I breathed, and my diaphragm softened, I felt how intolerable it was to face my own helplessness. As I did so, I thought of floating above the trees in that ravine. I reminded myself that this crisis was triggering and amplifying all the post-traumatic stresses of my fall. And, most important, I reminded myself just how lucky I was. I had been alive to see Devin's magnificent performance. I witnessed it unclouded by any symptoms of a brain injury. I paced the sidelines of the game under my own power and not from a wheelchair. My family and I were indeed blessed with a miracle. The awareness sobered me up as I walked into the school and toward the room where the meeting was being held.

Walking into the meeting, I felt a slight but perceptible clinch in my gut and was unable to feel my feet hit the ground. I actually focused on the physical pain I felt in my pelvis and back to ground myself. Taking a seat I scanned the room, but no one was paying attention to me. I relaxed a notch. The meeting began, and I continued to look around and found myself thinking that perhaps this experience wasn't an accident either but rather another opportunity offered to me to honor a change in the direction of my existence. Breathing deeply, I noticed the fire in my heart and the ache in my gut as I accepted this fateful situation as part of the recovery process.

I realized I wasn't answerable to these soccer league men or those of my own club, even though they had the power to appoint or discharge any coach in the league. I was only answerable to myself, for myself. The thought of giving up the team and my attachment to the boys was very painful, but I recognized that there was a recurring theme in my life since the accident. Repeatedly, I had been confronted with the option of either resisting or surrendering my fate to a power far greater and wiser than my own, the Beloved. Life was steering me toward acceptance and faith. The central focus of my life was shifting from "me" as either hero or victim, towards an inner calling that now asked to be lived. I was willing to renounce my role and image of coach knowing that my underlying "self" was at my dream's gate waiting for me.

Perhaps I thought, this experience with the soccer league was just another in a sequence of events that was snapping the chains that bound me to the past, while at the same time releasing me so that I could be helped along and supported, as in the dream, towards a destiny that would unfold as my life continued to renew itself. A wave of emotion crashed and washed over me as I sat there looking at the men before me, realizing again that conscious suffering clarifies real identity. My diaphragm softened, my hands unclenched, and the bile in my mouth dissolved.

I turned my attention to the head table. Listening deeply to each of the men, I heard not only their words but the subtleties behind them. Their breathing movements, inflections in their voices, pauses and facial expressions almost made me laugh. I couldn't believe I'd externalized onto these men the power to enrage within me a sense of enforced helplessness. Throughout my life I'd known what being helpless felt like, especially during the last eight months. Hundreds of times since the accident I had found and lost an internal locus of control for my life and right now had rediscovered it once again.

The meeting agenda now focused on new business, and I raised my hand. Introducing myself, I explained my dilemma regarding my club's directive to adhere to a fifty percent playing rule when neither the league nor other coaches in Division 1 adhered to that policy. As I spoke, some of the league men rubbed their temples or stared at me as if seemingly attempting to probe my mind. It was obvious that their position accustomed them to being obeyed without question.

The man in the center had a corpulent face and had remained impassive while I had addressed them. He spoke first. Our eyes locked. His response to me sounded rehearsed and had an air of arrogance.

"From this time forward," he said, "Division 1 will be eliminated. The new divisions will be Divisions 2, 3 and 4 and the substitution rule will apply to all divisions. I will have a memo sent out to all Division 1 coaches this week regarding this divisional change and emphasize that the substitution rule applies to all coaches."

In the unhesitating and smooth delivery of this statement it was apparent that the course of action had previously been decided on. The memo, I knew, would be ignored. Division 1 coaches and players would continue to see themselves as Division 1 teams and would play competitively, ignoring any substitution policy.

My commitment in this lifetime was to be all I could be, a commitment which extended to parenting and coaching. And as a coach for Devin and the boys, that commitment meant helping them thrive as individuals and as a team. I couldn't coach in an environment which discouraged excelling – winning. Nor could I coach in an environment which fomented duplicity, lauding the benefits of a substitution rule while turning a blind eye to the fact that all coaches blatantly ignored it.

I would see the coaching year through to its end. But at that point, Devin and I would move on. I would not ask him to deny his ability and competitive spirit. He would have no trouble finding another Division 1 team to play on and would eventually become an essential part of a team that would go on to win the New York State championship.

And while the anger still stirred in me for the petty politics and pettier men that had forced me out of a role I loved, my rage was dissipating. My fists remained unclenched. I was breathing. I had done what I could, and I would suffer the change and relinquish this course of my life to my Beloved. My trust and faith in life had come to include a mysterious and beloved depth that had within it an elemental organizing principle that set my life in motion for a purpose. I could not always comprehend that purpose, but I would honor it.

CHAPTER 31
Saved by a Pig

"Jack, Dad is in really bad shape. He is deteriorating rapidly." My sister Jane's voice was full of fear and urgency.

I had just returned with Walker from a romp in the woods. His exuberance at being outside had been typically unbounded, and I had opened deeply to the magnificent world around me. Trees had creaked and groaned, complaining as they surrendered to the insistent wind. My body, I had noticed, groaned while my metal parts creaked as I too surrendered to the changes in my life. The previous evening's league meeting still roiled within me, yet as I walked in the forest, I intuitively knew that the process I was involved in was bigger than I was. My ego was simply a bit player in a drama that would unfold with or without my help or resistance. Looking around, I was reminded by the bending trees to humbly trust the process regardless of how painful it might be. As I walked deeper into the forest I began to relax, allowing my mind to shift into neutral while my breathing deepened and my existence began to merge with the surrounding reality.

I tried to breathe as Jane filled me in on the details.

"When I got here yesterday," she continued, "his blood pressure was off the chart, and his breathing was labored. He could barely walk to the bathroom. I called his cardiologist right away.

He was great and was able to get Dad scheduled for an emergency electrocardiogram and an angiogram tomorrow at Massachusetts General Hospital. He's deteriorating rapidly. It doesn't look good."

When I finally exhaled, a wave of fear and sadness passed through me pulling behind it a lifetime of memories. I hung up, walked outside and stood facing the forest, my breath rooting me to the earth as I allowed the psychic winds to blow through me. After a moment, I sat down on a stone wall. Breathing deeply, I shifted into neutral, surrendered to the anguish in my heart and looked deeply into the forest for guidance and help. But the noise in my head and heart was too persistent and broke through my meditations

"Alice, I have bad news about Dad." She listened sympathetically over the phone and did her best to reassure me.

"Jack, please take the time to keep your physical therapy appointment. I know your back has been hurting, and there's no sense driving up there in any more pain than you need to. You will be there in plenty of time for your dad. But please take care of yourself too."

I packed, and with a heavy heart and my mind racing, I did stop by the rehab center. My physical therapists were very receptive to my situation and began working right away on the muscle spasms in my lower back and scar tissue throughout my gluteus and leg. When they were done, I had another therapist work on my shoulder and elbow.

"I'm sorry to hear about your father. I hope he will be OK."

"Thanks." I responded, thinking as they worked on me just how much we had accomplished together.

We had all worked through a lot of scar tissue and pushed my range of motion and extension beyond expectation, but there were still some real limitations. In the wake of so much positive recovery, it was sometimes easy to forget the extent of the vertebral damage that still existed in my back and the neurological damage I still suffered throughout my right shoulder and arm. The triathlon was less than a month away and everyone was working hard so that I could participate.

Breathe. Let the pain flow through me. Pangs of fear about my father reverberated through my being, as did the pain of the therapy. I turned into it, as I had learned to do, a process that had accelerated my healing.

When I could, I talked to other patients whose fear of pain or depression had significantly limited their progress. I would always talk with them about what my accident had taught me, and how thankful I was for the awareness and understanding I'd gained. When I could, I helped patients learn to open to let go of control, and to use their breath to create space around fear and pain.

As they worked my elbow and shoulder, and as I wondered how my father would fare, I thought about the very learnings I had tried to impart to my fellow patients. Stop grasping and identifying with every fear, wish or desire that passed through your mind. You are more than the content of your mind. Allow yourself to become the container, not just the content of the mind. In letting go of the contents, love can begin to arise and with it a deeper appreciation of life.

Later as I drove to Boston, I couldn't help but wonder what my father had been thinking when he drove to New York just eight months ago to visit me after my fall. He had driven south; I now drove north, both of us confronting the possibility of each other's death. Did his mind tap out fearful messages? Did he measure the distance in long slow breaths? As I drove, a hot intensity burned deep inside me, occasionally producing a tear as the miles ticked by. Images of him rubbing my feet, holding my hand, or my holding his split open, blood covered head in my lap, flashed through my mind. Was this crisis the unfolding of his life or the ending of it?

My inner life had been secondary to my outer life until the accident. Now the two realms had found each other. I wondered if they would for Dad.

When I arrived at my father's house, I found him resting in his den. He smiled noncommittally as I walked towards him. Jane and Kevin were already there sitting with him. Dad's exuberant, forceful personality that had made him seem larger than life when I was a boy was nowhere to be found. His appearance was disturbing, but not frightening.

"This is some way to get everyone to come home for a visit," I said.

"I'm flattered," he replied.

That was true. I could see it in his brown eyes. As we sat around and talked that night, it became blatantly apparent that Dad's sharp intellect and his zest for life had disappeared. What was left of the old soldier was a thin veneer, almost transparent, which now allowed Jane, Kevin and me to have visual access to his humanness. Something about the vulnerability of my father's humanness began working on me in a vague sort of way. Staying open and waiting, and not getting attached to my judging and fearful mind had become my method of dealing with a crisis. Learning to be in the moment, and to trust that the moment would bring to me what I needed, was very different from imposing something on the moment. My desire for Dad to live, and my fear of his death or judgments about his condition could have eclipsed this experience, but I didn't let them.

As I lay in bed, I began to reflect more on the inner personality of my father that was becoming more apparent. The fear and stress of the past several months had begun to break down the character and physical armor that had sustained and protected his vulnerable core. The sight of his humanness that night softened my heart, as the preciousness of his existence became more apparent to me. As it is with everyone my dad's inner life was multi-dimensional, multi-layered and teeming with various kinds of instincts. Although Dad had never shared the rich complexity of himself with me, I sensed its emergence might be near. The crisis dad was in was going to force him, as mine had me, to unlearn old ways of coping, open him up to outside influences, and create an opportunity for change.

But Dad had to master his internal, fearful state first, before it distorted his external judgment. I couldn't gauge how accurate his perception of his condition was as he had kept his feelings to himself. But you could sense he was struggling with it. He exuded an aura of tension and anxiety that was apparent to everyone in the room. I had hoped he would have been more receptive that evening, because I knew whatever a person does in a crisis frequently sets the stage for what follows. I fell asleep thinking this crisis was either going to kill him or bring forth a different man.

Jane, Kevin and I spent much of the next day sitting on worn upholstered chairs in a small hospital room. Dad had been taken for tests and procedures early in the day. The three of us spent much of the time sharing stories of growing up. It was apparent that each of us shared the same man but each of us also seemed to have a different father. Dad related to each of us differently. Wounded love seemed to be an inescapable aspect of our existence. Yet, the family memories we carried and shared that morning fostered a deep connection among the three of us.

When we finally saw Dad, his face was neither expressive nor passive. His once bright eyes were now opaque. Jane and Kevin talked with him while I ached with compassion as he appeared to have disappeared into himself. It was more than just the sight of him with his disheveled hair and sunken chest. I could sense his terror. Intuitively I felt as if I were in his body, sensing him slipping off the edge of the cliff with nothing to cling to but a prayer.

Over the course of the next hour we met with the head of thoracic surgery and the head of cardiac transplant surgery. There was a maelstrom of details about worn valves and clogged arteries, but the bottom line was direct and left little room for interpretation. Dad needed immediate action in the form of emergency room surgery. If he didn't, he would have a massive stroke or heart attack. About the only choice he really had was whether he wanted a pig valve or a synthetic one to replace the defective valve in his heart

As I watched Dad and listened to Jane and Kevin's conversation with him, I noticed his initial state of shock change. He was increasingly becoming more agitated and his eyes more fearful.

"I'll be fine," Dad kept saying, "I just came here for some tests. I'd like to go home now. I'll schedule the surgery for another time."

Initially I felt he was being irrational, and then I thought of my mother. He was actually trying to convince Jane and Kevin that by some act of willpower he could get up out of the bed and walk out of the hospital. Mom had done the same thing twenty years ago. She had died three months later.

Slowly I reached for dad's hand and held it lightly and warmly as I listened to Jane reiterate the frightful facts.

"Both doctors agree that if you leave here today, you'll be dead before you ever get a chance to return."

Pleading and with a tone of fragility Dad said, "But I only agreed to the tests."

His fears and vulnerability nearly broke my heart. Dad's mind and all our minds were conditioned by fears and beliefs. Whatever the unknown fate was that lay before Dad, I intuitively knew the surgery was the right direction. I sensed Dad's life was summoning him to grow, perhaps one last time, and to open and cooperate with his psyche's desire for him. But the strong forces of resistance from his personality were formidable. His hands were clenched tightly into fists, as if steeling himself against the inevitable would do some good. I watched as his inner emotional life, dominated by feelings of fear and powerlessness, threatened to overwhelm him. The memory of how fear used to squeeze my throat tighter when I resisted it came to mind. I knew that only by confronting the fears that were preying on him and twisting his mind and body could he find peace and perhaps a deeper meaning for his life.

Gently, slowly, I began to talk with him about what he'd seen me go through for the past eight months. He'd watched me learn to say "yes," to unclench my fists and open to the excruciating torment and terror of many moments. He'd seen me find hidden, within the pain and fear, a sacred dimension of life that had nourished my miraculous recovery. As he listened to me, he slowly unclenched his fists. I talked about shifting his mind into neutral, a choice which would make his journey through this crisis easier. Just as mine had been, his ego was in the process of being torn down to its bedrock. Behind the fearful mask that my dad now wore, I sensed a different man waiting to emerge.

As my awareness of my breath deepened, it seemed to strengthen the loving energy that was being directed towards him. As I continued to talk with him, I realized that there was nothing in the world that doesn't vibrate with Spirit. The more I talked the more something poured out through the center of my being. I couldn't see IT, hear IT, taste IT, touch IT or smell IT, but I could experience IT, and IT flooded me, moving loving energy through my body and to my father's.

Over the course of the next hour Dad moved through his resistance into an experience of defeat and resignation, and eventually into an acceptance of the need for surgery. He chose the pig valve. In great relief that the decision had been made, Jane, Kevin and I had some fun with him, making pig jokes before we decided to leave him alone with his demons. Surgery was scheduled for eight the next morning.

We were back in Dad's room early. He looked frightened, tired and pale after spending his first night in a hospital since his birth. He'd never missed a day of work due to illness. The only surgery he'd ever undergone was an emergency appendectomy in a field tent in the Philippines during World War II. We only had a few minutes to speak with him before they wheeled him away. Dad was now in the hands of the surgeons and that mysterious architect who had sustained his life for nearly eighty years. The three of us decided there were prayers to be said and silent messages to be sent to loved ones who had passed on, beseeching their intercession on Dad's behalf. Each of us took some time for ourselves. I knew my mother, Genevieve, would be "watching out" for dad, and I felt even more deeply that Dad's Beloved would be holding and sustaining him as my Beloved had sustained me.

Light emerges from darkness.

I took hold of the blue denim jacket of Devin's that I'd brought with me. As my mind recalled the sound of the gurney being rolled into the operation room with its bright lights and swirling masses of green, my fingers began sewing soccer patches on Devin's jacket, symbols of moments past. As I sewed, I realized that you couldn't experience the will to live unless you confronted death. The confrontation with death brings both consciousness and unconsciousness together – black and white, up and down, inner and outer coming together – making life so alive, so rich in emotion, and seemingly boundless. The awareness of God was still within me, and I sensed that my father would awaken with the same. I prayed that he'd survive the surgery and awaken, open to the broken-open vulnerable state he'd be in, and find, with his Beloved's help, the courage and strength to carry his weakness into life and redeem it from his shadowy depths.

After what seemed like a lifetime of waiting, a nurse slowly walked into the waiting room and softly announced that dad had been returned to the cardiac care unit a couple of hours ago. The three of us stood and silently followed her down a long hallway. As we walked along, the nurse explained that dad had still not regained consciousness and therefore remained on a ventilator. We found our bleached white father lying on a narrow bed surrounded by machines that either sustained him or monitored his vital signs. Walking up to him, I took a deep breath and reached out and gently took his feet in my hands.

I gradually relaxed and adjusted to the sight of Dad's body. I realized he had left his body while his chest had been split open and his heart scrutinized and modified by strangers with scalpels behind green masks. Probably, he had not yet returned. A thought then crossed my mind. I'd spent a lifetime trying to touch that vulnerable place in Dad's body but my attempts always failed because I could never get past his vigilant, heroic gatekeeper, at least not until mom died, and then I found only his lonely emptiness.

Standing there and looking at him, I felt as if I held my childhood in my hands. This disciplined, heroic adventurer who had never been tolerant of human frailties, now lay before me in a state of suspended animation. His feet seemed to ground me. I felt the nearby realm of heaven and sensed dad's ambivalence about crossing back over the bridge into this earthly, time-bound existence. Could he, would he, reach back into time and make Earth his home? Dad's essence was still being held within the Beloved's light.

The three of us took turns waiting for Dad to transition back into his body. While Kevin sat with him, Jane went to the nurses' station, and I took a walk. As I walked, I felt a profound reverence for the fragility of life. How much choice, power, or control did I *really* have? My psyche, which provided the energy for my existence, had become much more central to my grasp of a meaningful life. Dad's breath, like mine, was simply on loan. What God asks for in return for this gift of life is personal responsibility and a conscious relationship with the mystery. As I walked, I silently prayed that he would be able to hear me as I whispered into his ear, "Breathe, bear the unbearable, let your breath lead you back to us."

When I returned to Dad's room, Jane and Kevin sat expectantly. Our lily-white father had begun to stir, and his vital signs had begun to strengthen. We three sat there silently waiting. Slowly, like a new leaf unfurling in spring, Dad's eyes began to open. His consciousness was not yet earth-bound and still reflected heaven's power. Slowly I watched as his consciousness re-ignited his body. We stood at either side of him, looking down, smiling a silent, "Welcome back Dad."

Over the course of the next couple of hours, we talked with him softly, watching as more of him crossed back over the bridge. His face was open and appeared radiant. No ego obstructions seemed to veil his Beloved's energy. Dad's companion, heretofore hidden in its secret place, was now apparent. The vastness of the moment held me captive. Slowly I sat down, feeling almost as if I were in church, as I watched and listened to the childlike sense of wonder being expressed by Dad. There was no ego focus, but there was a sense of a palpable inner connection and dimension sustaining him. I could see he had not only been sustained by his Beloved psyche, but had awakened to it as well.

For the first few hours dad seemed unconscious to his body except when they took him off the ventilator. Yet, gradually I knew he would develop an inner awareness of painful sensations and symptoms. Looking at him, I wondered if he hadn't come back to redeem those repressed parts of himself and thus activate greater healing energy throughout his body and personality. I also knew that the sacred energy I was witnessing would not, by itself, heal his wounds. The transpersonal energy would support, perhaps accelerate his healing, but only if Dad consciously chose to remain open could he gain access to the healing archetypal energy system. He was so much bigger, wider than his ego bound pre-surgery personality; but it wouldn't last without a conscious surrendering to the essence within.

In a silent moment I asked a question. "Dad, it seemed to take you several hours to cross back over to this side where we were waiting. It was almost as if you were ambivalent about coming back into life. Why did you come back?"

He looked at me, his brown eyes still reflecting a childlike state of wonder and said, "For the children."

A shiver of knowingness moved through me. I knew his return was not only for his literal children and eight grandchildren but rather for all the children within him whose lives were abruptly altered by his father's early death. His answer brought a teary smile to my face as I tenderly rubbed his feet. Love had also brought me back to life and with it, suffering. Would he too discover that within the suffering was a tincture of love?

Dad stayed in the cardiac care unit for the next few days. Early Sunday morning I returned home to catch up with my family and coach the soccer game. Monday, after spending a meaningful day at my office with clients, I made the trip back to Boston. Jane, Kevin and I arrived at the cardiac care unit early Tuesday morning to escort Dad in the ambulance to the rehabilitative center. He would be staying at the center until he became ambulatory and again capable of being self-sufficient.

Dad's encounter with his essence continued to reflect, like the moon, its transpersonal light. The more time I spent with him, the more I felt as if we were walking backward through our lives together. Not only was I remembering and re-experiencing my accident, but for the first time I had access to my father's heart and feminine interior. Dad had become like a child again and in that state his essence was unfolding. The divine and human worlds were interfacing before my very eyes.

Over the course of the next few days the state of grace that Dad had been in began to ebb. Yet as the transpersonal energy began to recede, he picked up the slack and began carrying his pain and weakness into life, bearing the unbearable. A quality of humility was still evident in Dad, and I recognized this as the signature of the Beloved.

We talked frequently about the process of consciously choosing to remain open to his experience regardless of how humiliating or painful it seemed to be in the moment. That process was a heroic adventure of a different kind than any he'd taken in his lifetime. I had come to understand that my guilt, shame, weakness, failure and feelings of inadequacy, the garbage of my ego, could be reclaimed and converted into fertilizer – a powerful healing fertilizer that not only facilitated my healing but others' as well.

After spending two days with Dad, I headed back to New York for a couple of days. When I returned to Boston for the weekend, I saw that he had begun to restore balance to his life in ways that were familiar to him. I'd gently prod him, urging him to humbly remain open to his weakness even while he was getting stronger. I trusted in a vision of light and empowered him to do the same by actively re-engaging life from the inside out, calling forth that whole man.

Those days with my father were precious to me. I was able to nurture him, and he received that nurturing in ways that affirmed my love and life. We had started this dance step nearly nine months earlier when I had fallen, and it had become complete. Our masculine polarities now had a feminine feeling interior. The emergence of this interior feeling dimension was one of the most important events of our lives.

Dad remained at the rehab facility for three weeks. Jane, Kevin and I had our lives to live and although we'd call and continue to visit, the intensity of Dad's crisis was over and life had to resume in somewhat of an orderly fashion. Daily I said a prayer of thankfulness for Dad's return and the loving experiences that now connected the two of us. There was now a psychic weave between us and within us that would always stay connected to a larger dimension of life.

I brought the experience of my father's trauma and transformation into my family, my psychotherapy practice, my rehabilitation efforts, and art class. A week after returning from Dad's, I resumed my art classes. During the class, I was seized by a powerful force from within. I was looking at the body of a female model, but I saw another. A corridor seemed to open leading into my feminine interior. A quaking, shaking energy moved through me as time stopped. While my eyes glazed with emotion, I drew what was emerging from within through my hand, eye and breath. The curved tip of the chalk drew "HER" as I went back in time entering and coming through what would never change and yet was ever changing. The grains of charcoal seemed measured against the white paper in a balance I thought was incapable of reproducing.

Forty minutes later, as I stepped back from the easel, I saw "HER" with hips and breasts that were round with substance capable of conducting a dynamic energy in whose cyclic rhythm I could lose myself. I entitled the drawing The Goddess Within. I had the print framed and gave it to my father a couple of months later as a birthday gift to honor the Goddess who had sustained us both.

CHAPTER 32
The Last Triathlon

Swim 1K. Ride 20K. Run a 5K. June had arrived, and with it the eve of my Triathlon. I had been going over my bike, checking the seat height, handlebars, toe clips, tires, brakes and chain. It was ready.

Was I? I wondered.

My experience in the ravine had launched a state of inward revolution that left me less attached to outward accomplishments. But I needed to exorcise the trauma's ghosts of powerlessness, helplessness, shame, and guilt that continued to haunt me

Although my numerous doctors and physical therapists had given me the green light, Alice wasn't convinced and remained a continuous blinking yellow. Yes, I had spent hours in the pool, but that's not quite the same as swimming in a pack of exuberant and competitive triathletes. And while I hadn't been on a bike since the accident, I had logged plenty of hours on spin cycles. Also different than grinding it out on the open road, and I wondered how my pelvis might take to the potholes so typical of New York's back roads. As for the run, I would have to settle for as brisk of a walk as I could muster.

As I sat down on the grass beside the bike the tragedy, agonies, and solitude of the past nine months surged through me. On the eve of my triathlon I was feeling tremendously vulnerable. The event had given me something to reach for and five months of struggling to participate in the next day's event had become an incredible opportunity for recovery. It had allowed me to direct and use my pain in a meaningful way. This confronting of physical limitations toward a goal had cohesively united my life and giving it traction, direction and meaning.

But, as I sat there looking at my bike and off into the forest, I realized for the first time that the bold, passionate but naïve goal of the triathlon had not only focused me but equally protected me from the razor sharp mirrors I'd begun to encounter in moving back into life. How could I have been so blind? Wrapped up in my recovery, I had become obsessed with regaining mastery over my body and reestablishing that narrow sense of self confidence. It occurred to me at that moment that perhaps I was doing this in the "old" counter-dependent fashion. As necessary as this was in the present, I realized that Alice, the boys, my friends and clients, had at times all probably needed more from me than I was able to perceive. They had seen and understood what I couldn't, that I was limited in what I could give or attend to in them at that time. They had all graciously taken what I had to give, but protectively had restrained their need for more from me out of fear of compounding my feelings of inadequacy, guilt or failure.

I went to bed that night restless. Eventually I fell asleep but awoke at 4:30AM out of a dream. Looking at the clock, I got out of bed and made a pot of coffee. My night was over and it was time to prepare for the day. As the coffee brewed I sat down, pulled out a notebook and wrote down the dream.

> *I was in a doctor's office. Two doctors examined my entire body and then asked me to perform a number of movements and do certain exercises. The movements seemed natural and I easily completed them. As I did so, I begin to feel confident.*
>
> *The two doctors talked with each other and then turned to me and give me their permission to enter the triathlon. Feeling grateful and encouraged by the news, I turned to leave the office.*

Just as I reached the door one of the doctors asked me to get down on all fours and crawl. I looked at him for a moment to see if he was serious. He was, and I got down on all fours on the floor.

I began to crawl but I couldn't move my left leg. My two arms reached forward, and my right knee came forward, but not my left. Sweating and anxious, I began to pull myself around in front of the doctors, dragging my leg. A sense of panic, even despair set in, and as it did, I began clawing and pulling myself along hoping to wake up my leg, but it remained paralyzed.

I woke up feeling anxious and vulnerable. Lost in thought, forgetting time, I continued writing. As I did, I struggled with all the paradoxes of that dream. I had been confident and then vulnerable. I had been given the "all clear" from my doctors, yet was unable to crawl. I battered myself with questions about my working arms symbolizing confidence and the paralyzed leg my vulnerability. I wondered if that vulnerability would betray me if and when the physical suffering of the race became too intense. I might fall down, or worse, I could shut down. I prayed that my will and suffering, like Jack and Jackie (or the hero and the vulnerable man) within me, would find balance and bring forth their unique strengths at the same time. I feared for the first time that perhaps a synthesis of the two was not possible

As dawn ushered in a new day, my anxiety subsided. As I put down my pen, a quiet sense of conviction and confidence began to develop. I drank the rest of my coffee and attempted to eat breakfast, slowly and mindfully. Packing up, I left my sleeping family and drove to the triathlon site. Though they had told me they would love to attend, I didn't want to put them through all the possible trials and tribulations of that day. As I drove, I realized that beneath my belief that I had to run this race alone was a deep need for Alice, the boys, and my friends. But, I was frightened that I couldn't control the outcome of the event or their responses to it. I felt as if they could kill me by what they might or might not say. I was simply too dependent to allow them to see me struggle to regain myself. Again I was reminded just how thin skinned victims of trauma can be.

Arriving at the site, I parked and walked to the transition area. It was early and I was able to select a very accessible place to rack my bike. As I was racking it, I noticed a shroud of mist over Green Mountain Lake. The sun had not yet risen above the surrounding hills. I placed my wetsuit, towel, helmet, sneakers and bike shorts with extra padding on the ground. Noticing that the mysterious quality of the forest was not yet dissolved by light, I thought of my Beloved; always there, lying in darkness, awaiting the light of awareness from my broken open cry. There was a certain quality about this lake and the surrounding rolling hills which reminded me of my impermanence and the fact that it would all be here long after I was gone.

After checking my tire pressure, I walked over to the registration tent. Smiling volunteers were busy registering participants and inscribing numbers on their arms and legs. A friendly woman with sparkling eyes looked up at me from the table and welcomed me.

"Good morning" I said, "It looks like it's going to be a great day for the race. I'm Jack Weafer."

"Did you pre-register Jack?"

I told her I had, and she began flipping through her pages of participants. I was suddenly struck by the fact that I had not asked to be placed in the last wave when I had registered. My anxiety seemed to instantly pull up an experience from one of my first triathlons when I felt brutalized by the flurry of flying fists and feet as my wave hit the water and participants fought for position. I couldn't believe I hadn't considered protecting myself by making the request when I registered.

Cheerfully, the woman said: "Jack, your number is 326."

Sheepishly I looked at her and said: "Is it possible for me to be transferred to the last wave?"

The look I saw on her face made me realize she had never been asked this question before.

"I don't know," she said.

"I'm recovering from an accident, and to say the least, I think avoiding get kicked and swum over by the following waves would be a good idea."

Several volunteers who had overheard the request were now looking at me. Thinking to myself that show and tell normally works best to get a point across, I gestured toward the scars on my body. Self-consciously, I gave them a thirty-second summary of the accident. Ultimately the coordinator graciously placed me in the last wave where I could move along at my own pace.

Taking a few slow, deep breaths, I walked over to a grassy knoll and sat down. Although I was glad to be in the last wave, the process was unsettling. A level of anxiety flowing from vulnerability and doubt coursed through me. This state had become common in the past six months, but it rarely determined my direction. Sitting there, looking out on the lake, I began to discern "something" moving inside of me. It was a kaleidoscopic array of images passing across the landscape of my mind: being fed and bathed, pushed in the wheelchair, hospitals, treatment tables, adjunctive consults, feelings of dependency, powerlessness, helplessness and pain. A wave of emotion broke over me, and as it did the memory of the morning's dream returned. As the emotion subsided I again thought of my family and friends who wanted to be here to support me, but I needed to do this race alone and not be under their lovingly anxious protective eyes. I alone wanted to yield and bend today and still move forward.

I knew transitioning back into life would be gradual, even though I had created a rather dramatic experience for this stage of my recovery. I knew I was a long way from establishing a sense of safety and predictability in my life, but I had to know I could count on myself. Once I knew that, it would be much easier for me to again depend on my family and friends.

After doing about ten minutes of stretching, I got up and walked back to the transition area. The holding pen was now filled with hundreds of bikes. Un-racking mine, I shifted it into the best gear for departure from the transition area. Taking off my shorts, I put them on the towel and sprayed my arms and legs with vegetable oil. Now I could easily slip my wetsuit on and off over my bathing suit. The wetsuit was such an incredible asset for me. Wearing it compensated for my limited stroke and leg mechanics by lifting me up and allowing me to ride higher, thus making it easier to glide through the water.

Grabbing a banana and a bottle of water, I took one last glance around to note my location and headed back down to the lake. Several other participants, all in wetsuits and wearing numbered bathing caps, walked out between the rows of bikes and joined me. Looking at their strong athletic bodies initially invoked the thought that I'd bitten off more than I could chew. Excitedly chattering, they all seemed to be in high spirits and their excitement helped rekindle my own. We all seemed to look out over the lake at the same time and notice the red buoy marker catching the first light.

Two rowboats, each with two people in them, were positioning themselves on either side of the course. In the water alongside the boats were scuba divers. Although I'd never seen an accident occur in the water, their presence today was reassuring. For the first time I noticed the distance to the buoy from the shore and was both relieved and reminded that this was a "sprint triathlon" which consisted of a 1K swim, 20K bike and a 5K run. Though roughly half the distance of other triathlons I'd done, this one would be the most challenging.

Two paths met here today. Time was a circle, and where I stood today, I had stood a year ago. The path I'd taken to get here today was certainly more arduous than last year's but also more meaningful because I had lost what I once took for granted. The nerve damage throughout my right shoulder and arm, along with the hardware in the elbow made getting my stroke mechanics in sync almost impossible. Although my flutter kick had gotten a lot stronger, my legs were out of sync due to all the hardware in my pelvis, scar tissue and fractured vertebras. Putting it all together, while trying to stabilize myself in the water and get enough propulsive force, took an enormous amount of concentration and discipline.

As the announcer called the first wave to the water, a jolt of anxiety shot through my spine. I calmed myself by remembering that there were three separate starts and finishes, and in the transition areas I could attend to problems, clear my head, and prepare for the next event.

The first wave was now standing around in knee deep water anxiously awaiting the whistle. When it finally blew, the triathletes churned up the lake in relative ease. The next wave moved into the water excitedly, and three or four minutes later they too were off. Wave after wave of men and women moved across the lake steadfastly directed toward the red buoy. Enviously I watched how easily the first wave rounded the buoy and headed for the beach. They burst out of the water and raced toward the transition area, and with that movement, Jack triumphed as my ego captured the scent of competition.

My heart beat faster. I found myself starting to pace. Suddenly I heard a voice in my head say: "Be patient old friend. Not only are you still alive, but you walked here today. It wasn't long ago that you thought walking was a miracle." Appropriately chastened, I got my ego back under control and walked down to the water. The cold sand greeted me followed by the frosty water temperature of approximately 60 degrees. As the final wave gathered in the water, I splashed my face and tried to settle down my breathing. I got off to the side and looked up at the announcer.

My heart was pounding. The whistle blew.

In the fraction of a second when my body hit the water I knew I wouldn't go on autopilot today. The cold momentarily took my breath away and snapped me back to reality. As my head broke the surface, I simultaneously reached and kicked while attempting to regulate my breathing. I had imagined this moment for months, but suddenly it was real. Concentrating on my form and breathing, I tried not to tighten up, which would work against me. Other swimmers were a little off to my left, but I was staying even with them. The initial sense of clawing at the water's surface had subsided as I found an odd but steady rhythm.

After the first fifty yards my focus shifted from internal, analytical to external and experiential. No longer entangled in thoughts and feelings, my vulnerability decreased as I kept pace with the other swimmers. I felt close to myself, close to my body. My blood was flowing, heart beating, lactic acid building up, and I was happy simply holding my own. The buoy was in sight. I lined up with it and made some adjustments to my stroke.

About ten yards from the buoy, my lower back went into an intense spasm. When I suffered spasms, my entire pelvis corkscrewed because the right side of the lumbar vertebras were broken off. Focusing on my stroke, I adjusted my kick and tried to stretch out my right leg. As I rounded the buoy, pain began to shoot through my pelvis as the biomechanical and motor problems began to multiply. A voice came on in my head, but I silenced it, thinking too much analysis leads to paralysis. My upper body was doing its job but was beginning to feel the strain of having to compensate for the loss of my legs. Looking around, I noticed that I'd slipped to the back of the pack. My breathing had become more constricted as my lower back and now glutes became one massive, unyielding spasm. Switching over to the breast stroke, I focused on the swimmer in front of me. The distance between us lengthened. Knowing if I stopped it would be all over, I concentrated on my movement through the water.

Just as I felt I had regained some measure of control I was overcome by neurological pain stemming from my crushed brachial plexus. The burning lava moved across my right shoulder down the arm and extended through my thumb and right forefinger. Harnessing my will, I continued to awkwardly kick and stroke as my body began to knot up like a rubber band. I focused my concentration on the stroke and kick and tried to find some kind of rhythm.

Deep inside, the pain and my breath were one as some ancient will moved my body through the water. Choosing the pain, I leaned into it and became grateful for the epinephrine now flowing through my body.

"Keep moving. It's a lot easier than overcoming inertia and getting back in motion," my inner voice repeated.

Suddenly something had hold of my arm. Startled out of my reverie I snapped my head to the right to see a scuba diver. Peering out from behind the Plexiglas diver's mask was a set of brown eyes. To the right of him was the boat with volunteers who were keeping pace with us. Quickly I swung my head to the left and sure enough, there was the other diver and boat. How long had they been there? Both divers' eyes were fixed on me in a look that projected concern and reassurance. Something about the eyes was familiar. What was it? With regulators in their mouths they weren't talking. But with a gloved hand, one of the divers gestured towards the boat. Adjusting my stroke but continuing to swim I turned towards the people in the boat.

"Are you all right? Do you need any help?" My mind struggled to find the answer. The sincerity of the concern reverberated through me and fanned the embers of memories. My vision blurred, tears began to flow as the memory of other compassionate eyes and the tenderness behind them had come to my aide in the past. The policeman who found me in the ravine and the helicopter nurse, my angel of mercy, looked and cared as the divers and volunteers did today. There was no judgment in those eyes, no tone of criticism in the voice. Breathing deeply, I offered the same compassion to those parts of myself most in need of nourishment. As I did, a golden elixir flowed through me.

"I'm OK," I said with the next breath of air. "I'm in some pain, but it's from an old accident. Not entirely unexpected," I added.

The divers swam alongside of me, their two sets of eyes glued to my face.

"If you would like to stop we can help you aboard and bring you to shore."

"Oh God." Tears mingled with the lake as today's voice mingled with yesterday's and something erupted from deep inside of me. Their caring support began to derail my desperate attempt to regain self-respect. They didn't know how much I'd lost of parts of myself. They didn't understand how important it was to make it on my own. As I struggled for a breath, my tears dissolved into the lake, and I entrusted myself over to these people and the lake. No longer alone, I allowed the love to reach me today as it had in the ravine, sustaining me, energizing me. That day I was in God's hands. Today I was in my body.

I heard someone in the boat on a walkie-talkie. He was in touch with one of the race coordinators and was getting the full download of my condition.

"Just nine months ago?" I heard him ask. Their conversation continued for a few moments as I struggled to keep swimming. I was going to make the shore on my own.

The humiliation I'd attempted to avoid and the vulnerability I'd sought to protect dissolved into the lake. Time passed, and then all at once, my foot hit the bottom. I stood up and struggled to get my bearings. I heard the cheering before I saw the crowd. Twenty, thirty people, maybe more, stood down by the water along the shore. At first they stood silhouetted by the rising sun. But as I took a few steps forward I could see their smiles, although my vision was blurred by the tears which ran down my face. I turned to my right and left and nodded to the divers and people in the boats. I know their conversation with the race coordinator had led to this incredible wave of support. I felt as if I was in the center of a parade.

Hands trembling, heart thumping, I hobbled out of the water and up through the cheering crowd which parted, giving me access to the transition area. The irony was that I was last, but felt first. In that moment I felt something inside of me heal.

The experience was profound and re-engaged my determination to attempt to complete the race. Stripping off my wetsuit I reached for my towel. Although my body was still locked up and in pain, there was now also a wonderful, pulsating energy that sustained and nourished me. Pulling on my bike shorts I looked around and grabbed my sneakers. Leaning on the bike rack I dried my feet and put my on sneakers. I put on my helmet and un-racked my bike. After walking a few steps, I carefully climbed onto the saddle. As I began to pedal out of the transition area, I passed several volunteers who must have been down by the lake. They all stopped, turned and cheered while someone shouted, "Go for it!"

As volunteers directed me out onto the road, I struggled to establish a sense of balance with some pedal cadence. I could see clearly the first mile was relatively flat and used the time to stretch out and adjust to the saddle. My pedaling mechanics were not at all smooth or circular because I couldn't apply even pressure through the strike cycle. The next few miles had some gradual inclines with a beautiful view of rolling hills as far as the eyes could see. My back and glutes were still locked up, but I was most irritated by the six screws that came out from the base of my pelvis. They had both-ered me for months on a stationary bike, so I used a gel seat cover and bike pants with padding. That worked on the stationary bike, but outdoors, with my pelvis twisted so, there was no "comfortable" place to sit.

I passed a red barn and farm house on my right before I came to another hill and shifted into a lower gear. Staying in the saddle, I tried to find the power and strength in my hip extensors. Climb-ing out of the saddle was just too painful as I'd be driving the femur head up into metal plates and screws. As I crested the hill, I saw before me a number of turns. Now sitting upright, I'd lost some aerodynamic advantage but relieved some pressure in my back and regained some steering leverage. More leverage meant more power in the pedal stroke. I kept pulling my knees in when they'd drift out and I'd start to wobble from side to side. Coming around a bend I saw some riders in front of me. They had no idea I was behind them. Although I'd never gone down in a race, I'd seen other riders collide and in my condition the thought terrified me. The riders were braking rather than riding through the turns. What concerned me most was that they were changing lanes back and forth. We had just gotten through the turns and were coming up to a straightaway when the rider in front of me reached down for her water bottle and lost her line. Abruptly I swung way out to avoid her, over the double line and with an adrenaline burst sprinted past her and the other riders.

Once I passed the halfway point, I was even more determined to do the next six miles or so. As I came to a gradual hill I saw more riders in front of me. Simply seeing them encouraged me. I knew if I could keep them in my sight, I'd finish the course. As I worked my way up the hill the pain became intense again. Once the incline was over and we began our descent, I got a sudden hamstring cramp in my good leg. The cramp was due to compensating for my weaker leg throughout the previous incline. When I was back on a level surface, I tried to stand up and stretch out. In addition to the spasm and nerve pain my legs were filling up with lactic acid. The other racers had pulled a little ahead of me but the sight of them was magnetic. Going deep inside myself, yet aware of my surroundings, I drew on images from the swim to support myself. The images seemed to blur the pain and soften the fatigue.

Approaching what I thought was the last hill, I shifted gears early out of fear of possibly stalling out and having to shift later. Half-way up the hill with my heart racing, panting, muscles burning, I shifted down again to a lower gear. Both the mind and body needed to give and become receptive, absorbing whatever passed through. The images of the cheering crowd as I crawled out of the water once again strengthened my will. Reaching the top of the hill, I refocused as I began my descent. Feathering the brakes I was making sure of their grip. All at once I noticed a rider in front of me, and as we reached the level part of the road, I pulled alongside. With every fraction of muscular effort I had left, I stayed with him, and we crossed the finish line together.

By the time I racked my bike and began to pace myself on the run course, a number of participants were crossing the finish line. Judging by the cheers and the smiles on the participants' faces, you might have thought they had just completed the ironman competition. Smiling, I headed out on my race-walk trying to clear out a sense of rigor mortis which seemed to have taken possession of my legs. Mark, who was a race-walker, had spent time with me this past spring demonstrating the mechanics of the sport. Although I was not graceful, I was fortunate to be able to walk at all. The first mile took me down and through town. Although I was clearly one of the last participants, there were still people cheering us on and providing water. I was glad I had done so much cardiovascular training because at this point of the race my conditioning was pulling along all the other parts of me.

As I passed out of town and walked along the beautiful road, I realized how the accident had changed my life. The adversity in my life brought about by the accident had unmasked me, redefined me, and engaged latent and hidden resources within me. Today, in the lake, I felt unmasked again. My vulnerability was vivid, yet instead of burying it, I used it to move forward.

The volunteers' concern and acknowledgement supported me while allowing me to suffer and to liberate myself from the past. I was learning, painfully and deeply, that appearing normal physically was not a quality life. I could not ignore that something vital was still missing from myself – something without which happiness is not happiness at all. That something was the raw vulnerability I felt in the presence of others but could not show. Beneath the agitation, immersed in fear and lost in the shadow of the trauma, was the organic connection that Jackie had with loved ones. But he was still mostly cocooned. The willingness to bring Jackie out into the world, to be whole in the world not just by myself, was what Alice and the boys were really asking from me. It was frightening to entertain the reciprocal necessities that being in the world entailed. I could run the triathlon but I'd have to be willing to crawl.

Turning a bend in the road I saw two volunteers standing at the base of a hill. When I approached, one woman gave me a cup of water while the other said, "At the top of this hill is the finish line. You can do it."

Smiling, I said "Thanks for the encouragement!"

Leaning into the hill, up I went. Struggling and staggering I crested the hill. The finish line was no more than fifty yards in front of me. Unbidden tears ran down my face as the impotent fury of the last nine months was finally vented. The oppressive weight of my own self-doubt was finally being relieved by each leaden step.

People around me cheered and clapped as I flung my entire being across the finish line.

CHAPTER 33
Unfinished

There is something magical about the finish of a triathlon.

It's a wonderfully festive and well-orchestrated milestone, designed to celebrate the winner in every participant. There's an arch, an official clock, music, an announcer welcoming you across the line, volunteers with water and commemorative T-shirts for every athlete, the camaraderie of fellow participants, and for the last one hundred yards or so, the chute to the finish is lined with people cheering, and shouting encouragement and congratulations. The Finish is like a siren that draws you toward it as you close that last 100 yards. It imbues you with that last spike of energy to drive you forward, through the pain and exhaustion and to the finish.

In all my triathlons, I had never posted a slower time.

The pain in my shoulders and back was searing, and I still felt twisted from the swim.

Every partially rehabilitated bone, muscle and nerve in my body had clamored in protest throughout the run, raging especially for the last half mile of the event.

But I finished, and I had never felt a greater sense of victory.

I couldn't raise both arms completely above my head. But when I crossed that finish line, I raised my left arm high and my right one as best I could, tears streaking down my face. I thanked volunteers, graciously accepted the congratulations of strangers, and humbly and ever so gratefully breathed in and truly immersed myself in the moment.

And while I did raise my arms, it was not a chest pounding, "look at me," moment. I knew how vulnerable I had been and felt throughout the race. During the swim in particular, I had opened my heart to the love and care of the volunteers on and in the water around me, and for the entire race I had been carried in equal parts not only by the warrior, but the rediscovered child within me. I had needed them both.

So with humility, thanks, aches, pains, and gratitude, I made my way back to the transition area to collect my gear. I took a final look around and soaked up all the images and emotions still swirling powerfully within me. I had found the boldness to fully commit and totally surrender to a goal that had seemed so far beyond my reach just a few short months before. My Beloved had guided me and pressed toward me the passion and previously hidden resources I needed to realize this dream and make peace with the reassembled body I lived in. The finish of the triathlon had revealed that I could once again walk in the world with the vulnerabilities and limitations that had made me so self-conscious.

I had many physical challenges yet to overcome. But though I was not nearly as complete an athlete as I had once been, I was in many ways more complete. Perhaps what had been trying to be born in me through the accident was learning how to "crawl" and then walk in the world with the fullness of who I was.

The finish of that triathlon would make for a lovely bow tied neatly around my road to recovery. But while I didn't know how I would fare going into the race, I always knew it wasn't the end point for my learning, my healing, or my story. It was not the end of my physical therapy or psychotherapy sessions. It marked a transition point in some respects, but not a close.

As I walked my bike back to the car, I reflected on the thought that no single event could truly mark the completion of a traumatic recovery. And as I did, a chill shot through me. And there, just beneath the surface, I could sense the shadow of the ravine.

"What is it," I said out loud, "That persists and endures beyond an array of treatments and my best efforts to get over it? What is it that still haunts me with flashbacks and a host of symptoms? What happens if I can't fix it?"

I waited for an answer, but didn't have one. I knew that shadow would lurk within me revealing itself to me through dreams, circumstances, actions and reactions. I would simply have to let it in and continue to let that force work its way through my life.

I racked the bike and sat in the car, and suddenly felt exhausted. Between the pre-race anxiety, the lack of sleep, and the event itself, I was spent emotionally and physically. Sitting there, I wondered if the highs of the day's race had somehow engaged my journey's depths. Mixed in with my euphoria of finishing was a sense of vulnerability and gratitude.

I found myself praying.

"God, spare my family and me from any further suffering. Please allow us a time to heal and rebuild our lives. And if there is something more I need to learn from this experience, please be merciful."

I was an odd mix of pensive, elated, exhausted, and reflective as I drove home. And in the throes of that emotional mix, I turned onto our bumpy driveway. It triggered the memory of my ambulance ride not even nine months earlier.

"Wow!," I said to myself, "I am so incredibly blessed." I had been given my life back. For that moment, I knew in every corner of my being, that the gift of my life had within it an elixir that would sustain me throughout whatever was asked of me.

I wore my T-shirt from the Saturday event when I walked into my first physical therapy session the Monday after the triathlon. It would be a two-part day for me, with physical therapy followed by a session with Colin. David saw me, my T-shirt, put down his pen, and leaned back in his chair.

"Unbelievable," he said, "absolutely unbelievable. You did it." He was beaming.

I owed David, Maggie, and the others a huge debt of gratitude. And as I related the highlights of the race day, I let them know what their tremendous work meant to me.

"I would have thrown in the towel half way into the swim," Maggie told me, as I recounted what I had experienced in the lake.

"Believe me," I said, "I thought about it. But thanks to your amazing work, my body was there when I called on it. I can't begin to tell you how grateful I am for your amazing care. I would never have made it through the months of pain and self-doubt had it not been for you."

"You've come so unbelievably far in such a short time." David said. "Sometimes I can't believe what I write down in your chart."

As David spoke, Maggie was treating some of my severe muscle spasms with an electronic stimulation machine. The pain was intense, and I worked hard to relax, breath, say "yes," and not resist. David commented as he frequently did on how I didn't allow myself to succumb to the pain.

"Jack, you've somehow learned to swallow pain like a fish gulps water. I've watched you for six months not get pulled in and trapped in the pain throughout your body. Even watching you now, with the machine set on nearly its highest setting, the pain of these intense spasms never seems to really take hold of you and suffocate you like it does for so many patients here."

There was no easy response to his comment. I had never thought of myself as a fish gulping pain, but it was incredibly difficult to clearly articulate to others what I had discovered on the hellish journey following my fall.

People's eyes tended to roll when I described floating above my broken body and experiencing the unbounded love of the Beloved that had sustained me, especially during those first six weeks. And learning to say "yes" to pain and surrendering the ego's control is not a message that easily registers or resonates in western civilization. I wanted to help people escape the fear and isolation of pain and help them understand how turning toward it, not away, was the path to healing. But finding the words and process to let people know would take me time. It was a hard enough journey to live and understand, no less articulate to others. My trauma still lived within me, and even with the triathlon behind me, I still struggled with the pain. I had to work hard, stop resisting, and remind myself how love and compassion will always transcend suffering, and that those energies flow from God's mind towards all of us when we choose to suffer consciously.

"Will you do more triathlons?" Maggie asked.

I thought for a moment before answering.

"I don't think so," I replied. "I accomplished something with this one that I really needed. You know, for so long during my rehab it had seemed that whatever was around me was 'of life' and that I was not. That caused me unbearable pain. Now I know, at least in one small arena, that I can also be "of life" – granted, in less a heroic form than I'd been accustomed to in the past!"

I thought about my answer. The triathlon had been a great motivator for me, but I had also realized that I could no longer gallop through life at the pace to which I had been accustomed. The healing process of human reintegration after a trauma was much slower and more deliberate than I sometimes wanted it to be. And as true as that was physically, I knew it was even truer psycho-emotionally.

I left the rehab center that day and headed to my first session with Colin since he had helped our family back in December. I was ready, or so I thought, to begin to disentangle more of what the accident revealed which still lay embedded within me. I would have to find a balance between Jack with Jackie. I also wanted to accommodate my reemergence into life without losing my awareness of the state of being I had experienced in the Beloved's presence. And I really needed to continue reassembling my life and bring light to those traumatic shadows that still lived within me. I knew I would need as much help psychologically as I had physically,

As I drove, I was inadvertently reminded just how far I had to go as I approached the exit ramp to his office. With sirens blaring, two police cars raced by me on the shoulder. When I stopped at the top of the exit, I realized how hard my heart was pounding and how tight my breathing had become. My hands were clenched tightly on the wheel. As I waited for the light to change, I heard the thundering of a medevac helicopter as it flew over me. My adrenal gland went into overdrive.

I arrived for that first session tremendously agitated, the memories of my own trauma freshly surfaced by the sirens and helicopter. It was in that heightened state of anxiety that our sessions renewed, and I realized again just how much of the trauma still lay entrenched within me. As we began our first conversation, and I found my breath, I remember hoping that Colin would be able to do for me psychologically what David and crew had done for me physically. Coax the shattered and displaced facets of my psyche back into life and into a more consistent and regulated communication with each other. Help me to unzip myself from a traumatic womb and psychically reconnect the dismembered experiences that were held in my unconscious or repressed in my body. With Colin's guidance, I would continue to try and balance the vulnerable child with the warrior, mind and body, the tigers with the elephants within my dreams, Jack with Jackie.

"Moving back into life hasn't been easy, Colin. A cycle of fear and vulnerability still haunts me. I sense the tigers in the shadows. And as I cycle through these feelings, I can sense the warrior within me replace Jackie. It's an instinctual defense, I know, but I don't want to re-armor myself and run from my inner world. It's been a real struggle!"

Colin warned me that uncovering the traumatic experiences of my fall would be painful and difficult.

"I know. But in the long run, it's the only way I can see to unite these opposing forces within me, to bring Jack and Jackie together into the world."

We spoke of fears and vulnerability, states of unregulated hyper arousal, of moments of strength, love, acceptance and compassion. With tears in my eyes, I revisited for Colin my two greatest fears that had been so overwhelming for me. The first was being held captive not only to the terror in my body, but to the fear of being abused or neglected by professionals. It was terrifying to "not be seen." I had felt so unsafe. Once my trust was violated by the nurse who had withheld my morphine, I knew that to survive, I would have to have my wits about me. It had all felt so unpredictable, which had compounded my sense of helplessness. Every part of my experience had felt transparent. There had been no way to conceal my humiliation, even if I had tried. Truthfully, my fear of dying had been the easiest of my fears to deal with. It was living in that state of powerlessness that had been terrifying.

The second fear was my fear of losing my mind, and how closely this was tied to moments when I would clamp down and say "No!" instead of "Yes". With each painful moment of re-entering my body, my ego would say, "I can't do it!" I can't! No!" Then I would hear a voice say, "Yield. Don't want anything, don't expect anything, and don't resist anything. Just say Yes."

Every time I fought I would start to feel like I was losing my mind. When I said, "Yes", I would work my way toward my center, and once there I often felt the grace and relief of the Beloved.

"Throughout this process," I told him, "I have formulated a sort of prayer. It came from a dream and it has become a mantra for my work and for my life. It goes like this:

"In opening myself to the pain of life and loving,
I touch into God with awareness,
And I release myself into the suffering of all humanity
Which draws me into God's presence."

"It has become apparent to me," I told Colin, "that the true key to recovery and healing can only be found in the courage to open and yield inside-out into in the face of fear and uncertainty."

In that initial session with Colin and through all of our subsequent ones, upside down I went, feeling first, discovering the strength to allow myself to be turned inward rather than completely anchoring myself in some idea about who I am. Had I further developed only my grounded-ness as a man, the trauma's psychological scar tissue would not only have generated or compounded my existing symptoms, but also restricted the depth, creativity and meaningfulness that was enriching and becoming my life.

Through my continued work with Colin, a river of creativity began to flow from me, and through it, my psyche began to release those parts of me that had been trapped inside following my fall. Through writing, drawing, painting, carving, and the dreams that coursed through me, I began to retrieve and raise as many of the lost and traumatized parts of myself as I could. I wrote and rewrote my story, working arduously to accurately articulate the extremely personal, profound, and terrifying experiences of the year. And through the retelling of the events and their adjunctive dreams, I gradually began to knit together the torn fabric of myself in the world.

"You finished a triathlon!"

Of all the reactions to hearing my story, that is one of the most common. And while I remain infinitely grateful and joyful for that accomplishment, it was truly just a moment in a much more gradual and profound process. I was not complete when I loaded my gear into my car and put the bike on the rack before driving home. I was not only still physically disabled, but chards of psychic pain remained embedded in my body and unconsciousness. I would have to struggle with my memories and fears and remain open to my dreams if I were to bring true health and integration to my life and personality.

So I wrote. Through the written word and chronicling of my story, I relived, rediscovered and processed the darkest corners of my trauma.

And I drew, and I painted.

Images changed from literal to symbolic as Jackie pulled Jack deeper into the search to find and express the multifaceted experience of my year. Pulled onto the canvas were fabric, fur, metal, bone and wood. When that well was dry, I was drawn into making masks and later into working with animal skulls I found in the forest. It was as if I was embellishing "death" with new life.

And I dreamed, and recorded my accounts of those dreams.

I dreamed countless and varied images. The ravine. Falling. Helicopters. A woman crucified. A boy pulled from a dark and muddy sink hole. A host of others. And through them, deeper levels of the core fear and helplessness that resulted from the trauma began to flow back into my consciousness. As I continued to befriend my broken body and embrace the memories surfacing from my wounded mind, I became more open to the vulnerable feelings associated with the imminent danger and impending terror of confronting death in the ravine. There was no longer an urge to escape, nor was I contracting or grasping for the old heroic defenses.

I discovered I could open to and "hold" more of the suffering as well as renegotiate the intensity of energy embedded in my body. Talking with Colin and being fully present during our sessions with my own feelings, fears and memories reinforced a vertical connection downward within myself to the core of my being. It was there that I made an ever more profound connection with myself. I learned to develop compassion and love for myself that allowed me to live life more fully than I could ever have imagined before the fall.

The process was not easy. On some days I was open, optimistic, creative, and accepting. On others, I found myself angry, resentful, depressed, and resisting at every turn. Rehabilitation of my mind and body was challenging. Balancing Jack and Jackie was not a simple equation to resolve.

As I struggled with this experience, I began to realize how a kind of interdependence had been formed within me, between Jack and that sensitive, wounded inner child of the past, Jackie. Jack was now taking the initiative and moving into the cold, scary, silent and conflicted process of replaying the dictated cassette tapes of my dreams and accounts of the fall that filled a desk drawer. Jack could even sit and write for a while though he frequently fell into a void or became blocked. Yet, where there was once a wall between Jack and Jackie, there was now a permeable boundary that seemed sometimes relatively easy to cross. Jack could give Jackie a shovel, an image or emotion and off he'd go, frequently into the bowels of my being, and dig up a variety of experiences that brought tears or shaking anger into the moment. Jackie's little hand grew stronger in this process as this loving boy was allowed to grow and be seen and validated on a daily basis.

As I worked with my hands on a canvas, my consciousness would often swell with a rhythm of compassion or anger, creating unbidden moods which swung me around throughout the day. But through my struggling with dreams on a canvas, the movement into my interior was deepened. I felt I was seeing into the abyss created by the trauma.

> *I've taken this woman down from a cross!*
>
> *Other people are standing around me as I attend to her. I'm trying to get her a drink of water, and I can't understand why no one is helping me.*
>
> *There is so much emotion moving through me. I sense that these people are somehow ashamed of her or angry with her for some reason. As I hold her tenderly, I feel their disdain.*

As I discussed the dream with Colin, I realized how it pictured the struggle I'd had with my pain and suffering throughout the past year. A part of me had disdain for how I'd crucified myself as a man, husband, father, and professional through the accident. Yet another part of me, now in the face of judgment, was both receptive and responded to my tormented and tortured depth. I could bring water (life) and comfort to myself and in so doing allow myself to love again and re-attach to life and the people in it. The emotion in the dream helped me accept more deeply how suffering is not bad – it is life to be lived, and in the process our heart is redeemed. Suffering carries compassionate love as a friend to our depths. Later I went home and began to work with this image and tension on a large canvas.

The image that came forth of my holding her electrified my body and mind. The energy continued to be activated and released as I embraced the painful, visceral experience and brought it to life on the canvas. Over the course of the next several days, I returned to the canvas. Staying in the moment with my mind in neutral, I worked to express the experience. The inner realm seemed to enter the world by healing, deepening, and enriching my life. I thought to myself over those days, herein lies the energy I needed for changing, continue to invite it in. I began to look at life from the other side, the psyche, instead of exclusively Jack's view of the accident. What was me and what wasn't me was now always merging, making me sometimes less and other times more painfully human.

Creativity surged the more I allowed my dreams to be expressed in my artwork. Hard wooden masks that initially appeared fearsome and powerful became feminized with fur, pearls, fabric, bells and jewelry. I personally also softened more as this process opened me to new possibilities that I'd never before seen or felt. The creative process was revitalizing, breathing new life into me.

The direction of my dreams all pointed downward into the sinkholes of my mind or body. And the energies and potential trapped in these realms would remain unavailable to me until I became receptive to them. The writing, the artwork, and dreams became the vehicles allowing me access to the deep ocean of my being, surrendering everything for the hope of making contact with the life that awaited me within.

It seemed as if each dream arose from my interior like one unconsciousness spasm after another. My struggle was to protect myself from those frightening spasms and avoid my fears, or let them enter my consciousness, turn me upside down, inside out as they inject their powerful elixir into my life.

"Keep going! You're almost there."

A volunteer had shouted that to me and other runners as we came to that last rise in the Triathlon.

Almost there.

I had learned so much and had come so far. I knew in my very being that saying "Yes" to the moment was key to healing and living, but it was a lesson that sometimes almost inexplicably drifted out of reach, like the memory of a dream fading in the morning light. The psyche is a powerful agent and instinctively protects us from pain, urgently ushering us away from re-experiencing what was once unbearable agony, humiliation and trauma.

Almost there.

Some days a dream or image came into my being, and I effortlessly accepted it and let the fears flow through me. And with each cycle of these resurging emotions I would grow a little stronger and recover more and more parts of me that had been lost. But at other times I relapsed into moments when anger overwhelmed me, and I roared a vehement, "NO" to the pain and the broken condition I sometimes felt myself in. There were times I awoke from a vivid dream of trying to climb up from the ravine filled with such fear and dread that I closed my mind to the memory and turned my back on the moment. But while those moments certainly were markers on my path back into 'life,' I knew that fear, resistance, anger, and despair, were not the paths to healing.

And so I cycled through the memories, emotions and the fears as they percolated up from within the sinkholes of my psyche. As often as I could, I said "Yes," and came back into my body, felt the pain and used it to move on and gain a deeper sense of myself. I opened myself to my suffering, and in doing so, extended my human connectedness, not only making the pain more bearable and healing more possible, but connecting ever more strongly with the essence of being, the love and peace that resides within each of us.

My experience of being broken open had taught me to say, "Yes." yielding into my depths. The intention being to remain present, to ALL that was taking place, not denying or resisting, but remaining open to all that was inherent in my journey back into life.

One of the final dreams I shared with Colin was also one of the most profound. It illuminated for me the very essence of being, a vast Silence that sustains us all.

Unfinished

The whole Norwich football team is walking by the coaching staff and gathering on the train platform to await the arrival of the train that will take us to the Coast Guard Academy for the last game of the season. The game has always been one of the biggest of the year.

Coach Sabol calls me over as I walk by him. He looks me in the eye and ask,: "How's your back Jack, is physical therapy helping?"

"Yeah Coach, it feels much better."

He pauses and looks at me doubtfully and says, "Do you feel good enough to play?"

"Coach!" it sounds like I'm yelling. "I know I can play."

He's still looking at me and I blurt out, "Coach, you have never seen anyone as mad as I'll be if you consider sitting me on the bench. I know I'm ready to play. You'll see." His eyes still on me he slowly nods and says, "OK"

I walk out on the train platform. All my teammates are standing around and talking. I feel a tremendous solemn significance in the moment...the end of something that has been so important to me. I walk over and stand next to Carl, Bob, Frank and Fred, and say, "I can't believe this is our last college game."

But as we start talking, I begin to notice that there is a pervasive silence surrounding us. As I look around, I realize the train station is completely deserted. In fact, it's overgrown with weeds and brush. The trains are long gone. Shocked, I realize that the trains stopped running long ago.

As I awaken to this reality, my knees buckle and I drop onto the old platform realizing to my shock and horror that it's been thirty years since the trains came through the station, and I've been standing on the platform preparing to play a game that has been over for decades; that I've been living in the past, identified with the past!

Feeling split open with this awareness, a great silence envelops me, and a groan erupts from my belly while the silence pours into me, and I pour into the infinite, transcending silence.

On my knees I cry out, "Oh my God! Oh my God!"

I woke up soaked in sweat, feeling like my whole life had imploded into the Silence. I sense the past, which seems shattered and a future which is just Silence.

I opened my eyes to the predawn light and kept hearing "Oh my God! Oh my God!" repeating in my mind. I got out of bed, walked into the kitchen, sat down, and over the course of the next few hours, I wrote. My hand shook as a torrent of emotions flooded through me. Tears boiled up from inside me and rolled down my cheeks.

"It's so true!" I thought to myself. "I've been playing this role of the heroic warrior for thirty years. For decades my story has been about defining myself through conflict and opposition.

But there is so much more.

It was there on the old platform, the old ego platform that I began to notice how in the physical world the relationship between past and present is not absolute but is really relative, even arbitrary. It was there in the dream that my knees buckled, just like the death experience when I was knocked out of my ego in the ravine. There my consciousness was magnetically pulled back and forth between the light above and my body below. The Beloved surrounded me, the sustaining platform of my being. Everything had dissolved into the light and into that Silence.

Since my fall, my body has been the battlefield upon which love and fear wage war. I remember, like it was yesterday, being broken-open in the morning light and captured from within, yet swept outward up to the light and into the arms of the Beloved. The twinkling emerald green light held me, but its heat was too intense to endure. Yet, licked by the silent flame, my connection with life was restored. Broken-open, pride sacrificed, I yielded to its presence, that vast and all-encompassing silence, with open-hearted acceptance as the Beloved showed the way to forgiveness. Suffering kept me open as I learned compassion. Where my tears flowed, peace entered. My once haughty neck was happy to bow while my proud back willfully bent as the Beloved summoned the child who led the way for the man.

Almost there.

The energy of that dream stirred in me for days afterwards, and I wondered why my knowledge of the Beloved and that great sustaining silence ebbed and flowed within my consciousness. What would it take, I wondered, to fully anchor that sustaining realization into every moment of my awareness. Could I?

A few days later, I sat in Colin's office and re-read the dream to him.

"Colin," I said. "Before we talk about the dream I have to first thank you for your insights and loving guidance over the past fourteen years. If it was not for you and our work together, I would not have learned how to put my ego aside and become receptive to my dream-maker's communications. Over the years we have held the tension with a lot of powerful dreams and experiences while being moved to tears more times than I can count. But if it hadn't been for all our early work that allowed Jackie to be in my life and allowed me to gradually accept the vulnerability underneath my heroic identity, I could never have come through the accident the way I have over the past two years. I struggled both in myself and with you in this learning process but the experiences changed my life and may even have saved it".

Colin was silent for a long time, and I could tell he was very moved.

"Well, Jack," he said, "you have done an incredible amount of good work in this office, and I've felt privileged to be a part of it. It's changed me too. And you're right, the center of it was Jackie and the vulnerability he never could risk when you were little because of all the shame and humiliation he was subject to. He risked it here, you risked it here. But this dream... my God, what a statement from your unconscious. How do we understand this?"

"I'm not sure," I said, "but it had a profound effect on me and has left me with a number of questions that I can't find answers for. It seems to me I've needed my hero in order to push through the incredible pain of my recovery. Perhaps the great Silence is trying to tell me that the great ego-game is over. Or perhaps the Coach is an out-picturing of the Beloved who I met on the ground of my being, who allowed me permission to step back into life once again, to step back up onto the ego platform joining my team-mates." I thought for a moment.

"When the accident happened and my body was in the ravine I remember how intense the NO was when I had a vision and 'saw' Walker and then 'saw' my boys finding my body. Is there a 'choice' to come back? Is it possible I 'raged' my way back into life?"

"I think you did rage your way back into life, Jack," Colin said. "At least the heroic process of your recovery must have required incredible 'rage.' But it seemed to me it was rage in the sense Dylan Thomas meant 'rage' when he said, "Do not go gently into that good night, Rage, Rage against the dying of the light!" You weren't about to let the light go out! You were the poster child of recovery. No-one could believe it. It was like playing football through all that pain again, right?"

"So, if I read it right," he continued, "the dream seems to be saying that game is over, and maybe it has been for a long time. The heroic ego game, I mean. The new game maybe has to do with facing into a different pain, the pain of Jackie, and the joy you find on the other side of it. I think when the Coach gives you the nod he "knows" about the Silence you'll find on the platform. He knows you have to find it your own way."

"That feels right," I said.

"When Coach gives me permission to join my teammates on the platform, I'm relieved. But it's back on the platform that my ego recognizes the significance of this "time" in my life. It felt like my whole being was on the platform quietly understanding and opening to what surrounded me in the present moment. And then, in a purifying flash that cleansed my mind of any thought and my heart of any emotion, my knees buckled under the weight of the immeasurable profound awareness. Kneeling in a state of humility and open-hearted love, silence seeks only the torn-open cry from the child within all of us. Jackie, the child within the man became the transforming agent who brought relief and blessings into my shattered life."

I paused and took a deep breath.

"Had it not been for our earlier work, Colin, and the discovery of Jackie, I would not have known that the way through this suffering was to embrace the vulnerability underneath it, turning inward on my knees, and finding in my depths not only healing, but a transformative understanding of life. It's been an incredible journey."

"It sure has," Colin responded, shaking his head. "But I'd say we've been 'companioned' the whole way, wouldn't you?"

And we laughed one of our wonderful laughs.

As I drove home from our session, I was filled with a profound sense of gratitude. I thought of that great silence, the Beloved that sustains us all. I reflected on its Presence in the ravine, in the hospital, throughout my rehabilitation, at every stage of that triathlon, in my work, in my life and in my dreams.

I had come so far, and I smiled in the knowledge that there was no great finish with bells and cheering and commemorative t-shirts. The journey was within and ongoing. Binding us all and just beneath our consciousness was a vast and sustaining Presence, a silence and solitude of love and peace.

I prayed for the wisdom to hold that awareness in every moment of every day, and to sustain an unwavering faith that the Beloved would always be there, even when I fell.

CHAPTER 34
Circling Back

"I can't believe I'm here again."

I have heard that phrase countless times in my practice and in life in general. I've heard it said about relationships, finances, employment, family, health and every other aspect of our lives.

"Here I am again."

And so it was in the weeks, months, and years that followed my fall. I found that the process of healing and of fully reentering life had me cycling back through many different dimensions of my professional and personal life. But over time, I learned to stop uttering the phrase with incredulity, frustration, despair or anger. I came to realize that re-experiencing past elements of my life was not a random occurrence. The Universe was always up to something.

At some point along the way, "Here I am again," became a trigger for me to stop and think. The Universe may work in mysterious ways, but it always brought me back for a reason. There was always a lesson to be learned, re-learned, and then really learned.

Through my sessions with Colin, my dreams and my art, I perpetually worked my way through different layers of memories of my accident. And by revisiting those horrific moments, whether through dreams, conversations, or writings, the traumatic shadow they cast within me slowly started to diminish. In physical therapy and then in my own regimen in the gym, a similar process took place. I had good days and days plagued with such pain that I lost sight of any progress I had made. Frustration would surge in me when I felt I had regressed to a physical state I had been in days, weeks or even months earlier.

But each time I became entangled in the physical or emotional pain that so often felt like a setback, I worked hard to keep my heart and mind open, to say, "Yes" to the Universe, remain open to the moment, and not resist. I reminded myself that I was not alone. The Beloved was always there, and would always be there for me, even if I fell.

And so I circled back into life. A year after my accident, I was drawn back into coaching by a call from Frank, a neighboring town's soccer coach.

"Jack, it would be great if you could join me in coaching the Lions." The Lions was Devin's under-10 team.

I was flattered, but at the same time grimaced with the memory of appearing before the soccer board barely a year earlier. It was a different town, but that fact didn't leave me feeling any less vulnerable, and my anger with Zealot and Jones was still surprisingly palpable. But I accepted. Circling back through the coaching process would allow me to pursue something I loved to do with Devin, as well as alleviate some of the feelings of fragility and vulnerability that lingered within me. The reverberations from my accident and our shared soccer fate also remained embedded within Devin. So when I told him of the request to join the Lions I could 'hear' in his pleas for me to say "Yes" that there was also another opportunity for him to create a different outcome.

So I coached, and Devin and I made new friends and had a fabulous year of soccer. And the following year, when the soccer season ended, Frank, his son, Devin and I transitioned into wrestling.

Frank had been a more outstanding wrestler than I but we both loved the sport, which is as old as humankind. It's a team sport, but at its heart it's also an individual sport. Books and movies make it look simple, but the holds and moves are countless and difficult to execute. It is about touch and pressure, movement and feeling, instinct and experience, and sometimes two bodies and one mind.

Although I had rebuilt my private practice, I was only working three days a week, leaving me plenty of time to be with the boys at practice, matches and games. Devin, like Brendan, enjoyed wrestling and showed a natural talent. Brendan was an outstanding wrestler, team leader and a great wrestling mentor and role model for Devin. I was very happy to be spending a considerable amount of time with both my sons and their teammates. Sports for both boys were like soul vitamins. They affirmed their development, encouraged them to courageously struggle with their limitations while learning to access and develop their inner resources. I watched as their emotions, imagination and intellect were being enriched, giving them the confidence and strength to risk adversities while sustaining their developing sense of self.

We were all growing and healing, together and apart.

The next spring, I was asked to take over the town's middle school wrestling program. I accepted and then also became a New York State High School wrestling official. I kept my private practice flexible allowing me the time I needed to attend to my new responsibilities. I was replenished by the richness of family life, coaching, officiating, and being a therapist.

Life had fully recaptured me.

Brendan and Devin led the way as I got back into wrestling condition bone-by-bone, ligament-by-ligament, yielding to the pains and their rhythm with the joy of being centered back in the body. For me, coaching, like being a therapist, moved the ego aside, kept the heart open, and paid tribute to life as we turn into it. Although I still honored and processed dreams on a daily basis, my focus, energy, attention and intention was in life. And once again I could coach and help children develop through a sport. While Brendan was closing in on the school record for most high school wins, Devin was leading his middle school with an unbeaten record.

"Drop into your body! Establish a connection. Trust its intelligence and breathe!" These were some of the words I used when coaching. As I heard myself say them, I noticed I was using the map I had discovered in the process of suffering. During warm-ups, I would gently remind the boys to witness their experience in the moment without judgment. If they noticed any anxiety or discomfort, I instructed them how to breathe. If critical thoughts came up like "I can't do this", I reminded the boys to release them. I talked about making a commitment to practice and exploring wrestling with their whole being. Together we identified strengths, while at the same time, allowed vulnerabilities to be experienced as we all gained confidence in ourselves.

September 2001 began with continued hope and happiness. Brendan left for college, and Devin entered eighth grade. Brendan was looking forward to pursuing a major in psychology with the intention of becoming a sports psychologist. Devin had a wonderful summer season. His soccer team had won the New York State Division 1 Championship. He was looking forward to being back in school with his friends, playing soccer, and wrestling. Alice enjoyed her team of guidance counselors at the middle school and was looking forward to being back with them and 'her kids'.

For me September was, of course, a very special month. I celebrated not only new beginnings, but my 'extended time,' which I felt profoundly grateful for.

And then on the morning of September 11th, with the suddenness of falling into the ravine, our sense of family was lost for an extended moment as the first plane was violently crashed into the World Trade Center. The experience moved everyone's life aside drawing us into naked horror and suffering while we stood or sat paralyzed and incredulous in front of our television sets.

One moment it was a beautiful day with a sense of hopefulness and happiness. Then in an instant, all of our lives were suddenly clouded with uncertainty, impermanence, fear and grief.

That Thursday, I received a call from a business owner whose company was within a few blocks of Ground Zero. It was the first day that businesses within the red zone were allowed to re-open.

He stated that he was pleased that nearly all eighty employees had come into the office, but he felt frustrated and concerned. There was a general disinterest among people he'd spoken to in getting back to work. They reported being unable to concentrate or focus, and that the work now seemed meaningless. They were talking a lot about their fear, how they kept seeing violent and horrible images in their minds, things they had seen from looking out the windows. They felt helpless and angry.

"Jack, is there anything you can do to help?"

"I don't know," I replied, "but I'll try. I'll be there early tomorrow morning."

At 7:00a.m. on that rainy, Friday morning, a driver picked me up at my home. As we entered the city, I noticed there were American flags everywhere, as well as signs reading "Our prayers are with you". We passed command posts, Red Cross centers, food stations to feed and comfort workers, and what seemed like an endless wall with pictures of missing loved ones. People were also standing along the street holding up pictures of their own, faces pleading for help and mercy, asking if anyone had seen their husbands, wives, sisters, brothers, children and friends. But in so many faces, despite the grief and fear, you could also see a sense of resolve and determination. This grief stricken city was united.

We were stopped at the first checkpoint and were asked for identification. I sat crumpled in the back seat of the limo wiping the tears from my eyes that were wide-open, staring ahead toward the smoldering abyss in the distance. My defenses were burned away by the debris cloud. As we arrived at the office, I exited the car only to be enveloped by a burning, acrid, rubbery, and metallic smell. The terror and grief were now rendered real in my body. I felt the silent innate sacredness of all of those lives leap into me. Navigating heartbreak, I wordlessly walked inside at 8:30a.m. Though I felt totally unprepared for that moment, it became clear to me that I was not there solely by my own will. I also clearly sensed that I was not alone. The Presence I had experienced in the ravine, the Beloved, was with me and around me.

I knew from my brokenness in the ravine, that love's shadow was everywhere. There was purpose hidden in this horrific experience that was invisible, made visible in the surrendered plea of suffering that united us all.

I met the company's owners who said the employees where assembled and that they were relieved and grateful that I had come in to talk with them. As I introduced myself and looked out on the unmasked faces, I could see the shock, the shattering of beliefs and ideals that until three days ago had defined the story of their lives.

We were all captured by the moment and on our knees. Behind them, through a wall of windows the rain did little to obscure the smoke, ash, and heat from the smoldering remains of the World Trade Center. I instantly imagined what they might have witnessed or were still reliving in their dreams and flashbacks. This was not something that could be talked out or de-conditioned away in the moment. This 'problem' couldn't be solved, but their suffering needed to be addressed. All I had was what I knew; horror and spirit sit side by side, each embedded in the other. I met them where they were and where I once had been.

I spoke of seeing our own and each other's suffering with open hearts, our tears clearing our vision, rinsing away any sense of separateness and judgment. That Tuesday, our inner and outer worlds had collided, burning away defenses, tipping us ultimately into ourselves, and activating our inner "Yes." We could look outside ourselves for a source of our anger, stand frozen, or attempt to flee.

"Each of us," I explained, "has a stress threshold for what we can handle and this experience exceeded it. Everyone's threshold is a function of experiences that we've encountered but not necessarily resolved."

"I know," I continued, "that there is a voice in each of our heads that is screaming, 'why did this happen?' and 'what does this mean?' I can't answer those questions, but I do have the knowledge that we can choose to answer them and endure this alone - or together."

I related that I really didn't know what courage was until I learned to stay in my body with an open-heart while being held captive in my own personal hell. I began telling my story of six years ago, and how I was taken past my threshold, not nearly 'big enough' to handle the situation I had found myself in.

"I learned to say "Yes" and open myself to, rather than resist the experience. I learned to sacrifice my need for control and release myself from the anger that burned so deep within me. I found, in allowing myself to be broken-open and in turning into my suffering, I began to heal."

"As hard as it seems today, if we can choose to open our hearts and say 'yes' to what is within us, as well as surrounding us, we will be a touchstone for all those who died too tragically and so suddenly. We can become a point of solace and a place of oneness within the heat of this tragedy."

When I finished talking, I looked out into compassionate wet eyes. They had taken in the love and hope I'd offered. The group appeared knitted together, with their fears momentarily stilled. We stood as one in both our suffering and love. As my journey into this company unfolded, I found myself spending one day every two weeks for the next year meeting with the owner and employees. It became a very deep and meaningful experience working with this creative, intelligent and courageous group of men and women.

During that winter, Devin provided our family with many joyful moments. Although only an eighth-grader, he wrestled for the high school varsity team. He had an enchanted season ending it as one of the top wrestler's among 157 high schools.

But by the next summer, the time spent inside the red zone, in contact with myriad forms of traumatic symptoms, had begun to get trapped in my own body.

Dealing with this "charge" in my body and the inherent emotions was a challenge for me that required action. One way I decided to work with my experience was to build a bell tower with Al for those who died on September 11th, and a chimes tower for those first responders who had survived. I drew up a sketch with my friend Norm and then had a host of materials needed delivered to my home.

What followed was unexpected and beautiful. Frequently, as I stayed in my body, hammering nails or drilling holes, tears would begin flowing. The repetitive movement, combined with being mindful of the purpose, shifted my consciousness. Memories of being inside the red zone, images, sounds, feelings, even smells emerged into my awareness and moved out of my body. The heart-breaking, violent, wet turmoil was now being turned inside out.

Within a couple of weeks, a sixteen-by-sixteen foot bell tower stood in front of our home. A covered, forty foot walkway connected it to the chimes tower, which was nine by six feet and eighteen feet high. Another covered walkway of twenty-six feet connected the second tower to the garage. The roofline of the walkway intentionally flowed downward between the towers, twisting and turning, falling away every eight feet, like the tears I, and so very many others, had shed.

Once again, I had turned inward to the suffering and been open to sharing the pain, fear, and love with others. And once again, this time through the creativity of building, I had turned inward, said, "Yes" to the pain, healing and growing richer in spirit through the process.

Nearly two years later, in a night soccer game out on Long Island, Devin was involved in a collision with two other players in front of the net. It was late in the game and after eight. As the two other players got up he remained limp on the field. Though he would walk off the field after several minutes, he remained on the bench for the remainder of the game. As we were driving across the Whitestone Bridge, Devin was talking about the game when his speech became slurred and his vision was blurring.

"Dad I'm telling my arm to move and nothing is happening, same with my right leg. What's happening?"

I tried not to struggle with my fear. Staying in my body the best I could, I instructed Devin to do the same. I called Alice. In a blink of an eye, our life, which had begun to feel solid and continuous, had suddenly disappeared in waves of fear and confusion. Alice was calm and focused as we spoke, while I struggled to slow down my breathing. She was somehow able to embrace the uncertainty and remind me that there was no point in getting ahead of myself, that Devin's symptoms would be diagnosed and treated when we got to the hospital.

Although I tried to face Devin's condition as openly and honestly as I could, there remained another part of me burning in fear and helplessness. I kept hearing Alice's voice in my head, "The outcome is unknown, the consequences will be what they are, and we'll all deal with them." I took Devin to the nearest hospital. Once there it was decided that he needed to be transferred to the same trauma center I had been eight years earlier. What the hell was the magnetic pull back here? My mind was spinning like a top!

Every time I resisted, I energized the fear. The moment was irrevocable. I reached for the silence but only heard 'noise' while fear grabbed at my body. I knew Jackie was inside somewhere, connected to the Beloved's energies, but it felt impossible to yield that far, that deep, at that moment.

Relief and acceptance occur one moment at a time. Devin was diagnosed with a ruptured carotid artery and would remain in the intensive care unit of the medical center for a week. His condition was serious but stable.

And there we were again. A hospital. A serious injury with an uncertain outcome. Fear and love arose and dissolved for all, as did the ability to witness the process we were undergoing. As Devin's condition and prognosis became clearer, the experience began to feel less frightening. As the news of the accident spread, teammates and peers came to visit, bringing various treats, laughter and love.

For several years leading to that point, Devin had defended himself against the pain his success had caused him from his schoolmates' jealousy and competitiveness. His commitment to excellence had formed him into and honor student who was also a top athlete and musician. As the week wore on, he began to see his friends through fresh open-hearted eyes. Daily he grew softer, less defensive, yielding to the balloons, cards and caring visits, uniting him again with the peers he had thought he lost through his own competitive nature

Love's shadow appeared to be everywhere. Again I witnessed, as I had with Jackie's emergence, that there was nothing to do, analyze, or understand, there was only to open, feel and allow. Spirit, it appears, does not break through to mankind as much as it waits to be drawn in during an emergency.

For six months the balm of inactivity transformed Devin, reassembling him from the inside out. He re-entered his life in his brokenness. He remained connected to his depths, honoring what was offered while continuing to relax his repressing barriers. Saying "Yes" to the transformative event unexpectedly filled his life with love and happiness. He had learned to trust the moment, relinquishing his wariness and embracing his vulnerability. What he had been seeking found him as he lay still long enough for his innocence and love to reach him. When his high school soccer season began, he was back leading his team with a different perspective and as an open-hearted leader.

Once again, he was free to run. And once again our family relived the lessons we had begun to learn during my injury and recovery.

Just before Christmas the next year, I called my father, then eighty-five, and living alone in his home in Scituate, MA. There was no answer. After failing to reach him over the course of a few hours, I called my brother Kevin, who also lives in Scituate, and told him I was worried. He arrived at our father's home finding him unconscious at the foot of his bed.

My father had completely recovered from his open-heart surgery. His pig valve had served him well and life was reasonably comfortable and familiar for him. He had stopped playing golf as his knees hurt, and his eyesight had begun to fail. Yet always a soldier, he had marched on.

Sometime in the middle of the night prior to my call, he had gotten out of bed to go to the bathroom. As he walked across the bedroom floor, he tripped and fell. He fell hard. He tried for hours to get up, attempting to regain his balance and make it back to his bed. In the darkness, inches seemed like feet and feet like miles as he pulled himself along. He thrashed about and was bleeding. Over many hours, his blood traced a gruesome story of his struggle along the floor, walls and ceiling, before he fell unconscious.

Even at his advanced age, his life continued to be woven into moments of heroic action and grief. Just as he had fought and grieved for freedom with great and terrible intent during WWII, he continued to struggle for life itself. But after his fall and his struggle that night, his life would never again be as it once was.

Had he heard the Silence as I once had in the deep forest? Perhaps he did, and perhaps it too reminded him that there is life beyond. The Beloved is there in those moments when there is no hand to hold, no face to kiss.

When I arrived at the hospital the next day, Dad had regained consciousness but his health was failing

"Dad what happened last night?"

"I got up to go to the bathroom and fell. I kept trying to get back to bed but then somehow in my mind I was landing on Angaur."

"You were down for a long time till Kevin found you. Blood was everywhere. What was going on?"

He closed his eyes and paused, licking his parched lips. I held a glass of water with a straw in it and he took a few sips. He slowly opened his eyes looked at me for a second and then stared off.

"We were being shelled…machine gun fire was cutting us up to ribbons…I just kept digging…trying to get down…"

My tears were burning my face as I asked, "All night long?"
"Yes."

As fate would have it, that would be the last exchange I would have with my father. Over the next couple of weeks less and less of him came back into our world.

He talked very little about the war as is common to many men of that time and era. Decades before we had once discussed Viet Nam and WWII, and I asked him about his Bronze Star Arrowhead and ribbons. He was an army captain with the 321st Infantry, and he'd participated in the initial assault wave of an amphibious landing on Angaur Island, Palau Group in the Asiatic-Pacific Theater.

"It was a bloody battle," was all he had said about one of the most seminal moments of his life. Beyond that, he never talked about what had happened.

As I held his hand and listened, I remember thinking just how circular our lives are. There I was again at my ailing father's side, just as I had been when his valve had been replaced. And for the last conversation we would have together, he was recounting and in some ways reliving the traumatic battle that had been the catalyst for so much that defined him as a man. His life was woven into a great story of heroic actions and sadness. His ability to love had been trapped under his losses and fears, so many which had evolved from WWII. As I sat quietly with him, I reflected on all of the touch points of our relationship and his life and knew he was indeed greater than the story he lived or the emotion that defined them.

I sat with him for a long time as his medications kept him increasingly more diffused, slipping outside, then inside his body. I thought how fortunate it was for both of us that we each had lived this long. I was fathered by him. Loved him. Fought and rebelled against him. Abandoned him. And then loved him again, embracing all of him as both of our hearts had opened during my injury, his operations, and our recoveries. I touched his arm, chest and of course his feet, as he had mine when I was in the hospital, connecting, healing, and allowing the silence of love to flow.

I watched as he approached death's door. His pride was slowly stripped away transforming 'somebody' through the action of suffering into 'nobody.' It was the child I saw in him near the end, a sweet boy who was drawing closer and closer to the Beloved's sacred energy. As I sat with him for what would be our last moment together, a sacredness stirred within me. Jackie touched and held his daddy's feet one last time.

Dad was still breathing when I left, but though there was a hand for me to hold and a face to kiss, the dad I knew was no longer present. I returned to New York early that evening in a snowstorm. After Alice, Devin and I ate dinner, I went out to plow the driveway. The snow had stopped falling, the lights from the tractor reflected off the pure whiteness. The forest was immersed in darkness and silence. Just as I was making my last sweep up the larger of two hills in the driveway, there came through the forest what sounded like a freight train. A gust of wind hit my back so hard it bent me forward. My central nervous system lit up sending chills up my spine.

"Dad," I called out.

When I climbed into bed with Alice not too long after, I told her that I felt like I had a 'visitation' from my Dad, and felt it was as if he had stopped by on his way out. We turned off the light. I had just fallen asleep when the phone rang. It was Kevin.

"Dad died not too long ago," he quietly told me.

Alice and I held each other silently as a mixture of grief and awe eventually ushered us off to sleep.

In the months following his passing, I reflected how death, like trauma, shifts our boundaries and definitions of ourselves. We grieve, suffer, and often experience great anxiety, all of which disorients us from what we know, how we cope, and who we are. It seems especially true that after the death of a loved one the pieces of our lives never quite fit back together the way they once had. And there I was again, relearning the same 'secret' that my dreams frequently out-pictured, to simply allow and trust what was happening within my life and personality.

"Learn," the Universe repeated, "to yield to change, and accept the flow of life moment by moment." By remaining anchored in my body, open-hearted, love will in fact follow 'yes' into life.

In the first few years that followed my fall, I retained a palpable sense of my near death experience in the ravine. The light, the incredible lightness of being, the overwhelming and blissful sense of oneness with the universe, and the pure love I felt lived in me almost like a sixth sense. I could close my eyes and be swept up by it. The intensity of the Beloved lived just under the surface of my consciousness, and with just a little effort, I could recall it and in a sense relive it.

But reengaging and coming back into life was a struggle, and more of Jack resurfaced out of necessity as I built back my practice, coached, and found ways to feel secure and less vulnerable in social settings. As more years passed, Jack's resurgence unfortunately lead to less integration with Jackie and a more vague awareness of my state of being in the Beloved's presence. I never lost the memory. Writing my memoirs certainly sustained the description and truth of it, but I lost access to the deep experience of that brilliant and unconditional loving state. I can equate the sensation to waking from an extremely vivid dream, heart racing, excited, senses awakened. And in the course of the day, while the images remain, the aliveness of it and the sense of reality become harder and harder to maintain.

Winter sped by, and spring transformed into summer in what seemed like a heartbeat. By June, I had finished remodeling the kitchen of dad's place, which we had decided to keep for a summer home. Our family eagerly looked forward to the times we would spend together at the beach house. Devin was not yet back from college and Alice still had to finish the school year, so I decided on yet another project, that of replacing some windows and a skylight in our New York home. I would take advantage of an energy tax credit for upgrading doors and windows.

After an enjoyable Fourth of July weekend in Scituate with the entire family, the windows and skylight I had ordered finally arrived. Al and I, along with another carpenter, installed the windows by the end of that week, and I was looking forward to the coming Monday to finish the project by installing the skylight.

We were all in New York. I spent the day caulking the windows and painting the trim. It was a hot and humid day, and by five, I was finished and ready for a swim. And like so many of the swims I have taken in the lake, it was blissful. The air was heavy with the aroma of the forest, turkey vultures rode the thermals above me, and the spring fed water was clear, clean, and unbelievably refreshing after a day working in the sweltering heat. I dove in, just as I had done for some 30 years. I stretched out, adjusted my breathing and started swimming.

It was an easy meditative swim, just the sound of my breath and a flicker of light on the horizon. I surrendered to the lake, the experience was alive, ongoing and continuous. Three quarters of the way around the lake, I saw out of the corner of my eye the change in the light and shadow now in the forest. I changed up my stroke and went into a smooth, silent glide across the water's surface. A turtle's head broke the surface near the shore, and the bass started coming to the surface searching for dinner, their surface rings expanding and dissolving all around me.

I felt, as I often do when I swim, that I was just a breath moving along the surface of the water, a part of the mystery that lovingly surrounds me, embracing me. There was a joy there that I can only find in nature. I glided up to the shore, got out, grabbed my towel off the tree limb. When I finished putting on my sneakers, I slowly bowed to the sun and gave thanks.

As odd as it may sound, I honestly felt its pleasure in my pleasure of that moment. Walking home through the stillness of the forest, I felt a sense of peace, an openness and at one with all that surrounded me. That evening that sense of peace stayed with me, and as I lay in bed looking up at the stars, I gave thanks again for the day to the ongoing soundtrack of the tree frogs actively calling to each other.

I slowly and contentedly drifted off to sleep. And I began to dream.

I'm swimming around the lake. The light and water are soft, my body relaxed and open. For some reason I decide to stop swimming and just float on the water's surface. It's so peaceful and relaxing, I want to take a short nap.

As I'm lying on the surface, the warmth of the sun further relaxes me, and I just sink into it. Slowly, I continue to sink down into the water. At first, the descent is lovely, sinking into a soft watery world where the light is muted but beautiful.

But as the sky and horizon disappear, I keep sinking, drifting deeper. Still relaxed I feel a gentle embrace until the descent accelerates.

Suddenly, I feel a powerful pull downward. No longer gently embraced, I feel defenseless as I am seized and dragged downward. Nothing to hold on to, no clinging, no knowing, no bearings. Instinctively I gasp in helplessness as I reach for and struggle towards the surface. The contact is terrifying. Every bit of energy I have is reaching, swimming and struggling for the surface, for the world - for life.

I woke with my heart pounding, disoriented, and with the sense that the very bed sheets were trying to pull me down and under. It took several minutes to regain my bearings and my composure and realize it had all been a dream. It took me even longer before I could turn back into the memory and try to understand and come to terms with it.

I was happy. Everything in my life was truly good. I had no interest in circling back through some horrific depths in my dream or waking worlds. It took me over an hour before I was able to get back to sleep.

I woke to fear and resistance. I didn't care what that dream might be asking of me, I wanted no part of it. I knew that consciousness begins in the night and carries its shadow into day, but in those terms, I wanted no part of my night.

As I replayed my nightmarish descent, I thought to myself how fervently I did not want to say – never wanted to say – "Here I am again" about depths like that. I lay in bed and wondered just what the Universe was up to.

"Ignore the dream at my own peril." I thought. "I won't go swimming. I won't take a nap. I'll really, really pay attention."

Even in the morning light, as I lay in bed while Alice walked our dog, the dream felt threatening and hostile. Dread and anxiety percolated within me. With every ounce of strength I had, I tried to shut off my sense of fear and powerlessness. But I couldn't. I wasn't able to just block it out. My body simply wouldn't release the dream. So out of bed and into the day I went.

Over coffee, Alice and I discussed the dream.

"Sometimes the only thing more dangerous than dealing with a dream is to not dealing with a dream," I told her. We talked and laughed and decided to go to the gym and then out to breakfast.

"You drive," I told her, smiling. "No sense in taking any undo chances."

By the end of the day I felt quieter, even softer in my being. I didn't like the idea of looking over my shoulder, or being pulled back into the depths, and I knew enough to remain on my 'knees' and in my body.

Before I went to bed I asked Brendan if he'd give me a hand getting the skylight on the roof in the morning before he left for work.

"No problem, dad. It will be nice to get this project wrapped up."

I climbed into bed by Alice's side. I looked up through the skylight at the stars and gave thanks for the day.

"How are you doing," Alice asked.

"I've been here before," I said. "I just need to turn into the anxiety that lingers from that dream, trust the Universe, don't resist whatever it's trying to tell me."

"And how's that going?" she asked.

"I'm working on it."

I drew a deep breath, let it out slowly and then drifted off into a dreamless sleep.

CHAPTER 35
The Return

July 13, 2009 began as a classic summer day in New York. Blue. Hot. Humid. The temperature must have been pushing 90, though I can't say the heat really had anything to do with the turn of events that day. Brendan had indeed helped me get the skylight onto the roof, and Al and I had just finished lunch.

We were back on the roof making final preparations for the installation of the new skylight. I had just finished trimming back some shingles and took a couple of short steps back to survey our progress, I was careful to watch my position in relation to the roofline, but for some reason my perspective was thrown off. I took one step too many, and suddenly, incredulously, I was falling.

I fell 22 feet, landing on the deck feet first before slamming onto my back. My head missed two large clay pots by inches. For just a moment, the spark of my existence was outside my body, but then my life force groaned, burying itself deep within me. Bones were broken. I was bleeding profusely. A combination of pain and rage swept through me.

"I KNEW IT," I shouted. "A FUCKING WAKING NIGHT-MARE!"

Walls of pain and fear began to close in and my cursing increased. My dream from two nights earlier had foreshadowed the event, and I still couldn't stop it from happening!

"I KNEW IT!" I raged.

A combination of the sound of the tremendous boom as I hit the deck and my ensuing rage had Alice running out from the kitchen. From the roof Al shouted down for her to call 911.

"Jack, help is on the way." Alice's comforting words were clear and my rage began to subside.

I quieted down, and as I did everything seemed to slow down, even the waves of pain and fear. I released my breath and tried to yield to the moment, to say, "Yes." As I began to yield, a silence gripped me. It felt merciful but also had a profound and disturbing quality to it. I remember having this vivid sense that it was not 'my' body that moved through life but rather a life force that now moved through my brokenness. But I didn't want to submit to this force. My body felt like a battleground.

I heard police sirens.

Al was looking down from the roof and Alice was frozen at the top of the deck. Both were silent and completely stunned. I was staring up at the sky which I remember seemed too bright. I was smeared across the deck, a hundred feet away from where I was 13 years ago when I laid shattered in the ravine. I closed my eyes.

Above the screeching sirens, I heard chimes. There were eight wind chimes on the tower, a half dozen more off the deck, in the forest and down in the ravine. They seemed to stir in response to a breeze moving through the forest.

I sensed movement along the deck and slowly opened my eyes. Two policemen stood over me. I turned into the vulnerability, into the moment.

"Mr. Weafer," one of them asked. "Can you hear me OK?"

"Yes," I groaned. As I looked up, I noticed that one of the officer's had been at my side 13 years ago.

"The paramedics will be here soon. We're going to take care of you. I'm so sorry you're going through this again."

"Me too," I responded.

The paramedics arrived and I heard pieces of their conversation with Alice.

"He has multiple fractures and with a fall from this height, we can't be sure how badly he is hurt internally. We really need to medevac him to County Trauma Center."

"Are you sure that's necessary?" Alice's words captured my exact thoughts.

"Absolutely," they told her.

I let out a huge sigh and tried to keep my anxiety at bay. I couldn't believe it was all happening again. They strapped me securely to a board and loaded me onto the stretcher. The only thing I was able to move were my eyes as they began to carry me up the steps.

I sensed Devin before I saw him. He towered over Alice, his arm wrapped tight around her. They both wore solemn, troubled expressions. Tears poured down the side of my face and pooled in my ears. The pain was excruciating as they loaded me into the ambulance. With the siren blaring, they started the drive down the rough and bumpy driveway and onto the main road.

When they opened the doors of the ambulance, the brilliance of the afternoon light blinded me for a moment, causing me to squint and blink hard as they rolled me out and started to place me into the helicopter. I noticed Devin's elementary school off to my right.

"Oh my God," I groaned. Thirteen years ago Devin and his classmates had watched a virtual mirror image of that moment play out in front of them.

As we lifted off, I searched the faces of the two attending nurses looking for that angel of mercy from my past. But she wasn't there. Over the thundering of the helicopter's rotors, one of the nurses called to me.

"I understand you have flown with us before."

I responded with a weak smile. I had indeed but today was different than 13 years ago. I came back to my breath and as I did, a wave of humility washed over me. I thought to myself, "Not *my* will but T*hy* will be done." Damn!" My depths had called to me and I didn't want to go, but I couldn't separate myself from the moment. The moment held me captive, and the truth in that instant was terrifying. My breath came in waves. One moment it was tight and hot, the next moment wet with grief.

As we flew, waves of dread and adrenaline coursed through me. I was swept away by a palpable sense of gut wrenching fear. My awareness became diffused, trapped outside my body in the whooshing sound of the rotors. Grabbing hold of myself, I struggled to redirect my focus to witnessing the horror that was taking place rather than becoming trapped in it. Powerful and tight currents of pain, resistance, fear, and anger were fired up in a fierce struggle to control me.

Suddenly the helicopter abruptly jerked up and down. A spasm of pain seized me, and the sudden experience of being swept downward and upward by uncontrollable forces triggered the feeling from my recent dream of being pulled into the depths of the lake. Instantly an anguished dialogue began sweeping through my mind.

"Was that dream your summons?" I asked silently to the Universe.

"You spun that dream. Was there even a chance for me to escape Your dark abyss or was my fate already determined?" The one-sided dialogue raged inside my head.

"How am I supposed to respond? I know You must have some hidden purpose in returning me to this dreadful place, but all I can see and feel is pain and anger. What the hell do you want from me?! You ask too damn much of me! Every cell in my body is begging You for mercy. You have to show me Your intention so that I can deal with this nightmare."

I could see my helmeted companions talking. Their mouths were moving, but I couldn't hear anything over the thundering rotors. I closed my eyes again. My head was spinning like a top.

"Why the hell am I back here again?! Aren't there others who deserve this agony more than I do? Why not pull them down into their own dark abyss so that they can hear You too? Can You not distribute suffering evenly? Why me?!"

I lay there strapped to the board, the pain coursing through my body like fire. I felt helpless, alone, futilely grasping for any thought to help me stop my spiraling sense of fear and powerlessness. As I turned in, a sense of grief and sadness moved through my body. Tears began to flow as I struggled with the pain and parsed through a flurry of feelings, memories and images that were surging through me.

But I kept coming back to, "Why?"

Had I not properly honored the life that had been returned to me? I tried to live and love by the lessons I had learned in the ravine. I tried to give to others the same compassion and love I had received. Did I fail by not placing my writing about my sacred fall into the hands of others? Why was I allowed to return to my family while others I had known were not as fortunate. And then suddenly I realized that I had failed my Beloved because I never felt truly worthy of the Beloved's mercy in granting me the gift of life. I had never been worthy of that love.

"Not worthy," I repeated to myself. And with that sudden awareness, something that was embedded in me began to shift. I yielded to it and a sense of compassion moved through me. As my body surrendered, I recognized the Beloved's perfume from thirteen years ago. My mind stilled and I became aware of everything and nothing. Flowing through me was a powerful wet energy. With it came the thought that the Beloved 'wanted' me to touch this deep place with knowingness, to see and understand what I had not allowed.

Aligned with that movement, I absolutely knew that if I could remain open and present to the mystery, that all might end well for my family and me. I prayed, "Beloved I yield my body to You, my life again in Your hands for some purpose I do not understand but will bear." Immediately, I heard myself say "Yes" out loud.

The steady beat of the rotors changed and the helicopter began its landing approach. Yet with the descent, my fear became amplified and a strong NO surged up in my body like a growl.

Was I to trust and surrender to the moment or impotently resist? Should I open my heart with acceptance and compassion, or would I shut myself off and let myself be consumed by the pain and fear? I willed myself to embrace my vulnerability, knowing that to say, "No" would be to repress the life force that was flowing through me. My instinct told me it was in 'how' I approached what lay ahead that determined the flame's response.

The helicopter landed and my trek back through time continued. Doors popped open and I was once again overwhelmed with a swirl of uniforms and voices as I was unceremoniously shuttled from a stretcher to an operating table.

"Can you hear me? Can you tell us where it hurts? Do you have any sensation in your legs? Is your vision blurred? Do you know what date it is? What's your insurance provider and number? Is there someone we should contact?" Multiple voices, countless questions, each doctor or nurse shouting over the others to be heard.

"STOP! STOP! JUST STOP!" I roared. "I can't answer three or four questions at once!"

And everything stopped. After a few seconds of silence, a male voice from somewhere beyond my feet said, "He's right." The concentrated energy in the room realigned and the process resumed in a calmer manner.

Later, my body was lifted off the operating room table and placed in a hospital bed. As I was rolled into another room, the image of being in a crib in the jungle flashed through my mind. I was helpless, but vigilant, and silently I was pushed along, finally coming to rest in a small room in the ICU. I opened my eyes to the sound of Alice's quiet and calm voice.

"We're here. Devin and I are here."

They approached me, side by side, stopping at my feet. Deep within I felt my present and past collide. A consuming flash of biting, painful memories cut deeply through me. In an extraordinary way, it was a seamless mix of both now and thirteen years ago. Submerged, I reached for the moment's surface. Everything I knew, everything I was, became engaged in the moment. My body shuttered in silence. The silence was so big that I felt as if my heart was about to explode. Not a word was spoken, and in that moment, as my body gradually began to open, I felt comforted.

At that point, my will no longer felt as if it had to take control. My body softened and began to shake, and the moment seemed to pivot on fear and love. An influx of feeling and sensation on both a gross and subtle level joined the three of us in love, loss and uncertainty.

I chose love.

"I'm glad you're here."

"How are you doing Dad?"

"I feel cold...alone. Would you touch me?"

I could tell in their expressions that they knew how I felt. They only needed the invitation. As our hearts lay open, their touch released me. I turned into the experience and noticed how different that experience was from the one we shared thirteen years ago. Thirteen years ago, I felt displaced and outside of time, horrified by my vulnerability and closing myself off. Today I felt immersed in the 'now,' with a fairly open and willing heart.

"Looks like I'm just in time." A nurse had walked in. "How would a nice warm blanket feel right now?"

With warmth and attentiveness, she began to cover me with the blanket and tucked it in around me. Alice and Devin were massaging my feet.

"Dad, it's like lightning bolts shooting up my arms."

"Me too," said Alice.

We all laughed.

"I've got to let go for a second, Dad. The energy coming through your feet is just too intense".

Yielding to their love I plunged downward into the source of the lightening.

"When they were putting you in the ambulance Dad, I said to mom that what had just happened was destiny...now you will be able to finish your book."

I was speechless. Devin's comment struck me as profound. He knew nothing of my dream two days previous, yet somehow he instantly saw this holy mess as something of value.

Brendan arrived as the orderly was rolling me down the hall to take me to radiology. His presence, like his character, was strong and loving. The pain I felt had receded and the sadness lifted as my family walked along beside me.

"I have to go to radiology for x-rays and tests. It's going to be a long time," I told them. Time had passed quickly, and it was already early evening.

"Hang in there, Dad. You're going to be OK." As the doors to the elevator closed, Alice, Devin, and Brendan all repeated their loving wishes.

"I'll see you tomorrow," I called after them, and we began our descent into the hospital's bowels.

I felt as if I was being pulled downward by some powerful, threatening, sucking void that was taking possession of me. Different urges, needs and emotions instantly fired off inside of me. With both terror and a sense of awe, I realized my experience was exactly what I woke myself up from two nights ago. But it was no nightmare that I could simply blink away. With the knowledge that my greatest potential ally was my body, I tried to align with it and redirected my awareness to my breath. I took slow deep breaths and noticed how palpable, even predatory, the fear felt like in that moment. It was oppressive and potentially consuming and threatened to pull me under. The last time I had taken that descent, it had taken me years to put the pieces back together and reconnect my mind with my body

Wavering slightly under the weight of the pain and fear, I redirected my awareness to my physical and emotional body.

"Yield, align and engage!" I told myself. "Feel it and let it flow through."

My mouth was dry and my body was shaking. I felt more fear than shock. Suddenly a sharp pain swept across my chest. Heart attack! Fear came rushing back. Calming myself down, I realized that it was a band of fear squeezing my chest. Breathing directly into my heart, I tried to relieve the painful pressure. Slowly, the physical discomfort began to subside. As the force and grip on my heart began to soften, I recalled my family and the warm sensation of my tears. I became aware of my impermanence and my ego's assumption that it operated under its own powers. I was clearly a part of something larger than myself. With one hand on my heart and the other on my diaphragm, I concentrated on allowing the fear and tension to flow out of me. Breathing deeply, I relaxed my belly, saying "Yes" and yielding to the moment's experience. I prayed for the courage to give into myself without giving up on myself; I had done it before and prayed I could I do it again.

On the bottom floor, I was hurriedly swept along through a vast labyrinth of hallways and doors. The sound of the bed's wheels clattering along the floor below me was very loud. It was cold. It was the bodily sensation of being pulled forcefully along toward some terrifying experience that grabbed at my awareness. As that happened, I again felt pulled up and out of my body.

"Damn it!" I fought to regain my attention and reclaim my body as my own. "Concentrate on your senses now!" I yelled in my head.

I shifted my body and tried to center myself as the bed was being rolled along. As best I could, I focused hard on my senses. My hearing captured me first. As I listened more attentively to the bed's rolling wheels, I noticed how dimly lit the hallway was and how the air smelled stale. There was a taste of copper in my throat and I found myself returning to the moment. As I did, there was something about that area of the hospital that reverberated to my core.

I began to hear echoes coming off the walls, following me. It was as if there were trails of feelings following me, reaching out for me. A realization chilled me to the bone. I had no memory of being here. It dawned on me that thirteen years ago I was largely swept away by the near death experience. Maybe spirit wanted me here for no other reason than I wasn't here the last time! I had been, in fact, out of my mind and out of my body.

The hospital bed rolled to a stop. There was a woman sitting behind a desk.

"OK," I hear someone say. "Just put him up against the wall over there. Someone will come and get him when they are ready."

As the bed bumped up against the wall, some faint memory was triggered in my body. I could feel it but didn't know what it was. I broke out into a sweat. I tried to calm myself repeating in my head that I had gone through a lot of x-rays, CAT scans, and M.R.I.'s. and I would be OK, but my body was not calming down. A woman wearing surgical blues walked up to me and checked the band on my wrist.

"Hello, Jack. We are going to take some x-rays. I understand you fell off your roof."

I nodded, embarrassed. As she started to roll the bed into x-ray, my spine tingled.

"What were you doing up there?" she asked.

"Changing a skylight," I said.

When I saw the x-ray machine, my breath caught and electric currents began rippling through my body. I couldn't breathe and felt the onset of a complete panic attack. Another aide approached the bed, and the two of them rolled the bed up against the x-ray platform. As they did, I was overcome with a primal fear. From the moment they touched me, a powerful blazing set of sensations exploded throughout my body.

Images from thirteen years ago now thundered into my awareness sending charges through my body. They cascaded through me like a set of dominos, each image detonating a surge of pain up and down my spine.

"Oh God, Oh God" I screamed. "Please don't move me," I pleaded with tears in my eyes.

"I'm so sorry", the technician replied, "We have to."

"Please don't," I pleaded again as they slipped a board underneath my shattered body. Pain surged through me as I screamed and cried. As they lifted me onto the table, I felt as if I was once again crashing into the boulders in the ravine.

"I'm so sorry, but we have to move you again. I am so sorry."

My screams continued. I felt I was being torn apart.

The memories and images, once buried deep within me, came thundering back from my body into my mind.

"Stop!" I heard myself say out loud, and I realized that I was still in the hospital bed. No one had even touched me. But the process of being taken into the x-ray room had triggered pieces of a memory that had never fully surfaced for all these years. The technicians around my bed looked down at me somewhat puzzled.

"I just need a moment." I gathered myself back into the reality of the moment,

"I'm sorry," I said. "I just had a flashback to a very traumatic moment from the last time I was here. Can we do this together?"

The flashback had mercifully dissolved as quickly as it had surfaced.

"Sure," they said.

They helped me onto the table and I remembered how much more terrifying and chaotic it had been thirteen years ago. My body had been so much more shattered.

I lay on the table, forcing myself into the awareness of my bare back on the x-ray table. The table was cold, unfeeling, un-giving. As one technician adjusted me the other positioned the machine.

YIELD, ALIGN AND ENGAGE.

"Feel this moment, not the past," I told myself. The pain was intense, but it was the fear and the pain that was replaying in my body and head from thirteen years ago that was intensifying the agony I was experiencing at that moment. The old memories and fears were so intertwined with my fears and injuries from falling off the roof that I was having trouble determining exactly which reality was real. But I knew I had to claim my life, here and now.

"We are going to go into the other room over there. We can see you. Try not to move." I heard the technician's shoes squeak as she stepped away from the table.

I didn't want to move, not physically and not mentally. I wanted to stay in this moment. But as I lay on the table, and the very real pain pulsed through my pelvis and wrist in particular, I couldn't stem the series of memories that continued to stream through my awareness. I tried to remain centered and tried not resist, but the dreadful and almost hideous images were relentless.

"Now that wasn't so bad, was it?" The technician was back at my side.

"I'm not sure," I replied.

They started to reposition me for another x-ray, and as they did, something triggered the memory of my dream from that first night in the ER, thirteen years earlier. I recalled with amazing vividness being in a crib, carried on the elephant's back and away from the raging tigers.

I breathed in deeply and remembered how that dream had given me hope. It had relieved my despair in the midst of unimaginable darkness. I was reminded that I wasn't alone, that in fact I was safe. The dream had brought the awareness, memory and feelings of being with the Beloved back to me.

As I thought back on that dream, a hand touched my shoulder ever so lightly. It was the technician.

"I'll be right back. Hold, don't move."

With the technician once again off someplace else, I noticed the silence in the moment. The silence comforted me as I lay here. The terrifying inward movement that happened began to feel sacred. A sweeping sense of gratitude for the Beloved's protection and care of me thirteen years ago moved through me with incredible intensity. Tears welled up and I felt them rolling down my cheeks. The Beloved had given up its concealment in the jungle's wilderness and come down, uplifting both body and mind while sustaining my life. I had been grateful to be alive and grateful for its nourishing trans-personal energies. But for all my gratitude, I never fully understood the mystery.

The Beloved had carried me back into life and had mercifully led me away from the thrashing tigers of pain and fear that were trying to consume me. As I recovered over the next several years, I thought that I had suffered and 'humanized' those energies back into my life. I wanted to believe that I had honored the gift of life that was given to me by turning into the suffering while remaining open-hearted. Perhaps partially I did, but I realized as I lay on that table that there was so much more I had not been aware of.

"I'm sorry if this position hurts but we have several more views we have to take."

I simply nodded not feeling the need to explain the tears that rolled down my face. The compassion in the technician's voice pulled me backwards, again. New images burst into my mind. I saw several compassionate, kind and loving people who took care of me thirteen years ago. And as I saw them, I realized the cure for my terror and pain had been the love and compassion extended to me. A lot of people had done things for me to get me back on my feet and into life, and for that I was grateful. But, what cured me from the inside out was love.

How far, I wonder, could I extend that love to both myself and to others?

The x-rays seemed to go on forever, focusing on nearly every part of my body. In some positions the pain trickled through me, in other positions it was more like a thunderous roar. Time seemed to stand still, as my mind became quiet. I knew that staying in the moment was where the healing and the Beloved were found. Allowing my attention to embrace the pain that was taking place in my body, mind, and heart was the best medicine for me. There would be no resistance to my fear and vulnerability. I would stay in my experience, fully aware and accepting so as not to get trapped in it.

"We're done!" The technician seemed more worn down by the process than I was.

They moved me off the x-ray platform and back into the hospital bed. I can't express the gratitude I felt when I came in contact with the soft, yielding mattress. I was grateful, aware, in pain, but buoyed by my awareness of the Beloved. My mind and body felt aligned with what I was beginning to see as the purpose of this experience – of realigning myself with that vibrant and overwhelming awareness of the Beloved.

Over the next several hours, life continued to pull me between my past experience and what was then my current trauma. It was hard to maintain a single level of awareness. One moment I felt a sacred peace, and the next fear and uncertainty. But as I struggled to remain open, I did notice that the fear seemed to surface most significantly the more tired I became. And as the fear surfaced, my pain in turn spiked. Resistance pulled me down into the depths, accelerating and intensifying fear, pain, and despair.

"A nurse will be with you soon." I heard the words of an orderly as exhaustion overcame me and I fell asleep.

I awoke with a start to see a female nurse standing over me, checking my wrist and taking my pulse. There was an irritable restlessness about this woman that made me anxious. I was fearfully reminded of the nurse who had withheld my morphine that horrific night in the hospital many years earlier. She dropped my wrist and put a thermometer in my mouth.

"Are you in pain?" She pulled the thermometer out of my mouth and checked it.

"Some." I said. "Mostly, though, I'm really thirsty."

She seemed to consider that before answering. With something definitively less than a sense of joy, she responded.

"I'll see what I can do," she said, as she turned and walked out

"Shit, I can't believe this." I said out loud.

She evoked such memories of that sadistic nurse who had withheld my morphine that my adrenaline was pumping and my pulse pounding in my ears. Against my will, the images of that hellish night flooded my mind. I grimaced at the memory and how I had raged. I had raged at the betrayal of trust, at my helplessness, shame and powerlessness. I had raged at feeling dehumanized. But as those horrific hours had worn on, I had found myself turning in and starting to understand that any effort towards control on my part could not be sustained. My only choice had been to continue along the path to persevere and yield to myself without giving up on myself. I didn't understand then that I was affirming life in spite of suffering. But the process showed me what was real and enduring, revealing a deeper possibility of the way life can be lived from an undivided state of being. I fell into the center of the pain and the Beloved's Silence met me, incarnating through the painful sacrifice into life from the depths of my existence.

I had begun to calm down, reminding myself again that these images that were replaying from my past were indeed old memories.

"Calm down," I told myself. "Open yourself to the moment."

The nurse returned carrying water. In spite of myself, my pulse surged again. She placed a cup in front of my mouth, and I took a slow, long drink. She followed that with a couple of pills that I didn't even bother to ask about. Not a word was spoken. I wasn't about to get labeled as a troublemaker again.

She turned to leave, and without looking back over her shoulder said loudly, "Try to rest; a doctor will be here soon." And once again I drifted off to sleep.

"Jack?" A voice startled me awake. "How are you doing Jack?"

I was completely disoriented, having no idea where I was or who might be talking to me. But when I moved, the pain jolted my memory into place. The room was fairly dark, and I could tell it was evening, but even in the dim light from the hall I was beginning to recognize the face in front of me. His eyes were on me and something warm flickered in them. I recognized him with acute clarity.

"Dr. Asprinio?!"

I felt unfastened, wide open, with feelings of relief spreading and circulating throughout my body. His gentle warmth, strength and optimism were as evident as ever. I was actually afraid I might have been dreaming.

"You are Dr. Asprinio, right? I'm awake? You're the real thing?"

"You know, Jack, I have rarely seen my handiwork after a patient leaves my care and certainly never after 13 years. But I must say, for being a young surgeon when I met you, I did a remarkable job."

We both laughed.

"I had no idea that I was as capable and ingenious as I was back then, until I looked over your x-rays."

An innate, warmth spread throughout my body. A sense of relief and gratitude washed over me.

"Doc, I always was your biggest fan. Boy, am I glad to see you!"

"You were pretty amazing yourself back then. You certainly still have someone looking out for you. The work I did last time is intact and looks good, real good. But here's what we found. You have a half dozen enclosed fractures in your pelvis behind your pubis. There is a fracture in your sacrum and in your coccyx. The good news is we generally don't operate on those fractures as they heal by themselves over time. Your lumbar vertebrae look OK. No new damage, the old damage is still evident."

"I can't tell you how much of a relief it is to hear you say that," I said. "No one has told me anything, and I thought for sure I had blown out my pelvis again."

"The impact wasn't as severe as last time. You must have landed on your feet in such a way that the heads of your femurs were pointing inward not outward like the last time."

"OK, that sounds like the good news. What's the bad news?"

"Ah, the bad news. I have a list I'm afraid."

"I had a feeling," I replied. "Too much hurts for me to anticipate anything less."

"Well, you have three or four rib fractures. You broke your arm at the wrist. There is a fracture of both the ulna and radius and it looks like a couple of metacarpal ligaments snapped." He paused and I knew with certainty there was more coming.

"Well," I said, trying to find some humor in the situation, "I could have told you that. Tell me something I don't know."

"There is a rotator cuff tear in your left shoulder. There is also a labral tear and your biceps tendon is torn. The joint itself looks preserved. Your right shoulder suffered a bit more damage. That rotator cuff is also torn. But here your supraspinatus tendon is torn as well as the subscapularis tendon. There is also a lot of fluid in the shoulder but the joint looks intact."

I waited to make sure he was finished

"That's it?" I smiled weakly.

"That sounds manageable." I continued. "But if I'm going to walk out of here, I'll need my knees to work and I know they also took a hit."

He hesitated for a moment and then started laughing.

"Well if anyone could walk out of here in your condition, it's you. But you're correct in your assessment of your knees. They both had medial mariscal tears. It looks like your right knee had the greatest impact as there's what is called intense marrow edema and a small non-displaced fracture of the fibular head."

It was my turn to pause.

"Doctor, if all the fractures are enclosed and non-displaced, then in theory they are weight bearing. And if they are weight bearing then I could walk out of here.

The good doctor ran his hand through his thick dark hair while looking at me contemplating a verdict. I sensed his concern and ventured another question with a slight hardening in my voice.

"I've been around this block before. I know I'll have to show that I'm able to walk on my own. Would you schedule a PT evaluation for me tomorrow?"

He stared at me. I swore I could see the memory flash through his mind of the day thirteen years ago when I was walking down the hallway and he had shouted, "Does anyone have a video camera, this is a miracle!"

"Sure," he said.

I smiled. Taking in his confidence and looking deeply into his tired eyes, I thanked him.

As he left, I tried to subdue my churning mind but it was a losing battle. I was too awake and although the room was dark the light in the hallway crept in. Working hard to re-center myself, I heard a phrase in my mind. It's Solomon's comment that "Pride goeth before the destruction and a haughty spirit before the fall."

I awakened the next morning to see two men standing over me. I recognized one immediately as one of the doctors who had attended to me after my fall in the ravine. I recognized the same dead eyes and his detached and uncaring mannerisms. Among other things, the last time I had seen him, he had fallen asleep during a follow-up exam on my pulverized elbow. In that second, he snapped my elbow straight out and forward. The scream I had let out nearly knocked him backwards and off his stool.

"I understand your arm is broken at the wrist and I wanted to talk with you to schedule surgery," he said with the same sense of compassion or concern as he might use when scheduling an oil change for his car.

"I'll pass," I said, with my ego blaring.

He shrunk back defensively, with obviously no recollection of who I was. I sat up intently. He took a moment to regroup and started over.

"I'm not sure you understand. I'm a specialist in orthopedics and this is my resident. Your case was referred to me yesterday."

The resident looked unsettled. I knew he and the not-so-good doctor could feel my anger. It took a moment for my words to find their way through my building anger.

"I had an experience with you once that was nightmarish and have absolutely NO intention of repeating it," I said through clenched teeth.

His face was brimming with condescension. I guessed he was not used to being dismissed at 6:00AM, or at any time for that matter. He had nothing to say.

The resident looked at him and they turned and walked out. For a few minutes after they left, I found myself inwardly berating myself for not being more confronting. Then I remembered that the care for the pain is compassion, not ego. I knew that despicable doctor had his own demons but I didn't need to be a victim of them. The way into this hospital had been on my back. The way out, if I was getting out, would be on bended knees and with an open heart.

I hadn't eaten since lunch the day before, a few moments prior to my plummeting off of my roof. I devoured breakfast when it arrived and I knew I must have been either really famished or mentally unstable, because I thought the hospital food was wonderful.

By lunch, I was still hungry. Alice arrived just as lunch was delivered. She was subdued with a look on her face of concern and anxiety. Unease crept into her eyes. She studied my face and body language as I sat up.

"Hi Hon, have you eaten?" I asked. "Do you want to join me for lunch?"

She shook her head and with a great and somber sense of concern asked how I was.

"I feel good, really good," I said, staring down at the covered tray in front of me. I wanted to begin eating but I was stopped by the look on Alice's face.

She stared at me, certain something was very wrong. I could see by her look she was thinking a psych evaluation might be the next order of business. She had been completely thrown by my response. I could see her staring at the top of my head.

"Why don't they ever clean the blood out of your hair? This is a hospital, for God's sake. Last time you were here there was blood caked in your hair for weeks." She took a calming breath and looked from my matted hair, straight into my eyes.

"*Seriously*, Jack, how are you?"

I knew when I heard her say the word "seriously" that I was in trouble. That's her code word that she is getting really annoyed with me. She was fairly certain I wasn't giving her the straight answer. I looked down at the unopened lunch plates.

"Sit down and I'll tell you," I began. "I saw Dr. Asprinio last night."

"Really?"

"Yup. He says I've got a few issues that have to be attended to, but none that will keep me from having dinner at home with you and the boys tonight."

Her eyes went from mine to the rest of my body, rapidly scanning me from head to toe. She glared at me intently.

"Do NOT tease me," she warned.

"Alice, I'm serious. If I can demonstrate that I'm ambulatory by passing a physical therapy evaluation this afternoon, I'll be driving home with you."

Alice held me tightly and we cried together. I felt as if I had found life's hidden treasure. Once again, on my knees, I was bearing witness to life with an open heart and mind, paying tribute to life. Hidden in how we suffer, the meaning in life can be found by being fully present in life as it is. Our fate depends on the attitude we take. For me, "Yes" was and is the essential psychological factor in accepting oneself and life as it is.

Alice released me and settled into a chair facing me. There was still a somewhat puzzled look in her eyes. I looked down and took the lid off my lunch plate to see what was hidden within.

"Chicken, my favorite." Using my uninjured right hand, I began eating.

"Well, the pain doesn't seem to have diminished your appetite, and I can see you've quickly become right handed!"

I laughed, but was careful to swallow before I responded. I had no intention of repeating my choking episode.

"Yeah, it's a good sign," I said.

"I was so enraged yesterday," I continued. "The humiliation at not being able to prevent the fall from happening was too much. I felt so impotent in the pain's assault. It was all consuming and suddenly I was totally trapped, AGAIN!!"

"Jack, I have never experienced or imagined that you could ever be that enraged. I felt really bad for you. And it was scary."

"I'm so sorry. I never, ever, wanted you and the boys to have to go through anything like this again. The physical pain is secondary to the utter helplessness of not being able to avoid this experience or protect you and the boys from this kind of fear and pain again. I'm really sorry."

Alice nodded empathetically then her expression became serious.

"I don't blame you. I know you were careful, you've learned to be. But you're you. I knew after we talked about the dream that you and Al would be careful, so I let go. This is your life. Yet, I'm a part of it too, and this is now a part of me and the boys. We are part of this together, the good with the bad. We will share this painful fall with the same love we share all the wonderful, happy experiences we've enjoyed. We'll get through this together. We've done it before."

I was silent for a moment, grateful for her words and the love we shared that was behind them.

"Thank you," I told her. "Thank you."

And I went on to repeat just how sorry I was for putting the family through this ordeal again.

"You know I'll heal from this experience and learn from it. I own that responsibility. But your understanding, acceptance and love make it easier for me to focus on what I need to get done. We have both learned over the years that guilt and blame serve no purpose in healing. Nor do they help us to understand why things like this can and do happen; they just do. The fact is I stepped off the roof. But that action happened beyond any conscious intention on my part, that's for sure!"

There was a kind of wordless trust in Alice's eyes combined with something else that I couldn't quite put my finger on.

"Jack, I understand 'something' happened on the roof. I'm not upset with you. It's a miracle that you are not hurt worse than you are, but what's the point of it all? It just seems like a lot of pain and suffering to me."

"That's true Alice, there is pain and some suffering coming my way. I'm sorry I pulled you into this with me. Nobody wanted our summer to look like this. But at the moment, the point of it all is my walking out of here. After my encounter with that quack doctor this morning, I realized the nightmare I had three days ago was not only pointing forward towards 'something' happening in life, but it was also pointing backwards to something that had happened in life. I guess what I'm trying to say is that what happened thirteen years ago is definitely embedded in what's happening now."

Alice's empathy channel was open, but she watched me warily. I feared my clumsiness in saying the wrong thing. I needed both of us to understand why our lives were turned inside out again. If only I could clearly see the purpose and direction, then I could choose it, make it mine and work it through. Hopefully then we could all participate in an experience that I had to believe would make all of us more whole. The view of my experience from the 'outside' might look like the language of pathology - lack of boundaries or lack of self-structure - but before the moment faded, I needed to establish what the experience was for me.

Alice sat forward in her chair. She could commit selflessly if she trusted me and understood the process. We both knew there would be sacrifice for all of us. We would all need to find a way to be in it together and own our part of what was to come.

"Alice, all I can do is trust my gut instinct that providence has guided me, maybe all of us, back here for some purpose. Last night after Dr. Asprinio left, I was speculating on what that purpose could be. Perhaps no matter how hard I tried to resolve the last experience, there was more that needed to be relived in life, in action.

In hindsight, I now see the dream as calling me back into the abyss of ego dissolution and my terrified flight from it. This time was different in that I barely lost consciousness; there was no being swept up into the Beloved's rapture in a near death experience. This time, very soon after I hit the deck, I dissolved into the rage of becoming a victim of myself again. I knew I couldn't escape from the chaos and pain that awaited me. I was not swept up this time but cracked open into the ground of my life.

Suddenly a peaceful quality descended on me, and I again felt the presence of the Beloved. I acclimated to it through the forest breeze and the sound of the chimes. Feeling and hearing that relieved my sense of aloneness. At that moment, I felt as if I was a part of the Beloved and the Beloved was a part of me. I may have been in shock and my boundaries displaced, but in the heart of the chaos there was a sense of peace and in the center of the pain and terror, there was a comforting silence. In the deepest cells of my being I know this process, and I want to trust where it will lead me."

Alice listened intently. I could tell she understood what was shaping me and would embrace me on our journey forward.

"When I was on the deck looking at you, I didn't know how to help you or even how to be with you. But when I heard the chimes, I did notice you relax. Until Devin arrived, I just stood there, frozen."

Alice looked up directly into my eyes and sighed.

"I just don't know how you do it."

Practice makes perfect?" Alice didn't laugh. I tried a different tack.

"One thing I learned from my last visit here as a patient was how to suffer. Everything I kept learning in those first few years was to turn into the experience open heartedly, feel it, let go and engage life. What the experience really taught me was that fear can either destroy you or focus you. I'm trying to stay focused in it right now by continuing to yield inwardly while initiating outwardly.

Keeping or finding my center in the moment is the real emotional challenge. Actually the greatest difficulty I've had doing just that was last night in Radiology. In fact, just being taken down there, I felt as if my sense of self was being forcefully stripped away, which provoked a bit of a panic attack. Alice, it took everything I had just to stay somewhat grounded and remain present. Something got triggered in my body that was both familiar and terrifying. What finally came up was death's scent in a chilling awareness of my absolute aloneness and loss of identity and power."

The room fell silent. After a few moments, Alice softly replied.

"I don't know how you stayed conscious Jack. I probably would have just passed out!"

I looked at Alice and smiled. I realized my heart was open in a way that if I could stay accessible and exposed with her, I would continue to stay connected to my interior feelings where Jackie lived. This meant to me that I was on my 'knees' and aligned with what felt like this experience was asking of me.

"My self-preservation instinct was lit-up and mobilized. It was working overtime because I felt it was imperative to remain conscious. As I was about to be loaded onto the x-ray table, I was deluged by agonizing flashbacks from 13 years ago. There was a fierce terror of losing myself. Back then I didn't pass-out as much as I felt extinguished. The central defining moment now was a conscious, peaceful, secure awareness, as if the Beloved was watching and waiting for me.

It was different from the experience of the Beloved last time but it's still with me now in a soft and gentle pulsation."

Alice shook her head gently.

"I guess our being here could not be otherwise."

She studied me with a smile on her face, especially in her eyes.

"So for you there is a sacredness in suffering. It opens you. Me, I'd just rather not suffer."

I laughed, staring down at the array of empty plates in front of me.

"We are such opposites. You seem to glide through life, never breaking a bone, spraining a muscle. You're rarely in a bad mood. Our lessons have been so different in this lifetime. We know the ego's secret deep down, beneath all those layers, boundaries, beliefs and fears is that it knows it's an instrument, not the source of reality and life. How many times has my body needed to be broken and my pride displaced for me to have the humility to both respect and understand this process?"

Her eyes were alive with loving energy

"Oh, I can't count the number of times, but it's taken more than sixty years for you to 'get it'."

I ran a quick mental calculation.

"I think I get a free pass on the first ten years."

Our afternoon passed slowly. Alice and I talked and I had a visit from one of Brendan's old friends, Arnie's son Max. By early evening I was hungry again and looked up when a new face entered the room.

"I'm Jeff Miller, the physical therapist. I understand you'd like to go home today."

Our eyes locked, "I sure would."

"Of course," he said flatly, "I have your chart here and I've read the extent of your injuries. There is a protocol, formalities, which you need to go through to demonstrate you're capable of going home and being ambulatory."

I got myself into a sitting position before responding

"What do I need to do?"

He leaned in toward me and extended a cane.

"I need you to get out of bed and walk out into the hallway with me. You can use the cane if you feel the need."

"OK," I said resolutely, "Here we go."

I winced uncomfortably as I moved my pelvis to the edge of the bed. Immediately I stopped, realizing my intention was ahead of my body. Settling myself for a moment, I hung my feet over the side of the bed and slowly slid them down to the floor. Right away I was imagining what I would experience and I was not really settled in my body.

"Just do your best," Jeff said.

I glared at him. He seemed to be somewhere between uninterested and anxious about how to catch me if I were to fall. I also noticed Alice was studying me with a concerned expression on her face. I visualized again what I had to do and stood up.

In a millisecond, I went from anticipating pain to experiencing it. In the back of my pelvis I could feel how entangled that moment's pain was with the past.

I was gripped with the potent and 'wet' emotions of happiness and sadness.

The pain came and went in powerful waves, but there was an absence of fear. In moments, I felt my ego engaged and in other moments it was off to the side. I simply continued to walk, yield and think 'yes', as I allowed the sensations to move up and out of me. There was no withdrawing from the moment, but I felt how the pain's excitability began to change to anxiety and then aggression, the forces which combined to help pull me forward.

I stopped. Softening, I breathed in deeply.

"Are you OK?"

"Yep!" I said, but my awareness was deep inside looking to center myself. Noticing that the anxiety more than the pain was beginning to overtake me, I looked up and spoke directly to Jeff.

"Thank you." The humility I found grounded me. As I turned into my room, my heart was wide-open and compassion was flowing through me.

The first thing I saw was the luminous smiling faces of Alice and Max.

"Good job!!" They cheered.

A shroud of fatigue descended on me as I approached the bed. Both the suffering and the love met me and moved through my depths. Life without armor is a vulnerable but powerful thing.

I could feel Jeff's surprise at my accomplishment.

"Well done," he managed to say. "It will take an hour or so to process your evaluation, then you'll be on your way."

I felt a catch in my throat, nodded, and looked into his eyes

"Thank you."

A wave of gratitude and relief washed over my body as I sank down into the mattress.

Alice looked at me with her eyes brighter than I'd seen since her arrival in my room. I read the relief in them.

"The look on your face when you first stood up was a bit troubling, but it seemed like the pain was less as you started walking."

I gave her a long look.

"Well, not less just more real. I wasn't centered in my body when I stood up. I was in my head. Once I got down into it, the pain was very real, but it became its own cure. I just had to make space for it in an open-hearted way."

I made a steeple of my hands and nodded to both.

"Thanks for being the support team."

As we talked over the course of the next hour, a part of me was giving thanks to my body and that which lies within its refuge. Once again, embracing the suffering, I had come into the fullness of life. I knew there would be continued uncertainty going forward. The vividness and precariousness of the past day would fade. The experience and memory would draw me deeper towards the Beloved in the moments to come, but only if I could remain present in life. That, I knew was the lesson I had come to relearn.

An orderly pushed a wheelchair into the room.

"Is someone in here going home today?"

My heart beat happily. As Alice went to retrieve the car, Max and the orderly helped me into the wheelchair. As Max pushed me down the hallway to the elevator, I couldn't help but remember how his father, Arnie, had done the same thing for me thirteen years ago. Suffering was once again being mediated by love.

Alice pulled up in front of the hospital where we were waiting. After Max helped me into the car, he gave me a hug and looked me in the eyes.

"I love you," he said.

The journey home, after having been taken by medevac to the hospital the day before, felt sacred. There was an incredible sense of relief, gratitude and expansion in the moment. I wasn't even aware of pain. I only felt the sensory quality of the day turning to dusk and a very deep feeling of being a part of the fabric of life itself - a life that I was so grateful to be allowed to remain a part of.

As Alice turned into the driveway to our home, I rolled down the window beside me. Every cell in my body felt as if it had come alive. I took in the dappled light streaming through the forest, the smells and the sound of tree frogs. They all soothed me. I was home.

As we pulled up to the house, I looked through the windows and saw Devin setting the table and Brendan at the stove. Both boys came out with smiling faces.

"You're just in time for dinner, Dad."

I had difficulty getting my legs out of the car without provoking intense flashes of pain in my pelvis. Devin helped me out as Brendan went to get a chair from the table in the dining room. They decided to carry me in sitting on the chair and place me at the table. They both stood over six feet tall with powerful athletic bodies, so it was relatively easy for them to lift me up and take me for a ride.

As we are talked and enjoyed dinner, the conversation turned towards everyone's experience over the past twenty-four hours.

There was nothing romanticized, only a deep personal experience of each person. As I listened to what everyone went through, it was painful for me. In their love for me was a pronounced awareness of the sacrifice in loving another, a sacrifice I asked of them. Working through our emotions, hopes, and suffering of the day had been a labor of love for all of us. I could only offer them a humble reception and an embracing appreciation of their open-hearted expression.

At one point, Devin's fear was accompanied by anger.

"You know Dad, you are going to turn our home into a tomb unless you make some changes," he told us.

Nodding, Alice allowed the boys to speak, inviting them out. As I listened to them speak, I realized just how young they were thirteen years ago. Time had disappeared into a deep well, but Devin held the truth of his experience in the center of his being. Silently embracing the whole of his experience, I could only respond that I was sorry and that I knew I had a lot of work left to do.

His suffering, like Brendan's and Alice's, had no value unless I could consciously accept it, and in so doing, redeem its value. The respectful response seemed to allow the heat of his pain to dissipate. I suddenly realized, they had all stood close to death with me. Their love truly was the redemption of suffering from the inside out, a deep suffering love.

"Dad, no offense," Brendan chimed in, "but you have got to take a shower before you go to bed."

"Yeah," Devin added, "blood, roofing tar, and a lot of sweating before you landed on the deck just kind of screams, 'Shower'."

I agreed, but didn't have the balance or strength at that point to negotiate the shower on my own. So again, Devin and Brendan picked me up in the chair and carried me through the house into the master bathroom. Along the way, we stopped and without a sound, the three of us looked out through the walkway windows to the deck below. Inhaling, I looked up and saw where I had fallen through the cut-away in the roof between the buildings. Simultaneously, the broken decking where I landed caught my attention.

In that moment, I saw there was only one spot I could have landed, fallen backwards and not died. It was as if I had been placed in that exact spot. A chill shot through my body. Not one of us said a word.

It had been hot when I had fallen off the roof, and it was hot that night. The windows were open and the glass walls of the shower allowed me to look out through the window, past the ravine below, into the forest and the lake beyond. Brendan held me up as Devin washed me. A powerful awareness moved through me. Each of us as men was holding the truth of who we were in the center of our being at that moment. There are so few moments in life when the purity of intention is fully engaged in a single action. That was one of those moments. I will never be able to find the right words to truly capture my experience of my sons' presence, love and compassion. As the wet curves of the downward spray cleansed me, some parts of me felt as if they simply crumbled into their loving hands. The sound of the water, laughter and the forest removed the last of the day's fierceness.

As my sons carried me to bed, I was reminded of how precious it had once been for me to carry them to bed. The four of us talked for a long while about life and the summer ahead. Brendan and Devin went off to bed. Alice fell asleep beside me. And I lay awake, exhausted but unable to sleep.

As I lay in the darkness, I became acutely aware of the stillness that flowed through the forest and into our home. It seemed to touch and connect everything outside with all of us inside the house. It was so subtle yet so present that it pulled me into the equally subtle inner movement of the Beloved. Breathing deeply into this awareness brought tears to my eyes.

I was alive, and perhaps more alive at that moment than I had ever been. I had never lost the memory of the ravine and the Beloved, but as I lay in the silence that night, looking up at the expansive night sky and stars, I realized that over the years I had lost access to the experience of that unconditional loving state. But in that silence, I lay awake, fully bathed in the love of my family, the love of all the wonderful people who had carried me through terror and pain that had seemed unbearable, the love of my father, the love of Jack and Jackie, the love that is the ultimate truth and unity of all life.

Trust. Surrender. Choice. Allow one moment to dissolve into the next. The Beloved will always be with me, even when I fall. I had learned these lessons before, circling through them over the course of 13 years. But in the last twenty-four hours, I had lived them and touched them with an awareness and intensity I had not experienced since the ravine. Love, and my openness to it, had brought me home. This had been a lesson learned.

In the silence of the forest, under the light of the stars, with my family asleep beside and around me, I drifted peacefully to sleep.

When I awoke the next morning, I felt pain. And with it, I felt the unwelcome presence of fear and doubt. Alice had gotten up earlier and I lay there alone. I kept my eyes closed and breathed in deeply.

"I'm alive," I said to myself. "I'm home." And with those thoughts, I noticed how peaceful the forest was. I could feel the warm summer breeze through the window, hear the birds singing, and as I opened my eyes, I saw a squirrel that seemed to be watching me from a branch of a nearby hemlock, its bushy tail twitching.

Yes, parts of me hurt. But they would heal. And while fears and doubts would occasionally lap at the shores of my consciousness, I knew the Beloved would never allow them to consume me.

I carefully swiveled my legs to the side of the bed and sat up. The day was unfolding and I welcomed every moment of it with complete awareness, gratitude and an open-heart. I was truly present and breathed into my heart with mercy and awareness. I held Jackie close. I gave thanks to being home with my family, and my heart swelled as I knowingly recognized the Beloved in all that surrounded me, fully aware that I was blessed both to be loved and to be able to love.

Suddenly, I understood what Rumi really meant when he said, "Love wills that this word be brought forth." And I recalled Devin's perceptive comment that this occurred to fulfill my destiny and allow me to finish my book.

I looked out into the forest, listening to its sounds through the open window and the voices of my family from beyond the bedroom door.

"Thank you," I said out loud. "Thank you for this life, made sacred by the love that flows to and through us each and every day."

Acknowledgments

Sacred Fall was written over 15 years. I am grateful for many individuals who supported and facilitated this process.

I would like to thank the following doctors who assisted in reconnecting my mind and body with skill, compassion and a touch of humor. Dr. D. Aspirinio, Dr. M. Burruano, Dr. B. Erner, Dr. D. Fauser, Dr. D. Kalsched. Dr. J. Maher, Dr. F. Malmed, Dr. P. Mangiafico, Dr. A. Moran, Dr. J. Passick, Dr. K. Ranade, Dr. J. Schoenholtz, and my Angel of Mercy.

After fourteen years and four revisions of this story, I met Ed Manning. Ed spent months helping to rewrite and edit this work. His tireless brilliance brought this story to life in a way I never could. At critical junctures we could always count on his dreams guiding the editing process. I am eternally grateful for his sense of humor, clarity, and tenacity.

In an attempt to understand my experience and facilitate healing, Susan Cicelsky generously gave of her time in typing and retyping this book's many revisions.

Al Thomsen's kindness and patience while mentoring me in my home construction process, specifically in the building of the towers, helped me heal and develop in ways I could have never foreseen.

Norm Cicelsky, both friend and architect, taught me to trust my vision in the building process.

Frank Algier, Susan Cicelsky, Jon Goldberg, Michael Hennessy, Sarah Lee, Roseann Marciano, Steve Schatz and Nina Tentenbaum all read various revisions of this story and provided valuable suggestions and comments.

Most of all, I am deeply indebted to my family. My wife, Alice, and sons Brendan and Devin, not only shared this journey with me but supported and encouraged the telling of our story.

I am eternally grateful for their love and unwavering faith in me.

There were many people over the years, not identified between these pages, who heard me tell this story and encouraged me to write it down. It is their story as well as mine, that with the best of my ability, I pass on to you.

Made in the USA
Lexington, KY
23 April 2014

Made in the USA
Middletown, DE
07 October 2018